The Napo Runa
of Amazonian Ecuador

▶ ▶ ▶ ▶ *Interpretations of Culture in the New Millennium*

Norman E. Whitten Jr., General Editor

*A list of books in the series appears
at the end of the book.*

The Napo Runa
of Amazonian Ecuador

Michael Uzendoski

University of Illinois Press · Urbana and Chicago

For Edith and Sisa

1 2 3 4 5 C P 5 4 3 2 1
Library of Congress Cataloging-in-Publication Data
Uzendoski, Michael, 1968–
The Napo Runa of Amazonian Ecuador / Michael Uzendoski.
  p. cm. — (Interpretations of culture in the new millennium)
Includes bibliographical references and index.
ISBN 0-252-03007-9 (cloth : alk. paper)
ISBN 0-252-07255-3 (pbk. : alk. paper)
1. Quechua Indians—Napo River Valley (Ecuador and Peru)—
Social life and customs. 2. Quechua Indians—Napo River Valley
(Ecuador and Peru)—Government relations. 3. Indians, Treatment
of—Napo River Valley (Ecuador and Peru) 4. Napo River Valley
(Ecuador and Peru)—Ethnic relations. 5. Napo River Valley
(Ecuador and Peru)—Social life and customs. I. Title. II. Series.
F2230.2.K4U94   2005
305.898'3230866416—dc22   2005002627

Contents

List of Illustrations   vii

Preface   ix

Acknowledgments   xi

Introduction: Value and Ethnographic Translation   1

1. *Sinzhi Runa:* The Birth Process and the Development of the Will   25

2. The Poetics of Social Form   50

3. Ritual Marriage and Making Kin   69

4. The Transformation of Affinity into Consanguinity   95

5. Meat, Manioc Brew, and Desire   118

6. The Return of Jumandy: Value and the Indigenous Uprising of 2001   144

Glossary of Quichua Terms   167

Notes   171

References   181

Index   193

Illustrations

Maps

1. Ecuador 7

2. Amazonian Quichua Speakers in Ecuador 8

3. Political Map of the Amazonian Region of Ecuador 9

Figures

1. Kindred 64

2. Scale of Ritual Marriage Fiestas 76

3. Cari Parti Dancing 87

4. The In-Law in the Family Household 106

5. Runa Theory of Value 115

Plates

1. A Visaru and a Tocadur at a Wedding 75

2. Warmi Parti Dancing with Meat Gifts 92

3. Woman Preparing a Paca 124

4. Statue of Jumandy 146

Preface

This book, written in the humanistic tradition, addresses the interrelated problems of value, kinship, and historicity among the Napo Runa. In my struggle to convey these multifaceted anthropological problems, I have drawn on the work of the late Quechua writer, poet, and anthropologist José María Arguedas. Indigenous characters in Arguedas's works define themselves as spiritual-cosmic beings who are connected to the world, and especially nature, through an intense affectivity and aesthetic. These relations are not superstition but rather modes of perception by which people visualize their connections to the substances and powers of mythical forces that are essential to the materiality of things and to social process.

In thinking about Arguedas's work, I have become more cognizant of the aesthetics of power in Napo, an aesthetics that cannot be divorced from the processes by which power comes to be embodied. Personhood in Napo, as I will show, is defined by experiencing flows of power that derive from realities outside oneself. The Napo Runa define power as *ushai* but use other terms to describe it as well: *yachai* (knowledge), *causai* (life force), *samai* (breath or soul substance), and *urza* (force). The Runa describe especially powerful people as *sinzhi*, or "strong." Such people are especially skilled in eliciting *ushai* through their connections to ancestors, shamans, animals, the forest, and other powerful beings.

I also seek, however, to convey some of the subtle and complex dynamics by which *ushai* becomes a collective force of social action and historical consciousness. In this regard, I draw on the term *millennial* as it is developed in the recent volume *Millennial Ecuador: Critical Essays on Cultural Transformations and Social Dynamics* (2003), edited by Norman Whitten. I follow Whitten's use of *millennial* as an English metaphor for the Quichua concept of *pachacutic*—namely, transformation defined as "the return of space-time (chronotope) of a healthy past to that of a healthy future" (Whitten 2003:

x). In this reference to *pachacutic*, millennial events derive from the flow of *ushai*, the "underneath" or chthonic power that gives life to them.

I offer this dialectical tandem of power and transformation as an orienting tool to help readers appreciate the book's larger context. I spend the first six chapters presenting the symbolic, social, and material complexities of personhood as created and defined by the Napo Runa life cycle. This is *ushai*, power. The final chapter changes voice, for there I consider the millennial person in the context of a significant political and historical event of change, the indigenous uprising of 2001. As I will demonstrate, the events of 2001 were monumental for the Napo Runa. Not only did they lead to several casualties, but the significance of these events has created a flow of life force and memory from the past into the future. This is the *pachacutic*, the transformation.

Acknowledgments

Fieldwork for this project was supported by grants from the Fulbright Institute for International Education (1994), the Research Enablement Program (OSMC) under the Pew Charitable Trusts (1996–97), and the University of Virginia (1999) and by a teaching and research position with the Dirección Bilingüe Intercultural de Napo (1996–97). Subsequent trips to Ecuador were funded by Florida State University (2001) and a Fulbright Scholar Award (2002). In 2002 research was also facilitated by a teaching opportunity at the Facultad Latinoamericano de Ciencias Sociales (FLACSO) of Ecuador. I am grateful to all these organizations for their support. In total, I have spent approximately thirty months in Ecuador over the last ten years.

I offer the warmest thanks to Frederick Damon. No citation or acknowledgment herein can do justice to Fred's many intellectual gifts that have become part of my own thinking. I acknowledge my debt to the late Chris Crocker, whose vital soul has become something of this work. I thank George Mentore, who brought his entire family to visit my field site in 1996, a moment in time when we finally came to understand each other. I sincerely and most warmly thank the series editor, Norman Whitten, for pushing me to integrate more of my own experiences into the text. Norm was not simply an editor. He was both critical and supportive at the necessary moments and has done much to make this book stronger. I thank him for such generous and astute mentoring throughout the process.

I thank Fernando Santos-Granero, Jean-Guy Goulet, and Thomas Abercrombie for comments on the final chapter they made during the 2003 American Anthropological Association meetings. I also thank Chris Gregory for encouragement. I thank warmly the anonymous reviewers, whose critical insights have improved various aspects of the argument in no uncertain way.

There have been numerous others who must be thanked along the way:

Renault Neubauer, Luz María de la Torre, Frank Salomon, Carmen Chuquín, and others who helped me to learn Quichua. I would especially like to thank Professor Fernando García of FLACSO and the director of the Fulbright program in Ecuador, Susana Cabeza de Vaca. I also thank my two dear friends, Simon Bickler and Syed Ali, who spent a lot of time reading parts or entire chapters of this book. Others who have helped along the way are Carissa Neff, Cheryl Ward, Bill Parkinson, Brian Selmeski, Mark Becker, Tod Swanson, and Alexander King.

I also thank the many Napo Runa people who have contributed to this project and have helped me to understand something of their world. I would like to thank my parents, Don and Linda Uzendoski, and my two sisters, Kerry and Kathy, for much support and encouragement. Lastly, I especially thank my wife and my family in Ecuador, all of whom have contributed greatly to this cause. To the many people I have not mentioned I offer my apologies. While I have received much help along the way, I accept full and complete responsibilities for any errors or shortcomings.

The Napo Runa
of Amazonian Ecuador

Introduction:
Value and Ethnographic Translation

I remember standing with a group of Napo Runa men in a long, motorized dugout canoe at the edge of a wide, slow-moving river. The luscious, tall trees bent toward us, blocking out the rays of the newly risen morning sun.[1] Birds flew overhead, looping and singing, while insects buzzed and chirped. A fresh rain the night before had left the river dark, and intermittent clumps of debris from the shower moved steadily down it. Still cooled from the dimness and the passing rain, the air was crisp.

It was a Sunday during the first months of my fieldwork in Yacu Llacta,[2] and I had been invited to play in a soccer match with the men, who had joined a league in a nearby town. After shoving off, we moved slowly upriver, and I struggled to maintain my balance as the canoe rocked back and forth and the wind gusted. The men around me were talking in an animated manner, making jokes and commenting on current events. The conversation turned toward Runa men who had to miss the game because they were working in a nearby ecotourism hotel owned by a rich Swiss man whom the Runa called the "Suizo." The captain of the team, Jorge, complained that this foreigner was using both the region's natural resources and its people, whom he paid a pittance compared to the large amount of money his business generated. Jorge looked at me angrily and said, "Whites [*blancos*] don't understand what it means to live by sharing. We Runa people live by reciprocity [*pariju causana*]."[3] I appreciated Jorge's discourse about values and value conflicts as seen from the Runa perspective. Other people in the canoe, however, thought that Jorge's anger was directed at me, and they asked him to be quiet. This was the first time—but not the last—that the distrustfulness of others taught me something important about value.

This book resulted from my own personal inquiry into value. It is based on innumerable acts and experiences of living, participating, and talking about value and value conflicts within Napo Runa communities. Like others who have considered value from an anthropological perspective (Dumont 1977, 1980, 1982, 1986; T. Turner 1984, 1996; Munn 1986; Gregory 1997; Piot 1999; Damon 2002a, 2002b; Graeber 2001), I approach it as an ethnographic, theoretical, and intersubjective question (Jackson 1989, 1996). A beginning definition of value might be the "chains that link relations between things to relations between people" (Gregory 1997:12). Values are contained not in things by themselves but only in a total social context of people and things (Gregory 1982, 1997). As I argue in this book, value is not given in nature but produced by human action and intentionality (see Godelier 2000:260).

There is more at stake here than just another ethnography about a remote place in Upper Amazonia. I seek to shed light on how data from the Upper Amazon fit into recent debates about gifts and commodities (Gregory 1997; Appadurai 1986; Piot 1999; Humphrey and Hugh-Jones 1992; Bloch and Parry 1989), personhood and kinship (Valeri 1994; Strathern 1988, 1992; Rival and Whitehead 2001; Overing and Passes 2000; Weismantel 1995), exchange theory (Mayer 2002; Damon 2002a, 2002b), and Amazonianist debates about the social themes of conviviality and predation (Overing and Passes 2000; Viveiros de Castro 1992, 1996; Taylor 1993, 1996; Lorrain 2000; Santos-Granero 2000; Rivière 2000). I also address social theory and the problem of how other cultures view "society" (or sociality) itself. I approach the issue of sociality from the perspective of the native philosophy guiding reproduction, the native theory of kinship. I argue that the kinship and value forms discussed here represent a sophisticated Upper Amazonian political philosophy. This system has deep historical roots in the pre-Hispanic regional systems that once connected the people of this region to the Lower Napo and the Andean world through modes of circulation that included trade, marriage, and possibly adoption (see Uzendoski 2004a; Salomon 1986; Weismantel 1995; Kohn 2002a). The principles behind these Upper Amazonian social forms are not immediately obvious to the outsider, but they are as multifaceted and complex as the forms and structures of the capitalist world-system (Uzendoski 2004a).

In analyzing concepts of social form, value, and value metamorphosis, I take inspiration from Marx (1977), who showed how capitalism, seen through the lens of human action and labor, symbolically and materially transforms one set of categories (commodities and labor) into sets of other categories (equivalent form, money, and capital). Marx describes a productive system that produces not only things but also people, relations, and symbolic structures of meaning. I use Marx's notions of form, "relations," value, and especially value metamorphosis as general ideas that orient me to the relevant

Napo Runa concepts and analogues discovered through fieldwork (Damon 1980, 1983, 2002a, 2002b). Marx's philosophical method of study is indeed powerful. In my view of Marx, the symbolic categories of the system (forms) are "internally related" (Ollman 1976) to the system of production and are realized in the circulation processes organizing production and consumption. In other words, symbolic forms are internally related to production, consumption, and circulation.[4] As I will show through the Napo Runa case, society consists of not only the imaginary and symbolic realms but also the material relations of life production and the value forms that relate people to one another and to nature (Godelier 2000:62).

The social forms of value prevalent among indigenous communities in rural Napo differ significantly from the commodity principles of capitalistic relations. I use Chris Gregory's (1982, 1997) distinction between gift and commodity economies to capture some of these differences. Nonetheless, I think it is better to speak of gift and commodity modes (rather than economies), for people in almost all societies today participate in both forms of exchange. Commodities are alienable; they are produced and circulated as if they exist independent of people. Moreover, commodities are exchanged in the morally free space of capitalistic exchange: the market. The predominance of the market as a structure that organizes social relations around the circulation of commodities helps to explain why the concept of the commodity itself orders human relations as if they were things (Marx 1977:165–66), a social process described as "reification" (Strathern 1988:177; Lukács 1967). In other words, as Marx and others have shown, commodities transform human relationships into material ones: commodities are the most basic form of capitalism itself (Marx 1977; Gregory 1997; Strathern 1988; Damon 2002a; Uzendoski 2004a).

By contrast, the defining feature of gifts is that they are not alienable and function,[5] metaphorically and pragmatically, as conceptual extensions of people. Gifts assume and follow the social forms of persons. They are morally charged entities that create relations. Gregory (1982) has deployed the useful and rich analytical term *personification* to describe how gift exchange converts things into people. As I will show, processes of personification in Napo do not display the absence of things or a utopian rejection of materiality. In general, Amazonian peoples view the production, circulation, and consumption of things as essential to creating and reproducing people. Nonetheless, Amazonian conceptions of materiality and of things and their relationships to people are culturally distinct. Many of the animals, fish, plants, and trees that become things to be consumed are regarded as living beings with subjectivities (Descola 1992, 1996a, 1996b; Fausto 2000). Throughout the following chapters I will attempt to shed light on these various transformations of things and persons, subjectivity and objectivity.[6]

While personification gives insight into the way value is organized in Napo, Gregory's (1982) well-known model remains incomplete because it opposes people to things instead of articulating the relations between them. For example, the model makes the production of things seem nonproblematic in gift modes; similarly, the production of people is notably absent in the treatment of commodity modes. As the chapters here will show, the production of people among the Napo Runa depends heavily on the production of things and the manners in which they are produced, circulated, and consumed. Things are crucial to effect the metamorphoses of value that define people and create kinship relations in daily and ritual life. In addition, the Napo Runa find commodities to be necessary and desirable, for they depend on them to produce people.

Critics have argued that Gregory artificially separates gift and commodity forms as involving mutually exclusive mindsets (see, e.g., Appadurai 1986; Gell 1992; Bloch and Parry 1989; Hugh-Jones 1992).[7] His critics, however, seem to overlook or dismiss completely his discussion of personification, a model that not only occupies a central place in his work but also successfully explains the way in which many cultures organize value around the reproduction of people (Fausto 2000; see Damon 2002a for a recent discussion of Gregory's work). While the account here is informed by value theory as such, I must stress that my purpose is to show what value means from the perspective of the Runa. Specifically, the Runa have developed an elegant and complex ethnotheory of value that is simultaneously intersubjective, gendered, reproductive, and cosmological (Santos-Granero 1986; Descola 1992, 1996a; Lorrain 2000; T. Turner 1995). I will argue that value in this system can be shown to be a consistent pattern of thought and action modeled on a complex, multistranded theory of kinship and substance transformation.

Metaphors of Society

The main theoretical challenge for this book is translating Napo Runa concepts of social value that do not fit into the Eurocentric epistemologies of value that dominate classical and current theories about the social in non-Western societies. For example, Piot (1999) and Strathern (1988) have shown that accounts of non-Western cultures often assume European–North American notions of value in their application of commodity metaphors, subject-object relations, and personhood. In thinking about such epistemo-logical differences between Napo Runa sociality and those of classical social scientific theory, it is useful to change social metaphors and move away from the Durkheimian notion that societies are organisms. The organism metaphor implicitly posits that "society," as an abstract concept, encompasses West-ern "individuals"; the familiar forms of autonomous personhood (Dumont 1986) and implicit commodity relations are assumed as the basic elements of social life (Gregory 1997). One can often gain insights into other social philosophies, however, by seeking appropriate social metaphors from *within* the experiences and practices of the culture in question (Wagner 2001). These metaphors are sometimes expressed through everyday practices that seem to be trivial—what Bloch refers to as "what goes without saying" (Bloch 1992, 1998). Being often based in imagery rather than discourse, they resist verbal explanation and must be witnessed and experienced rather than explained (Wagner 1986:xiv).

I discovered an appropriate social metaphor of indigenous sociality in Napo over a series of weeks while learning to weave (*awana*) the net carrying bags (*shigra*) that people use to transport game, vegetable foods, fruits, and many other things. As I progressed in my task, I realized that the process of weaving, like the terminology itself, is an analogue to the reproduction of persons. Let me discuss how these bags are made.

Because shigra are woven downward, the central ring is first hung upside down from a wall by an attachment string. The net is expanded around the center point in a circular fashion, which creates the head (*uma*). The weaver continues to work downward through a process of expansion (making two loops out of a previous one) referred to as making children (*wawa rana*). When the body is finished, straps (*rigra,* or "arms") are attached. When the straps are extended in length and connected together, the bag is finished.

Weaving reflects personification. The analogy between the shigra and social life signals that social forms are not "given" but must be produced by people. It is no coincidence that, like weaving, people grow social forms as networks of relations in which almost everyone can trace some kind of a relation to everyone else. Like weavers, people make social forms by separating and connecting potentially infinite webs of relations. Social life, like weaving, makes cuts and ties up ends in strings of potentially infinite relations. The relevance of this native imagery, as an analogue to intersubjectivity and social-ity among the Runa, should become more salient throughout the following chapters.[8]

Getting There

No ethnography can be objective, and ethnographers do not cease to be human when they go into the field. As Michael Jackson relates, "lived experience overflows the boundaries of any one concept, any one person, or any one society" (1989:2). Our naïve habit of leaving out the ethnographer's lived experience and portraying ourselves as undisturbing observers is in fact a strategy for easing anxiety (Devereux 1967:3; Jackson 1989:4). While I explicitly acknowledge my participation and subjectivity in creating the knowledge this book represents, I do not make my subjectivity and self-reflexivity the focus. Rather, I focus on the social principles guiding intersubjectivity, or the pragmatic and conceptual processes by which people create and re-create themselves as viable social beings.

My journey to Ecuador began in the 1993 intensive Quichua program run by Frank Salomon and Carmen Chuquín at the University of Wisconsin–Madison. Not only did I learn Quichua grammar and vocabulary in this program; in addition, my teachers stressed that Quichua is linked to culture and that one cannot be divorced from the other. As I learned Quichua, I became fascinated that I lacked much of the implicit social and cultural knowledge to understand the words. The next summer the University of Virginia offered me departmental funding to study Quichua in Ecuador. Thanks to Renault Neubauer, a professor at the University of San Francisco de Quito, I came into contact with Luz María de la Torre, a linguist and indigenous leader from Otavalo. I studied Quichua with Luz María for almost the entire summer, acquiring a very basic command of the language. In my lessons Luz María reinforced the notion that Quichua is not merely a language but also a way of life, a way of seeing and acting in the world. This indigenous culture, she stressed, carries with it a great wisdom that is not appreciated by the dominant culture but is experienced and used daily by Quichua speakers.

On returning to the United States, I found out I had been selected to receive a Fulbright scholarship to begin a period of extended fieldwork among Quichua speakers. I was drawn to study Amazonian Quichua, mainly because I was interested in looking at highland-lowland cultural transformations. I returned to Ecuador (see map 1) with the intention of working in a Quichua-speaking indigenous community in the Napo region (see maps 2 and 3). Unfortunately, no one I met in Quito was willing to refer me to a specific fieldwork site. I met the people of Yacu Llacta through a tourist company that was owned and operated by community members. The tour introduced me to Amazonia and brought me into contact with the Napo Runa. I was surprised at the differences between the highland Quichua I had learned and the Napo dialect. Although people could understand what I said, they made fun of my pronunciation and vocabulary. After spending some days there, however, I offered to teach the guides and their families English in exchange for Quichua language and culture tutoring. They accepted this proposition.

After the tour my first days were spent helping out in a *minga* (collective labor party) for carrying stones, brought from the sandy and rocky areas of the Yacu Llacta River, to the site where they were building a basketball

Map 1. Ecuador (drawn by Stephen Holland; © Norman E. Whitten Jr., all rights reserved)

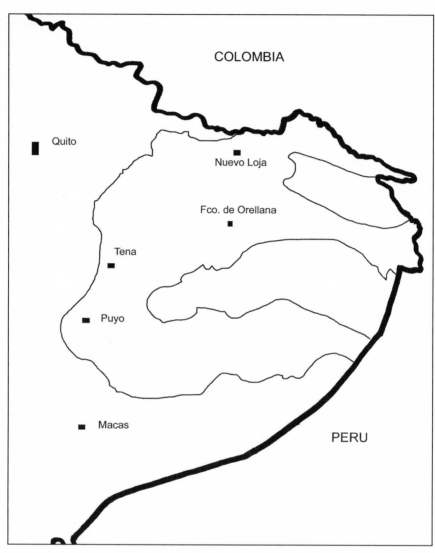

Map 2. Amazonian Quichua Speakers in Ecuador

COLOMBIA

Quito

Nuevo Loja
(Lago Agrio)

NAPO

SUCUMBIOS

Fco. de Orellana
(Coca)

Tena

ORELLANA

Puyo

PASTAZA

Macas

PERU

MORONA SANTIAGO

Map 3. Political Map of the Amazonian Region of Ecuador (adapted from Landá-
zuri 1989)

court. Because they held a minga two or three times a week, this presented an opportunity to demonstrate my willingness to help, which made a positive impression. Jorge, the community president at the time, appealed for people not to be lazy and threatened to impose fines on anyone who failed to show up. These fines were almost never enforced, however, and in response to the community need, each household sent at least one person (and manioc brew).[9] As people worked in the minga, they usually remained near family and friends. The social nature of the minga and the sharing of manioc brew made for a pleasant experience of *jumbi* (sweat) in which no one held the all-too-familiar sentiment of capitalist work: I'd rather be doing something else.

It was mainly through extensive participation and convivial living in Napo Runa culture that the data for this book were obtained. I entered the culture via the language, and my first year was spent gaining fluency in Napo Quichua and learning the important issues around which my hosts organized their lives. I spent that year pursuing questions of cosmology, myth narratives, and shamanism. However, I was deeply interested in nearly *everything* people did and how they did it. I was fascinated by morning bathing and table manners, by how people worked and spent free time, and by the stories they told. I was especially interested in fishing, which we did quite often. My many activities while in Yacu Llacta included helping the community to run its tourism business and build a museum and teaching people English. In return, the people of Yacu Llacta allowed me to live with them and to learn about their culture. I learned numerous things assisting with the tours, for we were able to walk for days in the forest, talking about plants, animals, and Napo Runa culture.

Another item of extreme interest to me was local gossip and everyday occurrences in the community. My solid foundation in Quichua language allowed me to follow most conversations after a relatively short period of time. Table manners were another issue, and learning to eat rainforest cuisine required a difficult adjustment at first. The social norms of this place demanded that I accept whatever food or drink was offered to me. Everything seemed strange, and I lacked the experience or tastes to appreciate the social norms associated with the food and drink. Drinking manioc brew became a necessity, since most daily activities and conversations featured it. I also had a few bad experiences with *aguardiente* (a distilled-alcohol beverage made from sugar cane), a substance I soon learned to consume with caution. I was exposed to many foods, including palm hearts, white cacao, caiman, palm grubs, and various kinds of fish and game. After some time I came to appreciate the taste and sociality of Amazonian cuisine. It became central to my experiences, relationships, and shared memories of the place.

After a while my life among the Runa became more complicated. I developed deeper and lasting relationships with my hosts and learned about their lives and values—and about my own, too. I discovered that our differences explained something about our common humanity and the human condition in general. The longer I stayed in the community, the more I realized that the Runa were changing me. Observing my many and subtle transformations, they judged that they were making me a better person. I learned new skills. My speaking abilities improved, and I developed joking relationships with people. I learned to walk through the forest—day or night—with fewer missteps, handle a machete without hurting myself, follow proper protocol in using the rivers and forest for disposing bodily wastes, and get around in a canoe without falling in the water. I learned to participate in the daily routine without having to be watched "like a child."

My Quichua host, Bancu, jokingly said to me one day: "Now you are not as much of a good-for-nothing person of European descent [mana valic rancia]." Although I had learned many of the difficult skills that are basic knowledge to most Quichua men, however, I never quite mastered them: I still sometimes tripped while walking in the forest, fell out of the canoe during fishing trips, and said the wrong things. This gap between my will to learn and my lack of success at being fully competent in Napo Runa culture made for many humorous situations. My Runa hosts constantly reminded me of my ambiguous status, mainly through joking and laughing. At times these jokes were painful and discouraging. At other times I enjoyed them and responded with my own humorous jibes.

The people I lived with were as surprised as I was, and even annoyed, when I succeeded in doing something they thought I could not or should not do. One day, bored, I took the fishing net and canoe upriver to see whether I could catch some *shikitu*, the small plentiful fish that feed on the algae lining the riverbed rocks. I was gone for hours and came back with what seemed like an embarrassingly small amount. I threw the bag of fish on the floor and proclaimed the trip a failure. Nevertheless, although I did not learn it at the time, this episode gained me the respect of my adoptive family in Yacu Llacta. I had become a producer of meat.

Toward the end of my first year of fieldwork, I had fallen in love with a bilingual and bicultural Quichua woman, Edith. This is not the place to recount the details of our private lives, but I will say that the decision to get married presented difficulties for both of us. For example, my host *ayllu* (family) had to acknowledge adopting me so as to provide the kinship relations necessary for an arrangement with Edith's ayllu and community. Later, as my kindred, my adoptive ayllu was obligated to assume, and enthusiastically accepted, the responsibility for completing the ritual fiestas of marriage so that the relationship would be legitimized. Our marriage became an intercommunity event, with the final ceremony uniting over three hundred people from my host community and Edith's, places that were over three hours apart (by bus and canoe). The process made me painfully aware that Runa marriage is not an individual but a relational affair in which people become the objects of other peoples' relationships. When my grant and visa ran out in the beginning of 1995, we returned to the United States, where I prepared my dissertation prospectus and sought funding to continue research and move on with our life together.

Eighteen months later we were able to return for my second period of field research. This time I had formulated different questions relating to complex issues surrounding everyday life. I saw that questions I had taken for granted in Yacu Llacta did not have easy answers. For example, when people referred to a *muntun* (extended-family household), how were these relationships conceptualized and constituted? I realized that people were not operating according to social principles of bounded groups; rather, they saw social life as fluid and relational, defined by pragmatic activities, concrete practices, and exchange. I turned my attention to the ways in which people create and produce social relations through the articulation of value forms.

When we returned to Ecuador, we decided to live in Ambatu Yacu, Edith's natal community. Ambatu Yacu is a rural community not far from a larger indigenous regional center, Pucara. The larger Pucara area was a good place to continue my research. Edith and I were asked by the community to work as English teachers in the bilingual, intercultural Quichua-Spanish school of Pucara. We began each day, sometimes long before dawn, with *wayusa* tea or manioc brew followed by fishing, weaving, or numerous other activities. We would then travel by foot or bicycle to Pucara, teach until the early afternoon, and return home. We spent the late afternoons and evenings tending crops, hunting and fishing, talking, building houses, and playing sports. In 1997 I fell ill with hepatitis A and typhoid fever and had to spend two weeks in the Catholic mission hospital in Archidona (where I received superb care). After recovering I returned to Ambatu Yacu to spend what time we had left and enjoy the vacation months away from teaching. In September we decided it was time to return to the United States.

Since 1997 I have returned to Ecuador multiple times and now consider

Napo to be my second home. Although coming and going is difficult, this constant movement has allowed me to reflect anthropologically on experiences in distinct cultural and physical worlds. As I have matured, I have worked my way deeper into the Napo Runa and anthropological life cycles. Time has given me new insights into kinship, marriage, and "adoption" from the Napo Runa perspective. My language skills and familiarity with stories and myths have grown. As an assistant professor I have had the opportunity to interact with students, teach about Amazonian cultures, and further reflect on and write ethnography. Furthermore, this book's ending presented itself only recently. The uprising of 2001, the focus of the final chapter, did not occur until after I had written my dissertation. Although I did not experience this event firsthand, my experience of its remembrance and memorialization inspired me to write about it.

Marriage to a local person in the community of study in itself need not give the researcher any advantage or disadvantage in fieldwork. Doing solid fieldwork requires that one first and foremost get a solid grasp of the local language, develop multiple and lasting interpersonal relationships, and pursue a research agenda that "fits" with the community's priorities. In Ecuador almost all the anthropologists who develop good relations with their indigenous research consultants are viewed as meaningful parts of those families with whom they work. As one indigenous leader from the highlands of Ecuador expressed to me, the problem is not the mere presence of anthropologists. Rather, he said, "the major problem is that they sometimes forget us. They don't realize how attached indigenous people become to them and how seriously we take it when we make them part of our families."

There is an assumption in the discipline that anthropologists need to maintain a "safe distance" from the people they study in the field (Geertz 1986:373). Distance is associated with professionalism, while closeness is associated with ethical impropriety. The pejorative phrase "going native" captures this stereotype of the anthropologist becoming too close to the native culture (E. Turner 1997). Distance and closeness, however, have little to do with professionalism. These rather vague terms fail to capture the nuances of anthropology as an intersubjective enterprise of mediating human relationships (Jackson 1998:97).

The American Anthropological Association's Code of Ethics provides precise language for thinking about the responsibilities that arise from one's personal and professional relationships with peoples and communities. The code states, "Anthropological researchers, teachers and practitioners are members of many different communities, each with its own moral rules or codes of ethics. Anthropologists have moral obligations as members of other groups, such as the family, religion, and community, as well as the profession." Anthropology is a unique profession in regard to ethics mainly because of the multiplicity of obligations to culturally diverse communities it entails. I fully agree with the idea, expressed in the code, that anthropologists' primary responsibilities lie with the people whose culture is being studied and, if appropriate, entail a commitment to promote their causes, an issue I return to and discuss in more detail in the final chapter.

Models of Identity in Napo

I once spent time in town with some young Quichua-speaking friends who began talking about how they liked to go into town, hang around discos, and drink and dance with other youth from Tena. I was surprised when they said that they had friends in town who thought that they were mestizos and did not know that they were Quichua speakers. One friend commented that this situation was difficult, for sometimes Quichua "just comes out by accident."

Many Quichua speakers who walk the streets of Tena are not easily identified as "indigenous" by appearance alone. Language is an important feature of identity, but almost all Quichua speakers also speak Spanish, and Quichua is not frequently spoken in urban public areas. There is also a growing (though certainly not dominant) population of indigenous youths who do not speak Quichua. Some urban youths whose parents speak Quichua do not consider themselves to be "natives," even if they, too, speak Quichua. I have heard people make statements such as "My mother is a native, but I am not." I have also heard urban Runa youths refer to Quichua-speaking girls from rural communities as *natis,* a derogatory term for "native." Many people of the older generation see urban life as problematic for Quichua ethnicity. They say, for example, that the Runa who live as white-mestizo people do are "weakened" because they eat city food and do not bathe in the cold rivers early in the morning.

Runa identities are complex and overlap with white-mestizo identities. This characteristic tension—of the white versus the indigenous and the rural versus the urban—has been a prominent feature of Runa identities in Upper Napo for centuries (Hudleson 1981; Oberem 1980; Macdonald 1979, 1999; Muratorio 1987, 1991). In the urban context, especially, it is difficult to see clear boundaries between Runa and mestizo cultural forms. Runa people, however, do not see themselves as an isolated group set off from the other populations with which they live. As I will try to show, Runa identities are defined by specific relational values and social forms rather than set within the abstract or essentialized idea of "being Runa."[10] These values and practices are rooted in forms of kinship, a complex that is often described or named as a muntun (literally a "pile or bunch" of relations, implying residence and consanguinity) or, synonymously, an ayllu.

Transculturation

The complexity of Amazonian Quichua social process can be found in the need to qualify the term *culture* as an analytical category when describing that process. For example, Hudleson (1981) has argued that lowland Quichua is a "transitional culture" that is moving from an authentic indigenous culture toward an acculturated mestizo one. The unidirectionality of this framework is problematic and assumes that Quichua identities are on a constant path toward acculturation and disappearance. As I will show, to assume that Napo Runa socioculture is simply disappearing in the face of the dominant culture is misinformed.

A more useful concept for describing Amazonian Quichua social process is transculturation (Oberem 1980),[11] which can be defined as "a shift in ethnic identity through intermarriage" (see Reeve 1985:16) and has roots in the fluid dynamics of Andean and Amazonian cultures (Uzendoski 2004a). Transculturation speaks to fluid boundaries across which identities are exchanged and transformed through intermarriage between different relational centers—which is also one of the defining characteristics of societies that archaeologists define as "tribal" (see Parkinson 2002:1–12). Social action among the Runa is persistently transcultural.

Amazonian Quichua might be thought of as a complex of multiple identities with *awallacta* (literally "highlander" but referring to white and mestizo people) and *auca* (savage) at the extremes (Reeve 1985). In the center stand other marriageable and exchangeable identities referred to as *Runapura*, meaning "humans among themselves"—under which fall various indigenous cultural and ethnic affiliations (such as Shuar, Pastaza Runa, and Otavalo). Reeve states that Runapura are "inherently kinsmen. They not only frequently intermarry, but are believed to share a common origin" (1985:22). In today's world of Upper Napo, indigenous people marry mainly those who would be classified as Runapura, but they marry people from the other categories, too. Increasing numbers of Runa are marrying mestizo people and even foreigners of European and North American descent. Transculturation is a two-way street, however, because seen from the Runa perspective, identities are not given but must be made (Viveiros de Castro 2001). Runa who marry outsiders do not simply lose their Runa identities, just as outsiders who marry in do not lose all their former identities. Former identities are consciously dissolved so that new ones can be built up. This dynamic of transcultural realities is generated by the symbolic, aesthetic, and ritual value forms of Napo Runa socioculture. Marriage among the Runa is essentially a transformative complex in which metamorphosis is made explicit as part of the value creation process.

Current Issues: Conviviality, Predation, and Value

I now briefly discuss some current issues in Native Amazonian studies to add further nuance to my larger argument about sociality and value. One topic provoking talk among Amazonianists is conviviality.[12] This talk springs from an innovative and insightful book edited by Joanna Overing and Alan Passes and entitled *The Anthropology of Love and Anger: The Aesthetics of Conviviality in Native Amazonia*.

In their preface the editors argue that Native Amazonian societies focus on the primary value of conviviality, which they define as "peacefulness, high morale and high affectivity, a metaphysics of human and non-human interconnectedness, a stress on kinship, good gifting-sharing, work relations and dialogue, a propensity for the informal and performative as against the formal and institutional, and an intense ethical and aesthetic valuing of sociable sociality" (Overing and Passes 2000:xiii). Conviviality here is offered as a dominant value among others, such as anger and hate. More broadly, the book adopts the theoretical position that Western frameworks of society distort the very processes they seek to comprehend. Alternative modes of theorization are thus required to better convey what society and social knowledge mean in Amazonian terms, a claim with which I agree completely. Working from this position, the fifteen essays in Overing and Passes's book demonstrate common philosophical principles of affective living that underlie various Native Amazonian cultures.

The editors, however, state that *all* Native Amazonian peoples hold as their practical and lived ideal "the tranquility of their social life and . . . the quality of its affective state of being" (Overing and Passes 2000:7; see also xii). Conviviality begins to break down here, for it is offered as a universal theoretical construct rather than as a value. While some peoples, such as the Amuesha, subscribe to complex ethnotheories of "love" that link the affective to the social and cosmological (see Santos-Granero 1991:201),[13] other Amazonian cultures view predatory themes as dominant in social life and cosmology (Viveiros de Castro 1992, 1996; Descola 1992, 1996a, 1996b; Taylor 1996). Descola (1996a:90), for example, has argued convincingly that "predation . . . appears to be the dominant value of the Jivaroan tribes of Eastern Ecuador and Peru." Herein lies the crux of the controversy. Whereas some Native Amazonians seem focused on values of love, others seem to be focused on hate (Taylor 1996).[14]

Conviviality undeniably captures something crucial about Native Amazonian modes of value and sociality. To dismiss it would be a mistake. Conviviality, for example, is a crucial and terribly important aspect of lived experience among the Runa. Nevertheless, conviviality and predation have yet to be analyzed sufficiently in theoretical terms. As Fernando Santos-Granero writes:

> Native Amazonian ideals about conviviality are not unattainable utopias. They find their fullest expression when settlements are growing, social relations are still close and intimate, and commonly held ideas still very much alive. But the ideals about the beautiful village and the perfect conviviality carry the seeds of their own destruction. . . . Larger settlements often promote internal conflicts. . . . What authors often fail to explain satisfactorily, however, is why this is so. (Santos-Granero 2000:283)

Value theory does seem to offer a more nuanced view of the relationship between conviviality and predation. Overing and Passes's (2000) use of conviviality as theory, I think, does not go far enough in problematizing the value question consonant with the work of current value theorists whose work I have mentioned earlier. The more convincing arguments about value are those that rigorously treat value as a problem of reproduction and internal relations rather than simply of individual traits. As Damon has argued, "discussions of the idea of value, independent of specific productive purposes and cycles, are bound to be murky, ultimately unsatisfactory, and at best just odd-job tools" (2002a:239).

This criticism is brawny, but the point helps to show why a lack of emphasis on production in convivality theory undermines its anthropological usefulness. Conviviality may be a "value," but it only scratches the surface of the value problem, which is more complex than any single kind of relation or emotional state (Rivière 2000:264). These arguments are equally applicable to predation theory, for predation is often only "the first moment" in the production of persons (Fausto 2000: 937). As I attempt to show in this book, even beginning to grasp what value might mean for the Napo Runa requires a multiplicity of perspectives and concepts that focus on confronting the native theory of reproduction.

Separations and Combinations: Substance Forms

The following chapters describe social action and reproduction in daily life
within rural Upper Napo. In describing and trying to translate social action,
I draw on a combination of concepts from Roy Wagner (1967), Frederick
Damon (1983, 1990), and Marilyn Strathern (1988). I take from Wagner the
notion that substance "relates" whereas exchange "defines." I will show
that the Runa invert this idea, however, for among them exchange relates
whereas substance defines. I take a circulatory perspective (i.e., an analysis
based on the totality of exchange) that reflects how people *transform* relations by building on previous sets of exchanges (Damon 1980, 1983, 1990).
I also use the distinction between same- and cross-substance versions of
relationships (Strathern 1988). Same-substance ties define relations within
the ayllu, whereas cross-substance relations create and combine relations
among *aylluguna* (pl. of *ayllu*).

Among Amazonian (and Andean) peoples, substances are understood to
give life as they flow through various domains: human, natural, and spiritual.
They are symbolically conceived and manifest in many practical domains.
Quichua speakers in Upper Napo talk about both *samai* (spirit or breath) and
yawar (blood) as essential substances of kinship. Samai, however, is within
all things that have life. As José Palacio states eloquently in *Muerte y vida
en el río Napo:* "All things and man have *samai*. . . . Vital energy in its different manifestations is *samai*. . . . The Napo Runa rarely speak of the soul,
and when they do it, it is in a lazy form. What they know and experience is
samai" (1991:15).[15]

From the Napo Runa point of view, physical substance includes spiritual
substance and vice versa; samai is the inner perspective of the material world
and the social person, a theme present throughout this book. Napo Runa
notions of substance are difficult to translate using the English language and
the Western concepts embedded in it. Long ago the famous anthropologist
Edmund Leach reminded us that "anthropologists . . . must re-examine
basic premises and realize that English language patterns of thought are not
a necessary model for the whole of human society" (1961:27).

My cultural analysis focuses on the Runa terms and categories analogous to
these anthropological theories, not the anthropological theories themselves.
The idea of substance itself is problematic, for the general understanding
of this term reflects the English-language thought pattern of biological re-
latedness (Schneider 1968). I have found that writing ethnography requires
the creative use of language, both in redefining the senses and meanings of

some English words and in using native terms. One term that I have chosen to redefine is *substance*.

To highlight translation difficulties with concepts of substance in South America, I draw on the work of the Quechua poet, novelist, and anthropologist José María Arguedas. In *Deep Rivers* the book's protagonist, Ernesto, speaks of the Inca walls as seething with energy and speaking to him. He likens the walls to a bloody river:

> The stones of the Inca wall were larger and stranger than I had imagined; they seemed to be bubbling up beneath the whitewashed second story. . . . Then I remembered the Quechua songs which continually repeat one pathetic phrase: *yawar mayu,* "bloody river"; *yawar unu,* "bloody water." . . . The wall was stationary, but all its lines were seething and its surface was as changeable as that of the flooding summer rivers which have similar crests near the center, where the current flows the swiftest and is the most terrifying. The Indians call these muddy rivers *yawar mayu* because when the sun shines on them they seem to glisten like blood. (Arguedas 1978:7)

By associating the river with blood, Arguedas evokes the idea that nature and humanity contain the same life essences; like blood, the river contains the energy that flows through all things. Ernesto is able to feel this underlying energy—the current—by touching the walls (which speak to him, too). The idea of a shared and constantly circulating life force reflects not only a cosmology of substance but also a predilection to personify human-nature and human-object relations. Such relations abound in *Deep Rivers,* and they are not simply superstition. For example, Ernesto is able to survive, psychologically and pragmatically, the harsh realities of racism and poverty found in highland Peru through his connection to the Andean "deep river."

An English translator of Arguedas's work, Francis Barraclough, told me of his difficulties in translating the terms and concepts of substance when moving from the South American ideas to English ones. For English, he told me, substance seems to imply weight and boundedness ("a man of substance"), whereas native concepts, such as those found in Arguedas's books, refer to flow. Barraclough once asked a Quechua speaker to bring him the *sustancia* (substance) of some potatoes. He thought she would bring him the potatoes themselves and was surprised when she brought him the water in which she had boiled them (Barrclough, personal letter, Dec. 12, 2002).

Translation

These complexities of translation might contain in them a lesson that speaks
to my particular humanistic view of doing anthropology. Anthropology has
always been shy of presenting the ethnographer's difficulties and struggles
in translating native forms. Indeed, the typical set of exchange and social
relations that underlie ethnographic work are not incorporated in the analysis itself. Cultural analyses are presented as finished and definitive works
about other cultures. I find something arrogant in this process. Moreover,
sometimes no one but the specialist can comprehend the bulk of the anthropological account.

Part of the difficultly lies in our unexamined assumptions about the exchanges between the anthropologist and the native during fieldwork. Much
of anthropology still goes by a colonialist folk model: the anthropologist gives
the natives manufactured or technological things (e.g., cigarettes, machetes,
beads, and money), and the "natives" give the ethnographer information
about their culture. These assumptions, and the implicit power relations that
define them, later become translated and reworked into ethnographies as an
objective account of the native culture in question. The boundaries between
native and ethnographer become reified and invented as an objectivity of
cultural boundaries in this process (Wagner 1981). Ethnographies appear as
things divorced from the social and symbolic processes and many exchanges
that create them.

The conditions of contemporary ethnographic fieldwork are not nearly so
"colonial," however, for native peoples are no longer as enamored of manufactured goods or as compelled by colonial structures to give information as
they may have been previously. Pierre Clastres, for example, speaks of that
earlier era when he relates how the Atchei were being "hunted" and killed
by whites while he lived with them on their "protector's" property, a white
man's hacienda. The Atchei could not escape Clastres. He writes, "I had to
bargain with death; with patience and cunning, using a little bribery (offers
of presents and food, all sorts of friendly gestures, and gentle, even unctu-
ous language), I had to break the Strangers' passive resistance, interfere with
their freedom, and make them talk. It took me about five months to do it"
(Clastres 1998:97).

Today the world is different, with many indigenous peoples having read
histories and anthropological accounts about them. Indigenous peoples make
movies, fight injustices, and promote their value systems and cultural forms.
These are not the powerless Atchei of Clastres's epoch. We might speak of

an indigenous renaissance, a "reconquista" to right the world's misunderstandings and crimes against the indigenous. From the first day I came to Yacu Llacta, for example, the success or failure of my project depended on my willingness to submit to Runa sociocultural norms and to reciprocate. I never received or gave something outside the context of a tangible social relationship—my every move was judged and watched carefully. Initially, as the account with Jorge shows, I was distrusted as a *rancia,* someone who takes more than he gives. Perhaps these new conditions of ethnography make visible and necessary the ethnographer's *subjectivity* in creating anthropological knowledge (see Wagner 2001:6–7).

I invoke subjectivity to suggest not that ethnographies must be fictions or biased but rather that they cannot be divorced from one's perspective and process of attaining knowledge, a perspective that changes throughout life in any event but especially through fieldwork experiences. Perhaps we might leave ethnographies as unfinished works of translation (Sammons and Sherzer 2000) rather than view them as totally objective, finished analyses. Like translations that try to translate untranslatable works (such as Arguedas's *Deep Rivers*), accounts of other cultures might make the interactions, conflicts, and intensity of ethnographic work more apparent and analyzable. We might also, as Goulet suggests, "experience this qualitatively different world of . . . spirits, and . . . incorporate such experiences in ethnographic accounts" (1994:16). Such an endeavor produces not a distancing or subordination of the other peoples and their cultures but a process of creating relations that shows the complexity of "knowing" culture. In leaving behind the idea that ethnographies are fully objective accounts of cultures, I am happy to acknowledge that the native people remain the experts and last authority on their systems of knowledge. I, the ethnographer, remain a humble apprentice of Napo Runa knowledge. In trying to know "them," I have also learned much about myself and the workings of the anthropological gaze on the other (Taussig 1993:16).

Presentation of the Book

This book presents various social perspectives on the Napo Runa system of producing value. In chapter 1 I describe the production of persons and masculine and feminine personhood through an examination of severing and connecting actions that begin at birth. I translate the beginning forms of substance relations associated with new life and parenthood and argue that the birth process itself shapes people into gendered beings with strong wills.

Napo Runa notions of "love," or *llakina,* are discussed in relation to these processes of soul and body formation. I hypothesize that Napo Runa notions of gender derive from masculine and feminine complementarity, a principle that is examined from contrasting perspectives of masculine dominance and feminine strength and their respective affective associations.

In chapter 2 I show that the forces of samai, substance, and convivial life are configured by an aesthetics of shape-shifting, the transformation into animal or other power alters. I analyze a myth, a song, evangelical Christian discourses, humor, and other forms of expression. Shape-shifting is demonstrated to be both a principle of shamanism and a concept inherent to Napo Runa notions of kinship and social process. With the ability to elicit transformative powers and substances from multiple worlds, Napo Runa aesthetic forms create people as entities defined by cosmic bodies.

In chapter 3 I elaborate on these transformative principles in the context of marriage rituals (*tapuna, pactachina,* and *bura*). Marriage is discussed as a theater for creating the main productive relationship in Napo Runa culture: the cross-substance relation of masculine and feminine complementarity. I show how the transformations of marriage are expressed through gift exchange, music, ritual action, and ritual discourse. I argue that marriage is the defining ritual among the Napo Runa and serves to transform not only people and their relational bodies but also entire communities. Marriage severs and recombines the relations that define ayllu and muntun networks of kinship.

In chapter 4 I examine the theory of value behind exchange behaviors (giving versus reciprocity) and look at further separations and unions that occur after marriage. Specifically, I analyze the same-substance relations of affinal incorporation, adoption, *compadrazgo* (ritual kinship), and marriage alliances. I argue that these forms of kinship are expressed through the transformation of substance via ritual action, sharing, and reciprocity. These forms guide the metamorphosis of affines into consanguines. I argue that these high-value relationships connect people to one another through woven networks of shared substance relations that span the region.

In chapter 5 I explore how personification is linked to the production of things and the overall theory of production, consumption, and circulation. I look at the system of exchange, circulation, and value creation as mediating and satisfying the desires of others. I argue that giving gifts of manioc brew and meat transforms kinship relations in both everyday and, especially, ritual contexts. Meat and manioc brew are complementary and gendered spheres of exchange. This configuration is patterned on the larger Napo Runa philosophy of producing life by mediating desires through exchanges of things and substances among complementary others. In this regard, masculine and feminine exchanges are central to everyday and ritual life.

In the book's final chapter I argue that significant political consequences are at stake in the way value is viewed. I analyze the February 2001 indigenous uprising in Napo in the context of the ways in which notions of value, person, and exchange permeate historical consciousness. Kinship is elucidated as defining not only social praxis but also historical consciousness and centuries of conflict with neocolonial forces. I explore how the Napo Runa person—one connected to others and nature through bodily cosmology—is inhabited by the subjectivity of *pachacutic* (transformation). I end by arguing that the Napo Runa person is transforming history, Napo province, other sectors of Ecuadorian society, and beyond. The book's final layer is the linkage of value to issues of subalternity (Gregory 1997; Piot 1999; Guha 1983) and concerns with indigenous social and economic self-determination (Whitten and Torres 1998; Whitten 1996, 2003; García 2001, 2002; Whitten, Whitten, and Chango 1997).

1

Sinzhi Runa: The Birth Process and the Development of the Will

> *They believe in metempsychosis. . . . when I asked an elder of the village who knew a little Spanish and was considered the most educated what he thought was the soul, he instantly answered me that it was a breath of air, that leaving the human body it entered into the body of an animal and when that died, it went into another body again.*
> —Gaetano Osculati (1846–48:96–97), traveler and scientist, interviewing a Napo Runa person about his concept of the soul

I begin by thinking through the tropes of "strengthening" (*sinzhiyachina*) and "straightening" (*dirichuyachina*) children. I heard these terms constantly in talk about children and their growth and states of social maturity. I later realized that they were linked to a greater philosophy of life involving relationships among internal and external states of personhood, cosmology, and social values. Sinzhiyachina and dirichuyachina reflect the problematic nature of translating implicit concepts of "what goes without saying" (see Bloch 1992, 1998) from one culture to another.[1] Napo Runa socioculture shapes birth and the upbringing of children through the development of the will, a social awareness and power it locates in the human heart (*shungu*). The will becomes visible ethnographically through an analysis of the way children are made into viable social beings with gendered identities. According to Napo Runa culture, the will is not "given" at birth. It inhabits the body but must be formed.

I learned about sinzhiyachina and dirichuyachina not only as people used these terms to describe their children and one another but also as they applied them to me. One day, while helping carry stones up a riverbank, I slipped and fell down the slope. A group of women laughed loudly at me, saying that I was a "child" because I could not "stand up straight" and hold my ground like a "man." They also said that I was "soft" and referred to my body as soft (*chuclu*). They said, "We have bodies that are taut. European people's bodies are soft corn." (Can wawara angui, api, chuclu. Ñucanchi tingli aichara charinchi, runaguna. Ranciaguna chuclu aichara charinaun.)

Once I learned these implicit concepts of hard versus soft and of adult-child relations, I was able to employ them myself. One day I responded to these same women, saying that I was not soft but rather "as strong [*sinzhi*] as the peach-palm [*chonta*] tree," a remark that was received with much laughter. I had also learned that the term *apayaya* means "a strong man." I would use this term often, in the way that young men would use it, to affirm that I, too, was not soft and that I was a man. The women soon turned my overuse of the word into another joke: they made it my *burlashuti* (Quichua nickname).

The Completed Person

In indigenous Napo, value is created through a dialectical process of divesting persons of certain properties, things, and relations so that new ones can be constructed (Strathern 1988; Mosko 1995; Piot 1999). My subject matter is the *completed person* and the modes of social action and reproduction that define the notion. Following La Fontaine, I define the completed person as "the product of a whole life" in which moral worth is not individual but resides in "the social form, which includes as a vital element the maintenance of continuity. The concept serves to fuse the finite span of a human life with the unlimited continuity of social forms, by identifying personhood with self-reproduction" (La Fontaine 1985:132).

The first point I take from La Fontaine is her focus on social forms of personhood, not the individual, as the unit of analysis. Furthermore, La Fontaine suggests that using the concept of the completed person means seeing how its continuous forms articulate with finite human lives. The completed person is a product of *reproduction,* the manner in which both humans and the social forms that define them persist over time.

With regard to the kinship forms of Upper Napo, the transformational steps of kinship identities reflect a dynamic view of personhood as composed of both finite and open-ended qualities. I see the basic unit of analysis as the specific social actions and relations that constitute personhood. Personhood begins as a parent-child substance relationship with the production of new life. To understand personhood as an *open-ended* category, however, I must first look at how people are reproduced as *finite* beings.

Runa Models of Growth: Strengthening and Straightening

Runa notions of growth and maturation center on tropes of strengthening and straightening the body. Runa people describe their babies as "soft" (*llullu*) and "little" (*shituwa*). This emphasis on softness represents experiences with babies' vulnerability and less well defined bodies. In Runa communities babies often fall ill and sometimes die. Of the many diseases that attack the young, those that cause diarrhea are of special concern.

The inability of babies to resist sickness is directly related to the proposition that they are less strengthened than adults and are relatively formless as physical and social beings. Babies are viewed as totally dominated by corporeal desires. They cannot talk, walk, or produce anything of value. They take up the time of their mothers and other relatives who watch them. They fall down and become injured easily. The characterization of babies as soft is more than just a description of their bodies, however. It is a statement about their personhood and psychological development.

When babies are described, people usually employ the term *causana* (to live) or *wañuna* (to die). The former connotes a state of health and vitality; the latter, a state of illness. Babies are "dying" just as often as they are "living," for illness is common. Babies also lack *iyai*, or thought. People believe that babies desire mainly nourishment, love, warmth, and safety. Mothers see the *chuchu* (breast) as the archetypal object of infant desire and believe maternal milk to be the ideal nourishment for babies. Moreover, mothers are constantly concerned with their babies' "antidesires," their inability to control excretion cycles or avoid illness. When babies are healthy, desire is normally the order of the moment. When babies are sick, however, antidesires become primary.

Like those in many cultures, Runa mothers say they begin to feel love for a child even before it is born, and they constantly touch it, talk to it, and speculate as to its future. The mother-child bond is the first and most intimate relation in Runa society. It is never forgotten. Runa children have only one "true" mother (*mama*), but lots of other women assist in the mothering role. This love, moreover, is not just a feeling. It is thought to make the child grow, to become strong. Babies who are not loved are said to be *pucchi,* or perennial runts, for love is thought to transfer bodily energy from mother to child. Love is a means of substance nourishment, a complement to bodily feeding directed at the development of strength.

Mother and baby stay in close bodily contact for most of the day. Mothers sleep with their babies and breast-feed them many times each day. Mothers carry their babies in an *aparinga,* a shoulder-slung cloth wrapping that keeps the baby snug against the mother's back. If the mother goes to work in the garden or to perform some task in the forest, she will remove the baby from the aparinga when she gets there and construct a makeshift hammock. She does this by placing two posts in the ground and suspending the aparinga between them. Mothers keep watch over their babies and periodically swing the hammock slowly to keep the child occupied and discourage insects. When the mother leaves, she must be careful to remove the posts and hide them, for it is believed that if they are left standing, a forest spirit (*supai*) may sense the child's presence and subsequently cause harm during the night.

The Birth of a Child

Pierre Clastres writes: "Every birth is experienced dramatically by the group as a whole. It is not simply the addition of an individual to one family, but a cause of imbalance between the world of men and the universe of invisible forces; it subverts an order that ritual must attempt to reestablish" (1998:16). Similarly, Napo Runa socioculture shapes the birth process in unique ways. In 2001 I returned to Yacu Llacta to visit the ayllu with which I had lived during most of 1994. Things had changed. My host brother, Galo, had gotten married while I had been away, and his wife was pregnant. As we talked over a bowl of manioc brew, I was told that Marta was expected to give birth any day. The ayllu was busy preparing for this important event and asked me to help. I decided to stay a few extra days.

Bancu, Galo's father, asked me to go to Santa Yacu, a community on the Napo River with a nursing station and an on-call doctor. The plan was to bring the doctor back to Yacu Llacta to assist in delivering Marta's child. Bancu's brother, a trained nurse, also lived in Santa Yacu, and we could pick up medical supplies there. Arriving after a few hours on a bus, we went to the nursing station. The doctor was not there, and no one knew when he would be back.

Rather than just return home, we decided to wait to see whether the doctor would come. The women of Santa Yacu remembered me from a wedding I had attended in their community years back. They offered us one, then another, and then yet another very large bowl of the manioc-banana brew called *warapu.* I drank these slowly while conversing about my life in the United States and Ambatu Yacu.

I tried to entertain them with the esoteric Quichua phrases and expressions I had learned. Bancu, an extremely knowledgeable person, had been teaching me "old" words not used much by young people. One such word, *tsiuca,* conveys someone who is dirty, as in "tsiuca runa" (dirty person). Another term, *quilonso,* expresses a lethargic person, as in "quilonso warmi" (lethargic woman). I also invoked the phrase *amushun* (let's drink together) a few times; this particularly powerful social term of dualism obligates another person to drink in mirror image with the speaker.

Unfortunately the doctor never returned. A bit dejected, we took the bus back to Yacu Llacta after buying the essential medical supplies: an injection to help induce labor, gauze bandages, and pain relievers. During the ride home, and full of manioc brew, I remember having a strong urge to relieve myself. I complained to Fermin quietly, "Ishpanayan" (I have to urinate). Bancu told me that I had to hold it, even if I were "dying." We finally arrived, I urinated, Bancu laughed, and we hiked home.

In the early morning Marta began the long process of labor. The house came alive and grew full of nervous energy and conversation. Someone had summoned a midwife, an elder woman from a neighboring household. No one ate breakfast. Marta, the midwife, was with the other women in a closed-off room. Bancu asked me to shave bits of a giant armadillo claw into a glass. Marta would drink an infusion of these shavings, which are said to make the child slide out easily. Bancu prepared the canoe in case of complications.

Afraid that something tragic might happen, I asked Bancu, "Why not take Marta to Tena so that she can give birth in the hospital?" I offered to pay the bill. Bancu responded, "We want her to give birth here in the forest our way. When we take our women to the hospital, the doctors there are too quick to cut them up. Our women are not like city folk. They need to be strong [sinzhi] to cultivate manioc." Bancu then told me that he would accept my offer only if there were complications.

Although I was not inside the birthing room, I caught glimpses of the events through the spaces in the bamboo walls. Marta's hands were tied to a beam in the roof, and her body was oriented vertically. The midwife was under Marta, poised to "catch" the child when it came out. Labor went on for a long time. It was Marta's first child, and the first delivery can be difficult. I remember that during some tense moments, I was asked to prepare manioc brew for Marta to drink. Galo told me, "Make some manioc brew for Marta! She will need the strength. Make sure that you make it thick, not watery!" I also asked the midwife if there would be complications. She responded, "I have delivered twelve babies successfully. This one will be all right. I measured the width of Marta's bones [showing me her hand], and they are fine. The baby will come." For many hours Marta had been soundless during the process. Runa women bear their pain silently. Only a few times did I hear her slight and muffled sounds of pain or discomfort, but most of the noise was made by the midwife and Bancu's ayllu. A few hours later a loud cry rang out, followed by the sound of fluids hitting the floor. A new life had emerged. It was a little girl, a "warmi wawa" (female child). I was asked whether I had a fresh razor blade, which I did, and they used it for cutting the umbilical cord. They then invited me into the room after the baby was washed and the miracle was over.

No one had eaten all day. During the final hours of Marta's labor, Bancu had killed a few chickens, and we had helped remove their feathers and prepare them for making soup. The men—Galo, Bancu, and myself—did all the cooking. Bancu said to me, laughing, "This is torture, torture [*tormintus, tormintus*]!" I still remember him chopping carrots awkwardly while Marta was in the final stages. I also remember having a deep admiration for this ayllu and the people involved. Bancu and his ayllu managed this stressful and risky process with a great amount of dignity and mutual respect. Never did I observe or hear of a single disagreement or moment of confusion. My presence, which might have been potentially disruptive during such an intimate moment, seemed natural. My respect for Bancu and his ayllu grew.

After Birth

Among the Runa newborn babies are wrapped in cloth bindings, called *chumbi,* when they are put to bed. When I asked people why they did this, they told me that the wrapping helps the babies to sleep at night and makes them grow straight, not crooked. They also told me that the wrappings help to concentrate and protect the baby's life force from the cold, spirits, and *mal aire* (evil wind). Another person commented that the wrappings represent the life force of the anaconda. The wrapping gives children a colorfully patterned outer skin that mimics the anaconda's. This mimetic connection is not trivial, for the anaconda is thought to be the originator of life itself and signifies the power of procreation. This relationship is sometimes evoked by likening the anaconda to the human penis. As Whitten and Whitten (1988:33) write, "Mythically, humans and the *amarun* [anaconda] share a common corporeal substance. The *amarun* is to the water world what the male human is to his household and to his family: the primary procreator." A fetus will float, kick, turn, and twist; consequently, as one pregnant woman remarked, "When in the womb, the baby feels like an anaconda." These associations are eloquent, aesthetic ways of stating the unique nature of children's bodies. They are not yet human. Closer to divinity, their softness and fluidity of form must be shaped into human substance by their parents and other relatives.

The Runa take great care to protect their "soft" babies. In the first month after birth, for example, a mother should not allow anyone but her husband to hold the child. People say that if she were to let another person hold her child, it will turn out to be *kibirishca* ("twisted"). The baby would cry a lot and turn blackish green, as would his or her feces. After this period other people are allowed to hold the child, but they must first ritually pass it, head first, through their legs. This action establishes a symbolic mothering bond—allowing "straightness" and health to pass between the child and the person wanting to hold it. Also, a mother must not wash her baby's clothing with any twisting motion, for it is believed that if the mother twists in the washing, the baby's growth will become twisted, too.

Babies are especially vulnerable to spirits and to ghosts called *aya*, which are more likely to be present at night, near burial sites, or close to fast-moving water. These locations are avoided for fear that they will cause illness to the child. Mothers must be careful not bathe their babies often, for the cold of the water and its elements weakens them. Moreover, mothers must abide by dietary rules referred to as *sasina* ("to follow taboo"). For two weeks they should eat only the meat of free-range chickens and other birds,[2] because "birds sleep well at night." Should the mother eat nocturnal game, it is said, the baby will mimetically acquire the animals' qualities, staying up all night without sleeping.

Fathers abide by couvade restrictions also termed sasina.[3] Some days after the birth of Galo's daughter, a group of men were playing a pickup soccer game. Galo, normally a strong player, was dressed for the game yet sat on the sidelines. I asked, "Galo, why aren't you playing? Are you injured?" He responded, "Sasinimi," or "I am fasting." Galo meant he was not playing because of the recent birth of his daughter. The Runa understand the concept of sasina to mean, typically, abstention from specific kinds of game, heavy physical activity, and sex. Runa men say that these restrictions were observed for months in the past, but abstention is still practiced for at least a few weeks after the birth of a child.

At first I considered Galo's behavior to be trivial. Nevertheless, this simple act and the commentary with it can be shown to represent, in a most casual but esoteric way, the whole of Napo Runa cosmology and social philosophy of kinship. Fasting constitutes a way of mediating not just a birth but also the substance and circulatory forms surrounding the new life and body that the birth brings into the world. For example, Métraux summarizes the couvade with reference to Native Amazonian views on cosmology, personhood, and the body: "The observance of 'couvade' restrictions often have been interpreted by Indians themselves as an expression of the close bond between the father and the infant's clinging soul" (1949:374). In other words, the couvade and the substance and health of the soul are intertwined.

The couvade demonstrates the complex cosmological and symbolic principles of animism in Amazonia and the circulation of energy between visible and invisible realms. It is part of a larger complex of views and beliefs about cosmology, personhood, society, and the body. During the sasina period Runa fathers and mothers resist eating anything that could harm or damage the child. They say that if the restrictions are not followed, the child will develop improperly. The child might grow crooked, turn colors, or become weak and ill from diarrhea or another sickness. The couvade is thought to spiritually feed the child, a process described as *pucuchina* (to make grow), the transference of vital energy or "breath" from parents to child. In the logic of the symbolism, the parents' abstention feeds and strengthens the child's soul substance, or samai. Rival (1998), too, has argued that the couvade links a father to his child, and to its mother, by a substance tie that is independent of marriage and residence. Rival's point is insightful: the couvade marks the creation of a new human life that complicates the boundaries of consanguineal versus affinal distinctions that hover over a new marriage. It differentiates the parents from previous statuses of less-complete personhood (Rival 1998:633). The couvade is a birth right of kinship itself.

The Runa do not cut a child's hair before it reaches its second year, for they believe that the baby would turn out *upa shimi*, or mute, were they to do so. As a child develops, people will comment on its development and begin to say that the "meat has taken" ("aicha aparishca"). The presence of "meat"—bulk rather than thinness—on a child is a sign of health (Runa people like plump babies, but their infants rarely appear fat). After cutting the child's hair, it is appropriate to begin looking for *compadres* (coparents): the *marcamama*, or godmother, and the *marcayaya*, or godfather (see chapter 4).

Adolescence

When children are old enough, the Runa say, they should be made to bathe in a cold river during the early morning hours. According to the Runa, children, especially boys, should pound the water with their fists as they bathe in the cold water. They should bathe in the middle of the river, not near the side.

It is also thought that one should squat in the water and grab hold of small black stones as a means of acquiring strength. This ritualistic bathing gets the blood flowing, and the river itself is thought to strengthen body and soul.

It is also emphasized that children should not sleep too much or be lazy (*killa*). People punish children who sleep too much or avoid doing domestic tasks. Older relatives living nearby, especially the father's and mother's siblings, tease children and provide coparenting in this way. Adults make fun of children who are troublesome, curious, meddlesome, too talkative, or demanding. They call children such names as "puñui siki" (sleepy head), "mishki siki" (sweet tooth), "killa wawa" (lazy child), and "iris illa" (bothersome), among others. To teach in this way is *burlana,* a kind of joking that might be translated as "making fun of" or "shaming."

Burlana: Teaching by Humor and Shame

Parents make fun of and shame their children, but to a lesser degree than the children's siblings and affines do. Aunts' and uncles' relations to nephews and nieces are special in this regard. In Spanish people generally refer to an adult occupying a pole in this asymmetrical relation as *tío* or *tía*. The relationship includes each parent's siblings as well their siblings' spouses. Usually, however, certain aunts and uncles will take a special interest in a given nephew or niece, with location determining this. Some parents further solidify the secondary parenting role of their siblings and siblings' spouses by making them godparents.

Guillu used to tease his older sister's child, Añangu, about his sweet tooth. Guillu made fun of Añangu at evening meals by asking him if he wanted a caramel stick, then if he wanted a sucker, then if he wanted a cookie, and so on. Añangu would grow more upset with each candy named, causing Guillu to laugh. Guillu always finished his list with the *chocobanana,* one of the sweets Añangu liked most. When Guillu got to chocobanana, Añangu would always explode with rage. Among other things, he would cry and threaten to punch Guillu. Añangu knew when he was being teased, but he was powerless to avenge himself. His moment of rage inevitably produced a roar of laughter in the kitchen. Once Guillu had produced a reaction in Añangu, he would stop, and Añangu's mother would then comfort him. Guillu would repeat the ritual in a few days, and each new performance would provoke as much laughter as had the last.

Children learn to employ similar tactics as they mature. I was surprised to find that a group of young brothers, sisters, and cousins of three to six years old had already developed a series of *burla,* or "joke," names for one another. In Ambatu Yacu I heard children referring to each other as *awallacta* (highlander), *varón* (male), *chuchola* (a mispronunciation of *chucula,* a mashed banana drink), and various other burla names.

Punishment

The Runa use humor to point out aspects of unwanted behavior, but they believe that punishment, too, is sometimes essential to making children "strong" and teaching them respect (*respeto*). During my fieldwork I saw many examples of child castigation and heard many stories of adults recounting the punishments they received as children. The Quichua say that they now punish their children less than before, but the punishments I observed were vigorously applied.[4] Runa parents punish their children not because they are mean but rather because they believe that punishment is necessary to instill proper values, behavior, and mindfulness. Parents say that their children are "soft," and punishment is necessary to strengthen their bodies and minds—to make them sinzhi—as well as to teach them to listen to their parents (*uyana*). Parents also note that, by punishing their children, they are making them "straight," or dirichu.

The most common punishment is to spank the child or slap his or her hand. Some women prefer to pinch the child's earlobe with their fingernails. Children wail loudly during and after such punishment, even if the physical pain is minimal. Mothers then send the child away and threaten more punishment if the crying continues.

A more serious punishment is to put capsicum pepper in the mouth, on the lips, or in the eyes. Capsicum plants (*uchu*) abound, and all aylluguna cultivate them in relative abundance. Normally uchu is placed in the mouth or on the lips if the child is unruly during a meal or does not wish to eat. Mothers sometimes put a tiny bit of uchu on their nipples to "punish" a child that demands breast milk too often. Little children do not receive capsicum in the eyes; this punishment is reserved for active and unruly older children, and its administration takes on a visible character. Punished children are sent running to the river to wash out their eyes, and they cry dramatically. They will then sit down and cry until the pepper's "life force" (*causai*) dies down.

Another common punishment is to strike the child with the stems and leaves of *chini,* a plant with stinging nettles. Chini grows abundantly in a variety of species and stinging powers, and it is always found near houses. I have heard stories of parents first hitting their children with chini and then applying capsicum pepper to the eyes. These common kinds of punishment stand out as defining memories in people's lives.

Once children reach the age of five or six, they begin contributing to the household by fetching things, and other expectations are placed on them as they get older. Boys usually fetch water, firewood, and heavier items. Girls are expected to help in the kitchen, wash dishes, and watch younger siblings. Children are taught responsibility for all their tasks, and they are punished if they disobey their parents' orders or if they make an error (*pandachina*). Children are punished for laziness, lying (*llulla*), stealing (*shuwa*), improper eating, and a host of other transgressions.

Children are rarely punished for fighting among themselves, and those in a given area always display a pecking order. Children know whom they can hit and whom they cannot; that is, they are aware of their superiority or subordination to other children. Fights rarely occur, however, and when they do, they do not last long. Such fights are always followed by a lot of crying from the loser. Parents sometimes punish the "winner" for hitting a smaller sibling or cousin, but more likely the parents will punish the "loser" for crying. I heard parents say that they tolerate a small degree of fighting among their children so that they learn to defend themselves. A weak child will be abused, beaten up, and harassed constantly if not capable of fighting back. People seek to raise willful and strong children, not meek or passive ones.

In the mid-nineteenth century Osculati observed a similar ritual use of tobacco and chini in the punishment of children. He writes of uchu, "It is brutal, the way that they punish their boys. . . . Most of the time they finish by throwing pepper into the eyes of the offender, leaving him completely blind for several hours and able to escape the pain only after washing thoroughly in the river" (Osculati 1846–48:100–101).

Adults told me many tales of their childhood punishments. I was surprised that almost all remembered these painful experiences as positive and "loving" (*llakina*). They believe that uchu improves eyesight, mainly night vision, and that its odor wards off evil spirits and jaguars. The chini's nettles contain a liquid with medicinal properties. The plant is believed to have a general cleansing effect on the body and be good for the muscles. It is also used ritualistically before hunting or shamanistic rituals. People associate these "punishments" with strengthening and maturation. These memories of punishment, mockery, and fighting all go into the way people conceptualize their inner strength, which they receive through the love and toughness of their parents and other elders.

The Notion of Soul and Body

The circulatory relation between the parent and the child begins at conception. The Runa do not believe that conception is a matter merely of fertilization. They believe that the man "puts" the baby into the woman's womb, and the woman's substance combines with man's in the long process of forming and finishing the child. For example, a few people told me that after a baby is conceived, the man must continue to have sex with the woman so that "the child will grow strong." Others claimed the exact opposite, that sex should be stopped so that "the child can grow well"—although both strategies trade on the idea that a child "pulls" out the father's energy. Either way, behind Runa notions of growth lies the idea that the baby, as a bodily form, contains the incipient manifestation of its parents' combined vital energies (Tomoeda 1993). Again, *samai* means "vital energy," but the term connotes soul substance, too. The Runa feel that sexual substances are manifestations of one's life force. Women encompass and "cook" semen, thereby creating and shaping new life. Linked to this idea is the complaint I often heard from men: that sex makes them feel "tired" and drained.

In the creation of a new life, blood (*yawar*) and breath create a substance shared between parent and child. This opposition roughly corresponds to a notion of body and soul, but not the Western dichotomy, for the Runa do not philosophically separate the two realms. The soul is simply the inner perspective of the body (Viveiros de Castro 1998). The notion that people inherit a simultaneously corporeal and spiritual substance from their parents differs markedly from related Western notions. In the Runa world "religion" lies within the domain of kinship and animates the notion of personhood.

The Runa concept of soul is complex. Nowadays many Runa use the Spanish word *alma* to convey the idea of the soul, even if they are speaking Quichua. I have found, however, that they use this term to mean something other than the Western notion of an individual, bounded soul. When I asked people to translate it into Quichua, they used *samai*, but they sometimes qualified the idea of breath by saying that a soul is a concentration of "inner breath" (ucu samai). The term *alma* stresses a concentration of vital energy, yet with an implicit understanding that soul energy circulates among people and natural beings. As I have discussed elsewhere (Uzendoski 2003), Runa Christians see their souls as originating in a kind of kinship relationship to God and God's "breath." To speak of samai is to stress a circulatory notion of the soul as stretching across kinship pathways, time, and space. Both *alma* and *samai* refer to the same theory of the soul, but the terms convey different nuances, mainly because alma has powerful linguistic associations with Christianity. Other terms that refer to the soul connote the same idea of a flowing vital energy that inhabits the body: causai, *urza* (strength), and *yachai* (knowledge). While these terms have their nuances, they are basically interchangeable with *samai*.

The Runa word for "soul" is thus a virtually untranslatable term that presents larger issues about the way people view spirit, substance, life, and death. I proposed translating the soul concept as a concentration of breath. In writing about the Pastaza Runa, by contrast, Whitten (1976:56; 1985:108) translates *soul* or *soul substance* as *aya* (pl., *ayaguna*), a term that can mean "a spirit," too. The Napo Runa, however, use this term exclusively in reference to the wandering spirit of a deceased person. In Napo there are many myths about the ayaguna, who are said to harass and sometimes kill people, and ayaguna are not easily differentiated from supai, or wandering spirits. People are troubled by ayaguna and have various means for driving them away, such as clipping off and burning pubic hair (ullu ilma), a manifestation of one's sexual energy thought to work as a kind of repellent. In Napo people expressed aya as an entity leaving the body after death; the aya is a concentration of samai that exits the deceased body, a soul without a body. I never heard anyone speak of inheriting or acquiring an aya as part of his or her own internal soul substance. I heard of people acquiring samai, causai, urza, and yachai, but the predominant term used to describe the soul in Napo is *samai*. The Pastaza Runa, by contrast, seem to emphasize aya.

I am convinced that Whitten and I are speaking of the same underlying concept of the soul, but the terminology varies across the region. Indeed, the Quichua dialects of the Napo Runa and the Pastaza Runa differ more in vocabulary than in grammar. These dialects are mutually intelligible, however, and the Napo Runa and Pastaza Runa have been interacting with each other for centuries. One area of this interaction is shamanism. As one shaman commented, "We have been trading samai with the Pastaza Runa since the beginning of time." As Whitten's work and my discussion show, the terms *samai* and *aya* denote related concepts within a picture of a complex reality in which souls circulate among people and animals through time and space. The crux of the issue is that there are meaningful linguistic nuances, and perhaps aesthetic ones, in the way Quichua speakers talk about and describe the soul, a promising topic for future research.

Descola includes the notions of the soul and substance within his definition of circulatory animistic systems: "Basic to many Amazonian animic systems is a view of the universe as a gigantic closed circuit within which there is a

constant circulation of the substances, souls, and identities held to be necessary for the conservation of the world and the perpetuation of the social
order" (1992:116).

The animism Descola describes speaks to the larger problem of external or
material form versus inner or spiritual essence. Native Amazonians view the
relationship between external body and internal substance as circulatory, a
kind of "feedback" relationship in which neither the visible nor the invisible
is the primary realm. Meaning unfolds from their continued opposition and
relation.

In the Napo Runa vernacular, the term *aya* represents a particular phase
of soul circulation—the release of concentrated samai on death or within
an alternative reality (e.g., dreaming or hallucinogenic experiences) from a
body. An aya is a wandering spirit with no visible form in normal reality. I
heard a person say that people who go to sleep become "light" because the
aya goes out during dreaming, a "dreaming" death. I constantly asked people
whether aya is something like a soul, and my queries were always rebuffed.
Bancu, for example, told me that ayaguna are spirits, not souls.

Vital Energy and the Corporeal "Envelope": Toward the Concept of the Will

This brief discussion of the soul allows me to form some hypotheses about
the Runa view of the relationships among maturation, sexual relations, and
desire. Implicit to the sasina restrictions of a recent birth is the idea that the
control of desire in one subject is essential to the regulation of vital energy in
another, especially young babies.[5] The Runa conceptualize this strengthening process through an idiom of managing desire in relationships. As I have
shown, sasina restrictions are couched in a logic that portrays the control of
alimentary and sexual desires as fostering the maturation of soft vital energy.
This energy also becomes more resistant to illness and outside pathogens,
such as mal aire, and the attacks of spirits and shamans. Furthermore, people
perceive children as soft because they seem unable to control their desires
and act on impulse.

The Runa believe that invisible energy circulates among people, animals,
and spirits. One way to conceptualize this unseen level of vital energy is to
think of it as a Platonic Form. Vitality can be seen as the mental model of
energy, the Form behind maturation. Like a Form, the Runa notion has a
shape to it, that of an unseen conceptual relationship between the mediation

of desires of parents and their young. Here, however, we must part company with the Platonic theory of the Forms, for Plato's ideal of perception is based on a "rational" theory of knowledge. The Runa, in contrast, base their theory of perception on a different kind of philosophy of being, one perhaps closer to what Viveiros de Castro (1998) has termed "perspectivism." Perspectivism (like the animism of Philippe Descola [1992, 1996a]) is the idea that "the manifest form of each species is a mere envelope (a 'clothing') which conceals an internal human form, usually only visible to the eyes of the particular species or to certain trans-specific beings such as shamans. This internal form is the 'soul' or 'spirit' [vital energy] of the animal: an intentionality or subjectivity formally identical to human consciousness, materializable, let us say, in human bodily schema concealed behind an animal mask" (Viveiros de Castro 1998:471).

The crucial difference between the Platonic theory of the Forms and Native Amazonian perspectivism is the spatial location of unseen reality. For Plato, the Forms occupy a separate, purely noumenal domain. In the analogy of the cave in the *Republic,* the Forms are likened to the reality behind those manipulating the shadows. The Forms are mere knowledge, for there is no relationship of energy transference between the two levels of reality. For Native Amazonians, however, the unseen level of reality is connected to external appearances by energy. Vital energy *internally* animates and circulates through all things with visible and nonvisible form.

Viveiros de Castro (1998) posits that, for Native Amazonians, animals and humans are covered by an exterior—the "clothing" or "envelope"—that conceals their internal vital energy. The vital energy animates and gives life. The exterior, however, is neither superficial nor meant to hide the true substance of a person. The external form of a being is an object of continual refabrication and purpose—the external "animal clothes" of shamans can be likened to "diving gear and space suits," not carnival masks (Viveiros de Castro 1998:482). The body/soul distinction is thus not an ontological discontinuity, as it is in most Western philosophy (Viveiros de Castro 1998:482), but rather a relationship between external form and internal substance.

Perspectivism relates to my discussion as follows: the people indigenous to Napo see external appearances—not only bodies but also behavior—as fabrications that reflect individuals' internal states of being, specifically their vital energy. For example, children behave the way they do because their internal energy causes them to act in an immature way. Children have weak constitutions. As I have argued, people believe that children's "soft" bodies and behaviors represent their relative lack of vital energy.

The converse is also held to be true: internal energy can be influenced by external factors and events. For example, illness can weaken or destroy the vital energy of a child. Just as softness makes a child susceptible to forest spirits, so too can a lack of nourishment lead to illness. Vital energy can also be restored through ritual healing; the two levels—internal and external—are conceptualized as being in a dynamic relationship, and one level is thought to reflect and influence the other. Neither is necessarily the more dominant or the more fundamental.

I have already provided examples showing how the Runa perceive vital energy in the temporary and transforming "envelope" of a child's body, but this extends beyond physical aspects to include children's proclivities to be dominated by their desires and antidesires. Children are fidgety, lazy, and troublesome, and they eat almost anything, often doing so in socially unacceptable ways. Children frequently become ill, too, and require attention to heal them. Joking and punishment are ways in which parents believe they can influence and shape the vital energy of children to produce a favorable trajectory of development. When babies become children, parents begin the task of shaping them into proper social beings. They talk about transforming childlike desires into a social will, described as *shungu* (heart), the social manifestation of the process of strengthening and straightening vital energy.

In the context of Runa life, one's will is one's ability to manage desires, but I have not fully defined this useful concept. Will can be defined as "a capacity for judgment and choice, an ability to entertain as points of reference both a consciousness of selfhood and a consciousness of social relationships" (Strathern 1988:90). The will is not just an awareness of one's dependency on the social relationships that define morality and personhood but also a consciousness of socially regulating desires in the value-creation process. In forming the will, personhood takes on a dialectical and "encompassing" relation to desire (T. Turner 1984). Reflecting this idea, people in Napo discern between behaviors that are associated with the will and those that are associated with desire when raising children. Without developed wills, children are not yet completed persons. They must be transformed from their soft (llullu) states.

Bodily Forms: Runa Notions of Will and Desire

In Quichua usage, the will and desire can be differentiated by their associations with different parts of the body. The will is associated with the most important organ in Runa cultural physiology, the heart. People describe thoughtfulness as having an "ali shungu" (a good heart). The will is thought to emanate from the heart, which is also taken to be the central organ of bodily feeling and perception. The heart is a kind of social eye, but thought, or iyai, is located in the head. The heart as a social organ is the center of vital energy. People sometimes describe people who act stupid as "iyai illac" (without thought), but nobody would say that someone is without heart. Sad or sick people describe states of malaise as having a "hurting heart" ("shungu nanana" or "shungu nanchina"). These are all common ways of describing how people feel by referring to their hearts.

Desire, on the other hand, is associated with the genitals, the tongue, and the stomach. The realm of desire is rich with cross-figurative expressions of male and female genitalia and food. The objects of alimentary desires are talked about as being sweet and leaving the stomach in a good state of fullness. People describe sexual pleasure in the same way, as producing the sensation of sweetness and leaving one feeling full. Gustatory and sexual pleasure are associated as the objects of similar kinds of desires.

Whitten (1985:108), too, has defined the heart as the bodily instrument of the will. He posits that one's samai is the "force of one's will," which originates in the heart and defines one's inner strength. The will allows one to influence others, as in making someone recognize the beauty of the music one is playing. Whitten asserts that, as with the perspectivism discussed earlier, the proof of the will's influence lies mainly in the way others perceive it, not only in its intrinsic characteristics. This notion of inner strength and its perceptions are linked to the idea of beauty (*suma*), which Whitten (1985:108) defines as a capacity within oneself. Suma is the means by which one's influence is expressed and experienced; it derives from the power of one's will.

At one level, the will is this kind of social awareness of the way one is perceived by others. At another level, the will is conceptualized as the source of influence and inner strength. These two ideas are interrelated, however, for influence depends on social awareness, and social awareness depends on having an influence on others. As the will develops, the part that is characterized as "social awareness" becomes encompassed by the part that "influences." Thus in childhood the focus is on awareness; in adulthood the focus is on influence. One must learn what beauty is before producing it.

The concept of a will—which begins as social awareness—is the key to building character in persons so that social values feel and seem natural. This theme—how to instill appropriate social values in persons—is common in many civilizations, although the nature and conceptions of those values necessarily change from one group to the next. For example, in Plato's Republic, the concepts of the soul (passions, spirit, and reason) are primary, and the souls must be ordered and arranged in a hierarchical fashion so that reason dominates. This ordered arrangement is crucial, argues Plato, to achieve the social ideals of classical Greece. In a similar way, people in Upper Napo are concerned with the concept of a will (equally as complex as the ancient Greek concept of soul) and in creating people who have "strong" wills. Creating people with strong wills leads to love, a "good ayllu," a good house, and a good community, the primary ideals of daily life in indigenous Napo.

Gendering the Will

Before vital energy is straightened and strengthened in specific social pathways, it retains an androgynous or "soft," nongendered form. As children mature, they develop masculine- or feminine-oriented wills. That is, as children become adults, they learn that they must contribute to the household just as adults do. People tell stories about realizing their gender-specific wills. A man will often tell stories of his first solo hunting trip or learning to hunt at his father's side. As boys mature, they learn not only to hunt but also to fish with traps and nets. They learn how to handle machetes and axes and to carry heavy loads. Little by little, boys increase their skills and knowledge in the productive bases of masculinity.

Women, by contrast, start realizing a gender-specific will at an earlier age. They begin by helping to garden, to prepare food, and eventually to prepare manioc brew and cook. Young boys, too, will help in these tasks; that is, they perform domestic and feminine tasks, which means that boys pass through a phase of femininity before they become masculine persons. As they mature, men and women gain different spiritual powers and qualities. Women receive various *paju*, or special magical powers. Above all, women pass on to their daughters, nieces, and granddaughters "lumu paju" (manioc power), which stimulates manioc to grow abundantly in the gardens. The paju is transferred in a very informal ritual, so that the power passes into the recipient's body. The recipient tugs on the donor's finger until the joints crack, signaling the transference of energy. The donor then spiritually "cleanses" the recipient and passes her breath by blowing on top of the recipient's head. This practice allows the younger generation to acquire feminine spiritual substance that makes them strong and wise. Other paju that I observed included the power of massage (fixing of twisted joints) and others for attacking specific sources of illness, such as mal aire. Almost all women have at least lumu paju.

Boys and young men also receive the samai of their fathers, uncles, and other senior members of the ayllu. To cure a sick child, a shaman will transfer his breath to the child to reinforce its weak vital energy. Fathers also pass on their breath to their sons to make them stronger. When the sons are older, fathers give them hunting charms, knowledge, and magical objects. I witnessed Bancu give his sons various magical objects, including stones from the caiman's stomach (which were swallowed), the tooth of a boa (kept in a pocket), and his samai (blown into the tops of their heads using cigarettes).

In previous epochs both boys and girls mimetically captured the vital energy of mythical jaguars by consuming the *puma yuyu* plant. In 1994 I participated in a puma yuyu ritual intended to increase vital energy and strengthen the will (see Uzendoski 1999). People emphasized that it is better to take puma yuyu from an early age, for its consumption constitutes a life process by which one gradually gains more power. Becoming a powerful shaman might eventually lead to the ability to shape-shift into a jaguar and enter a permanent jaguar state in death. I was surprised to learn that the "owner" of the puma yuyu plants we took was thought to have this ability. She reportedly had turned into a jaguar on a few occasions, and people noted that her faced looked feline.

Boys develop their masculine wills through bouts of drinking and the masculine behavior associated with it. Runa men who drink feel that drunkenness is an expression mainly of will, not desire. For example, I was once drinking with the men from Yacu Llacta after a soccer match in Ahuano. We stayed for a fiesta being put on by a campaigning politician's backers. These outdoor fiestas always entail free music, usually the modern Runa music called "Runa Paju," and abundant *cachiwa* (aguardiente). The cachiwa is often mixed with heated cinnamon or wayusa tea to make it more drinkable and to encourage women to participate. In this case the strong drink allowed Jorge to continue my education in Runa values. As I was drinking with him, I commented on the cachiwa's terrible taste, making a face to show my displeasure. He explained why the Runa drink such bad-tasting alcohol: "We do not drink for pleasure. We drink cachiwa because we are strong [sinzhi]." He then made me drink another cup with him while showing no displeasure. Drinking is a social action associated with being a *cari* (man). I will analyze drinking and its association with the spirit world and divine power in more detail later in the book; at this point it suffices to note that drinking is a specific and salient gendering action.

As young people mature, they move from androgyny to being gendered. The key transformations in this process deal with developing the masculine or feminine will, becoming a cari or a *warmi* (woman). The process of developing a masculine will thus entails divesting feminine aspects of being and enhancing masculinity. The inverse is true of femininity: to become feminine is to divest oneself of masculine essences. The Runa say that some men are "like women" and some women are "like men." These phrases are sometimes said in jest, but at other times they are serious characterizations.

Napo Runa culture contains men who develop feminine wills rather than masculine ones. In addition, women sometimes develop masculine wills. Ciricha provides an example. Her husband had died years earlier, leaving her with two children. Rather than move in with relatives, Ciricha decided to build her own home and provide for her household, a somewhat unique arrangement. In Yacu Llacta she was one of the best at fishing, and she occasionally hunted. She thus performed productive actions associated with masculinity as well as femininity. She was both mother and "father" to her children, and people often called her a "man-woman" (cari-warmi).

Masculine women and feminine men would be labeled "others" in Western societies. Among the Runa, however, these combinations of sex and gender are seen as socially acceptable. Many feminine men become respected members of communities, often serving as teachers and leaders. One such person is a leader in an evangelical church. Tessmann's related observation regarding the Napo Runa is noteworthy, mainly because of its early date (1930). Tessmann writes: "[Sexual] relations between boys are common. These occur in the forest. Authentic homosexuals don't exist. But they [the homosexuals] are not detested but rather tolerated" (1999:141). Tessman here struggles with the complexity of Napo Runa gender forms that do not easily translate into Western notions of homosexuality. He imposes Western assumptions of its negativity rather than acknowledge the Runa preference for viewing difference as value neutral. Tessmann's statement, however, shows that alternative genders have been part of Napo Runa culture for quite some time.

Feminine men and masculine women are often mocked, but so is everyone else in Runa society. Jokes about sex and sexuality abound. It took me some time to get used to living in a culture where sex is not thought of as "dirty" and where many people, especially grandmothers, openly make fun of one's sexuality. We might characterize the Runa as a sex-affirming rather than a sex-rejecting society. For example, I know of no truly "dirty" words or jokes in Amazonian Quichua.

The Napo Runa Theory of Gender

Gender relationships among the indigenous Napo are complex and not understandable through a Western conceptual framework of individuals forming a matrimonial union. Gender relationships in Napo are ideally complementary in the sense that life is not possible without masculine-feminine combinations. Masculine and feminine are contrary yet complementary forces that together make a greater whole. For example, one man explained to me that he and his wife were not separate people but rather different forms of the *same* person. Such an understanding strips the sense from Western notions of patriarchy and feminism, which are predicated on the cognitive and social assumption that people are distinct beings related by the domination of one over the other. If I am the masculine or feminine version of someone else, my identity and consciousness are not individual but rather relational. This ideal is expressed in many ways in daily and ritual life in Napo, as will become evident throughout this book.

After I presented this idea of gender complementarity to a class about Amazonian peoples, a student challenged me by saying that he thought of his relationship with his girlfriend as equally complementary. "We also think of ourselves as the same person," he said, "so I don't see how your idea is unique." At first I was taken aback by the contention that I had mistaken a universal idea of gender relations for a culturally unique practice. After some thought, however, I decided that I was not mistaken, but my answer required me to translate between the social forms of individualism and the social forms of Napo Runa culture. Individualism, a social phenomenon associated with the social needs of capitalism, allows people to conceptualize romantic relationships in many ideal forms, but it limits relational complementarity as a pragmatic, social ideal. Marx (1972:222–23, 1977), for example, has shown that individualism is linked to capital's social needs for workers who sell their labor to owners. "Capital," he writes, "announces from the outset a new epoch in the process of social production" (Marx 1977:274), one in which individuals alienate their labor to the market. Among the Runa, by contrast, gender complementarity goes far beyond the mere conceptual. It is pragmatically woven into the circuit of production and consumption and the circulation of things and people, sexuality, and desire itself. The social forms of personification in Napo Runa society, as I will show throughout this book, follow complex pathways and transformations of genderedness and complementarity.

Masculine Dominance: Violence and Complementarity

While complementarity is emphasized in Napo Runa socioculture, masculinity is the dominant gender force. Masculinity is defined by hunting and other forms of predation and by the capacity for violence. Masculine dominance is legitimated by its association with stronger spiritual power and the origins of life. Men control violence. A Napo Runa woman once told me that her husband had beat her "only one time." I asked why. She responded that she had fallen down while walking in the forest when pregnant, thus endangering the life of their future child. I wondered, however, why this woman was not angry that her husband had beaten her. On the contrary, she accepted it as legitimate. While one can hear stories such as this one, other women speak of husbands who beat them often and in an abusive manner.

From the perspective of Runa socioculture, a measured amount of masculine violence is viewed as legitimate when it is directed at socializing a young wife. This violence is described as "punishing" (*libachina*) and "teaching" (*yachachina*), the latter a euphemism that, like all portrayals of legitimate violence, emphasizes positive outcomes. This violence is directed and conceptualized as molding the woman around her man so that she becomes publicly and personally subordinated to his will (Descola 1996b). When men beat their wives in an abusive manner, it is described as *macana* (to beat up) rather than yachachina. Ideally masculine violence is socially regulated by the ayllu so that spousal conflicts are made central to the concerns of the larger group. In general, the Runa view macana as an immoral and destructive form of behavior.

Beyond controlling violence, men are thought to have more knowledge and spiritual power, or yachai, than women. This asymmetry reflects a principle set forth by Godelier (1999, 2000), who demonstrates that male social dominance is tied to men's connections to the sacred through specific kinds of bodily forms and sexualities associated with origins. This principle explains in a general way why men dominate women in Runa socioculture. Men are more closely and significantly (but not exclusively) associated with the origins of life and knowledge.

Beyond Dominance

Nevertheless, the proposition of masculine dominance within Runa socioculture raises some complex issues, for there is no accurate Quichua counterpart to this concept. Perhaps the closest analogue to the idea that men are dominant beings is simply the verb *cariyana* (which I translate as "to become masculine") and its many derivatives (see Lyons 2003).[6] This term, like other gender terms, is used to describe both men and women, but it represents masculine qualities and behaviors.

The term *cariyana* connotes both bravery and intelligence in the face of danger or death. I heard people describe others as "cari" or "cari tucuna" when they went hunting or fishing at night; crossed dangerous rivers; performed feats of strength or skill; or, in other contexts, established and implemented an effective plan of action in a dangerous situation. In Napo the word *cari* is linked to the idea of creating and sustaining life in an orderly fashion.

The mythology of the Napo Runa also helps reveal further meanings of the term *cari*. Napo Runa mythology centers on two culture heroes, the Cuillurguna, who are twin boys. There are numerous stories that feature the Cuillurguna, and the myth cycle explains the many transformations of the forest that took place in mythical times (see Uzendoski 1999). One narrative about the twins, for example, relates how they were able to give birth to themselves after their mother was killed by jaguars. The narrator highlights the twins' power to escape an otherwise certain death, describing them as "being masculine" (*cariyashami*).

This myth associates cari with strength, life, and intelligence in the face of death. The twins stories are in fact a kind of origin statement about Runa masculinity itself. The twins incorporate jaguar essence into their beings; they are breast-fed by the jaguar mother and, like the jaguars, are great hunters. Nonetheless, their wildness is converted into an order. The twins kill many animals that prey on humans (jaguars, anacondas, hawks, and others) to create a space for humans to live. They are said to make "space-time" (*lugar*) for life.

Another revealing narrative that invokes cari speaks of a young man who is not afraid of a blood-sucking spirit, or aya, that is harassing the community at night. The man states, "Carimi ani [I am a man]" to show that he is not afraid. The young man eventually defeats the predatory spirit, but only after it sucks the blood out of one of his children. The larger message of the story is that the more intelligent course of action would have been to eliminate the threat of the aya beforehand, perhaps by fleeing, performing a ritual cleansing, or consulting a shaman. This tale shows the ambiguous nature of masculine wildness. Without intelligence, masculinity leads to disorder and possible death rather than order and life. The narrator ends by indicating that the young man is not fully a masculine person, for he calls him a "malta runa" (young person) rather than an apayaya (strong elder man).

This story of a man not yet fully a man suggests a tension between masculinity and androgyny in Runa socioculture. Although he aspires to masculinity, the young man is still located between masculine maturity and the androgyny of his young life. In Runa terms, he would be "mana cari," or not (yet) a man, a phrase that is often used in the context of actions that are masculine in intent but not performed effectively. This usage contrasts with describing someone as warmi, (like) a woman. This absence is associated with incompleteness and the "softer" stages of human maturation.

My discussion of cari supports the notion that, in the context of larger Amazonia, it is worth rethinking concepts of "masculine dominance," a phrase that assumes an individualistic perspective of noncomplementary genders (Strathern 1988:57). Indeed, in the Runa context the notion of dominance does not convey the underlying interdependence conceptualized among masculine and feminine combinations.[7] Furthermore, masculinity's dependence on and inseparability from femininity makes masculine dominance a fragile proposition in Napo Runa society. One endlessly repeated theme I encountered in speech, song, and myth was that masculine wildness, bravery, and destructive power allow for the creation and maintenance of order. Nevertheless, this theme is also challenged by its equally present opposite: that without femininity and feminine strength, order soon becomes disorder and masculinity itself loses all potency; it paradoxically becomes mana cari, its own negation.

Conclusion

Now that I have looked at the ways in which Napo Runa socioculture shapes the birth process and directs the raising of children into gendered beings with strong wills, as well as the philosophical notions (animism or perspectivism) on which Runa ideas of parenthood and the creation of new human life are based, I will summarize some of the salient points. The philosophical basis of Runa personhood is a dynamic relationship between internal states of being (samai, or vital energy) and external ones (*aicha*, or "flesh") in which a substance is exchanged between the spiritual and the physical realms in a kind of feedback loop. In other words, divinity and humanity do not occupy separate ontological domains. Divinity is part of the everyday business of continuing human life: it allows one to heal, to hunt, to grow food, and to strengthen the wills of growing children. Substance relations are the primary idiom by which people begin to relate to others. Value is created through this process of converting things into children and developing children into social persons in the continuous or timeless nature of samai strength that permeates Napo Runa socioculture. As I will show in the next chapter, these notions of somatic and spiritual transformation are part of the aesthetic and cosmological patterning of everyday perception and reality, a patterning that more clearly shows the qualities of gender complementary and transformation. For the Runa, these principles form the cornerstone of value and kinship.

2

The Poetics of Social Form

According to the Amazonian Quichua, mythical space-time (*unai*) is centered within human awareness and inhabits the body. Unai is a source of both knowledge (*yachai*) and power (*ushai*). Quichua people experience unai through dreams, storytelling, music, ritual, sickness, curing, and many other contexts. As Whitten and Whitten write, "*Unai* is always with us. It exists in the present and will continue into the future. It is the source of mythology, of visionary reality, of some dreams, and of enduring tradition" (1988:30). Unai is a means of perceiving the world, especially the rainforest. It is not a mere "concept." It is a somatic, millennial, pragmatic, and aesthetic quality of the human condition.

In 1994 I accompanied some people visiting a shaman during their eco-tour of Yacu Llacta. I translated for the shaman as he showed the tourists his collection of plants, medicines, and curing procedures. He took out a small vial that contained *wanduc* (*Brugmansia suaveolens*), a hallucinogen. He implored the tourists and me to take a small taste: "It is a small amount. Nothing will happen." It was late in the afternoon, and the tourists soon retired to their cabana. I walked alone along the river's edge, following a familiar trail. Soon I noticed that the leaves on the trees were coming alive. They began dancing back and forth, as if responding to a rhythm. Later that night I had a similar vision. I was watching a particular tree in which the leaves became serpents that ran up and down the branches and trunk. After a few trips up and down, the serpents turned back into leaves again, and the process began anew. I was both amazed and frightened by these experiences, which in no way seemed to be hallucinations.

A few days later I related my experiences to Bancu. When I told him about the leaves, he became animated. "What you saw was the life force [*causai*] of the forest. The leaves on the trees were greeting you, telling you that they were alive." After these experiences I continually thought about the leaves on the trees and perceived them differently. The forest was no longer simply a "natural" entity. When I saw the leaves, I remembered them as living, shape-shifting beings. I had witnessed the most basic principle of unai—that the world is composed of an ancient cosmic energy that is constantly recycled as it changes form. In Quichua this notion is expressed through the term *tucuna* (transformation).[1] The principle is not only aesthetic but also shamanic. With regard to the Canelos Quichua culture, Whitten and Whitten have written, "Their art is guided by the very concepts and culturally conceived force fields that undergird shamanic control" (1988:24).

These experiences gave me fresh insights into the aesthetics and cosmological principles of Napo Runa myth,[2] for most myths feature shape-shifting themes. By sharing myths, people become millennial beings defined by common pathways of substance transmission that extend into the unai world and beyond. Indeed, unlike accounts from anthropologists and historians, the history that the Runa tell of themselves goes back to the beginning of time and humanity. Runa origin stories posit the presence and power of shape-shifting not only as a means of perceiving the world but also as the theory of kinship itself.[3] I will now examine one such origin narrative, which I heard from a man named Lucas.

Izhu, or the Great Flood

According to the Runa, the first people to inhabit the earth survived a great flood, the "Izhu Punzha." The Runa conceptualize the Izhu as the Amazonian equivalent to the Bible's Great Flood. They call the Izhu "our story" and take the biblical version to recount events that happened concurrently in the Middle East. When I asked people to tell me a story of the Great Flood, they sometimes recounted the biblical story of Noah's ark in Quichua. At other times they recounted the myth of the Izhu.

> There was a great flood called *Izhu* in the beginning times where the water exploded. My "father's fathers," who were powerful shamans, were there to see it. There were two mountains back then, Sumaco and Chiuta. Sumaco was taller, boastful, and confident. Chiuta was smaller, quiet, and humble [*umbas*]. As the water rose, Chiuta and Sumaco

began to grow. Sumaco taunted Chiuta, but Chiuta didn't respond. Then Chiuta grew more, higher and higher [*awai*], higher and higher, and in doing so became taller than Sumaco. He defeated Sumaco, who became completely covered with water, and won the battle. The water was very destructive. It turned the savage people [*auca*] over and over as they drowned in the gushing waters. My father's fathers were saved on top of Chiuta, where they planted some cacao, which still stands there today. If it weren't for them, then we wouldn't be here today. It was because of their actions that we have reproduced.

This Izhu myth is rife with transformation imagery and sound symbolism[4] (Nuckolls 1996, 2000), words whose sounds directly link them to images. One such word is *tun* used to convey the "explosion" of water, for it conveys the idea of something becoming filled or dark. It thus forcefully conveys the world's transformation from a state of order to one of chaos. Sound-symbolic words that evoke turning and repetitive phrases also simulate the power and rhythm of destructive water (*tian*). Not only is Sumaco covered; the auca are carried away in the destruction. The end of the story centers on reproduction and the construction of a new world from chaotic destruction. Lucas states that his "father's fathers" were saved by Chiuta, for they fled the rising waters by climbing to the top.

The myth is spatially structured by a further image that is not easily translated. The narrator often employs the term *palca* (branch) to describe the shape or form of the mountains. At first I was confused by this term, for I had heard it used only in reference to trees, "yura palca." It was finally explained to me that *palca* can also refer to any V shape created by a space between things—in the case of the myth, the valley between the mountains. The narrator describes the space between the mountains as "chi chaupi shungu palca [the middle-heart palca]." By choosing these words, Lucas creates imagery of duality and unity between Sumaco and Chiuta as opposed yet connected peaks. The "branching" here refers to the lines created by the form of the peaks and valleys.

The use of the term *palca* probably creates associations with the branches of trees, for Quichua storytellers often use words and images in multiple figurative and metaphorical ways. One such association is that of mountains to trees. Indeed, the use of the term *palca* resonates with the way the Runa talk about trees. In the story Chiuta "grows" as a tree does and thus becomes a sort of tree of life for Lucas's ancestors.

The poetics and meaning of this myth reflect a clear transformation of Andean and Amazonian mythical realities. Myths dealing with the tree of

life are common in Amazonia (see Narby 1998), just as myths about mountain creators are prevalent in the Andean world. Indeed, the spectacular
iconography of shamanistic visionary art displayed in Luna and Amaringo's
(1991) book reveals the common theme of trees "growing" and flowing into
human beings (see especially visions 30 and 35). The Chiuta-Sumaco myth
shows a conceptual flow between mountain creator beings of the Andean
world and these primordial trees of Amazonia, both of which are associated
with life-giving processes. In Upper Napo, Amazonian mountains become
shape-shifting trees of life.

There is a further imagery central to the story. Because the term *palca*
can refer to the vagina, too, it genders the valley as feminine. The valley
contrasts with the phallic symbolism of the growing mountain, and the two
spaces engage in symbolic, cosmic sex. The sex is represented by the violent
actions of the water. Regina Harrison (1989:163) has argued that spume
(*puscu*), always present during floods, is a powerful symbol of sexual power
in both Amazonia and the Andes. She notes that such foam is associated with
"loosening" a woman's bonds to one lover so that another has access to her
(163–64). Through this imagery, powerful and chaotic cosmological sex (of
the unai beings) destroys and remakes the world into a new order.

Myth, however, holds little meaning if divorced from the sociality of the
present.[5] Lucas makes the point about his fathers' living through the flood.
Lucas again connects the teller and all the listeners to the fathers when he
says, "From there we reproduced." The last section of the myth focuses on
reproduction and reiterates this theme by using the first-person plural repeatedly, as in "it is from doing so we have gotten away," indicating a collapse
of subjectivity between Lucas's fathers and the larger community. The myth
narrative conveys the message that kinship is a "deep river" of millennial being, one in which substance flows from unai and the Upper Napo landscape
to the current generation.

As I discussed in the previous chapter, people associate masculine presence
with strength and making life possible. These principles manifest themselves
not only in kinship and myth but also in the way the Napo Runa conceptualize
history and later historical epochs. Quichua narratives usually feature a shaman or shamanic being who mediates the forces of transformation between
epochs and is motivated by extreme love. Here, Lucas's "father" is the shape-
shifter who, like Chiuta himself, allows humanity to continue out of the Izhu
and into the current time. Lucas's father embodies the shamanic power of his
paternal line, and Lucas freely interchanges "father" with "father's father."
The continuance of power is noted by collapsing singular and plural subjects,

indicating the idea of many bodies within one body throughout time-space. The myth shows the power of Lucas's father as defined by the water he "tested" in the Izhu and by the implicit substance connection he has with Chiuta. Like Chiuta, Lucas's father is a creator of order and a shape-shifter in the Napo Runa sense of somatic power and transformation.

Notions of Power: Shape-Shifting and Embodiment

I take the idea of shape-shifting from Candace Slater (2002), who has used the idea to describe Amazonian views on corporeal and identity transformations. She defines a shape-shifter as "a creature or natural entity (a lake, river, mineral, type of vegetation) that is able to change its outward form at will and that eschews any fixed identity" (Slater 2002:16). Generally this concept works well as a way of thinking about and translating Napo Runa ideas of bodily transformation. As I showed in an earlier discussion of the soul, the Napo Runa view the body as a corporeal envelope that contains an inner essence of samai. Over the course of one's life, one's body must change form and become strengthened. The flesh, or aicha, is the location of the body's power.

This idea of shape-shifting requires some fine-tuning, however, for the Napo Runa concept of corporeal transformation is more subtle and nuanced. While the Napo Runa sometimes speak of turning into animals in the sense of literally taking on an animal shape, talk of shape-shifting more often conveys the idea of taking the corporeal substance of animals into one's own flesh. Shape-shifting describes the embodiment of the inner essence of animals and other beings as power, but the external shape, the corporeal "envelope," can remain human in appearance. Shamans look human, but they possess powerful animal bodies made up of transformed flesh. It is only during ritual acts or dreaming that people become animal others and experience the world as an "animal" or take on the shape of an animal. So my emphasis in using the idea of shape-shifting is to highlight power's embodiment as articulated through the animistic subjectivity of animals, birds, and other beings.

Feminine Shape-Shifting and Quichua Women's Songs

Feminine shape-shifting and power are central themes of women's songs. These songs, like myth, are events that connect people to unai. In 2001 I videotaped a women's song performed by Jacinta Andi. For years Jacinta had sent my wife and me gifts of food, usually plantains, manioc, and manioc brew. In return we visited her at least once a year and brought her gifts of food and sometimes clothes from the United States.

Arriving at Jacinta's house, we spent a good deal of time talking, drinking manioc brew, and catching up on the major events of our lives. Jacinta was very sad that her husband was ill and that she was living apart from her children. Other relatives stood in the doorway, commenting and taking part in the events. Vats of fermenting *vinillu,* a kind of manioc wine, were off to the side, put there in preparation for the annual fiesta of Pucara.

Jacinta told a story of her past. She explained how in the beginning times people had only canoes to get around, using poles to push them against the current. When the men got tired (or drunk), the women had to take over. She talked about her strength in performing many tasks. She talked, too, about how she always had manioc brew ready to serve and how she always made her man happy (*cushi*). Jacinta affirmed that the "love" (*llakina*) of her parents manifested as her knowledge and her strength. This strength, or yachai, was located in her heart (*shungu*), and it defined her being. The power of her will revealed itself through her competence as a feminine person, in nourishing not only her husband and children but also visitors. Jacinta also had the gift of foresight. She mentioned that she was able to foresee the needs and desires of her husband without his having to ask.

Jacinta was moved to sing only after her relatives had implored her for some time. Jacinta's niece, whom she called her "daughter," mentioned that it would be important for the ayllu to have a video recording of her "to remember her by after she dies." Jacinta then began to introduce her song. She stated that she was going to sing about her travels downriver (Lower Napo). She revealed that her song was about turning into a dove when her husband abandoned her. Jacinta then began to sing, relating how, after the abandonment, she turned into a dove and chased him. Not realizing that his wife had become a bird, her husband chased the dove with his rifle. He tried to shoot her, but she escaped. Jacinta repeated many times that she was a "dove woman," one who flies high in the clouds and near the sun. The strength of her high-pitched voice and the rhythmic pattern of the song overwhelmed and shocked my senses.

After she had finished, Jacinta rested, and a few moments of total silence followed. The silence felt concentrated. She then began to sing another song, one that conveyed her experiences as a woman who gathered rubber during "cauchu timpo," or the rubber time. The song opened up into a related message of Jacinta's being a woman of extensive travels, a "puric warmi" (walking or traveling woman). She sang about her love for her husband, as demonstrated in their shared times of drinking vinillu and warapu, both fermented beverages, adding, "As our little deaths approach, only then will we leave doing this." By the end of the song Jacinta was thinking of her son, who was not living with her. Such thoughts made her sad, and she began to cry after she finished singing. Everyone again remained silent for a good while. After some time, however, conversation resumed and Jacinta's sadness was lifted.

Both songs are structured by shape-shifting patterns. In the first song, Jacinta, left in Lower Napo by her husband, turns into a dove to catch up to him. When she reaches her husband, he tries to shoot her, but she outwits and escapes him. Jacinta is not angry at her husband for his masculine "blindness" and injustice. She remains faithful to her complementary relation to her husband's needs and desires. Jacinta's song reveals a Runa subjectivity of being, one based on eliciting power (ushai) in transforming discord into complementary "love." Indeed, as both songs reveal, Jacinta has been many things during her life, a dove woman, a rubber-gathering woman, a traveling woman, and a loving wife. These different forms show the power of her "soul" and social will. The theme of feminine power in the songs resonates with Jacinta's status as a very loved and wise elder in the community, a woman who continues to nourish those around her.[6]

Many other women's songs I heard in the Upper Tena region further associate feminine power with birds. Some, for example, speak of a woman's being a "kindi warmi" (hummingbird woman), a "nina siccha" (another kind of bird), or a "patu warmi" (duck woman). In another song a woman transforms into a hummingbird and describes herself as a "puyu warmi" (cloud woman); she moves between heaven and earth, land and water. Along the way she visits many flowers (*sisauna*), finally descending on her husband (see Uzendoski, Hertica, and Calapucha forthcoming).

I am not the only one to have noticed the association of women with birds in Ecuadorian Amazonia. In 1920 Karsten mentioned that "women [commonly] direct their songs to certain colorful birds of the forest, which they personify and with which they converse. . . . These songs appear to be quite numerous" (1998:372–73). The association of women with doves is also a salient theme in the myths and songs of other Quichua speakers of the Amazon and the Andes. Juan Santos Ortíz de Villalba (1993:151) presents a Spanish translation of an original Quichua song titled "Dove of the Sea," collected among Amazonian Quichua speakers of Lower Napo. *Canciones indígenas en los Andes ecuatorianos* (1996:38), a collection of indigenous songs from the Ecuadorian Andes, contains a highland love song from Otavalo in which feminine beauty is associated with the dove. In the Huarochirí manuscript (Salomon and Urioste 1991:49) the mythical creator god Vira Cocha seduces one of Pacha Camac's two daughters, but the other escapes by turning into a dove and flying away. The name of the woman's mother, Urpay Wachac, means "she who gives birth to doves."

Perhaps Salomon and Urioste can provide some insight into the social dynamics of women as birds through their interpretation of the mythology of gender relations. They write, "Marriage myths are myths of social dynamics. . . . They express not only an ideal of productive and reproductive union, but also an image of the many tensions involved in creating such a union" (Salomon and Urioste 1991:9–10). Among the Napo Runa as well, marriage involves both conflict and complementarity. Like a bird, a woman must "fly" from her natal kin networks, separating from them and recombining into the ayllu-muntun of her husband. Jacinta's first song reveals that Runa marriages are acknowledged struggles of conflicting forces: masculine and feminine, hunter and hunted, woman's ayllu and man's ayllu, and other such complementary oppositions. At the same time, her songs further show that her dove powers are in the end turned toward complementarity and a loving relationship with her husband. Conflict itself is transformed into positive emotional states (see Overing and Passes 2000:5–6).

Shamanism, Evangelical Protestantism, and Shape-Shifting

I associate shamanism with the aesthetics and social forms of shape-shifting. Indeed, as I see it, both Lucas and Jacinta are shamans, for they are socially recognized as especially powerful and adept shape-shifters. In making such a statement, I am rethinking traditional understandings of the category of "shaman" (*yachac* in the Napo jargon; pl., *yachacguna*) to include other types of healers and persons who may or may not identify themselves as shamans: musicians, joke tellers, and those who practice evangelical Christianity. As a shape-shifter, a shaman is someone who has mastered aesthetic forms that represent the unseen forces and powers that define the human condition and the human body. The term *shaman*, a universally accepted and globally popular term, does not fully capture how people in Napo conceptualize shamanism as an aesthetics of power and bodily transformation.

Indeed, the term *shaman* has come to indicate a certain sort of person, setting a boundary between those who have a special status and those who do not. I prefer to focus on practice rather than essence. In Napo, that is, people are more focused on doing shamanism than on identifying who may or may not be a shaman (Campbell 1989; Kohn 2002b:337). For example, many people who I later discovered were shamans often denied to me, and to others, that they were yachacguna. The reasons for resisting a fixed and public identity as a yachac are complex, but people often told me that to proclaim oneself as a yachac is to endanger not only one's own life but the lives of one's ayllu. The yachacguna are thought to have the power to kill as well as heal, doing the former sometimes through their mere anger. Because most sicknesses and deaths among those indigenous to Napo are thought to be caused by the ill will or anger of a shaman, to proclaim oneself as such is to risk being associated and attacked for the tragedies of others.

The following terms are used to describe people with shamanic qualities: *pajuyuc runa* (someone who has a *paju*, or specialized magical power), *curandero* (Spanish for "curer"), and *ductur* (Spanish for "doctor"). In addition, the terms "sinzhi runa" (strong man/person) or "sinzhi warmi" (strong woman) imply someone with shamanistic power. This person may or may not be considered a yachac. In Avila priests are considered to have shamanistic powers and are associate with the shamanic term *miricu* (Kohn 2002b:338–39). Evangelicals, called *ciricuna* in Quichua, conceptualize their powers in terms of Napo Runa shape-shifting but differentiate and oppose themselves to the practices of the yachac shamans. Evangelicals base their power on God's "breath" (*Diospac samai*) rather than the forces emanating from the spirits of the underworld (*ucupacha*). As one evangelical leader stated:

> We are like the powerful shaman bancu. A bancu is the most powerful kind of yachac. The spirits [supai] reside within him. He is their seat. Whereas the bancu gets his power from the supai, we get our power from God. God inhabits us just as the spirits inhabit the bancu. In the beginning times God took his breath [samai] and blew it onto a book. In so doing he created the Bible as a manifestation of his power. This is why the Bible has power. It contains God's samai.

Evangelicals in Napo consider their practices to be a kind of "spiritual armor" (Whitehead 2002) against dark shamanism and malevolent spirits that cause sickness and death. Like shamans, evangelicals consider themselves to be spiritually powerful beings (sinzhi runa). Evangelical power is linked to strict bodily practices, however, particularly abstention from getting drunk, dancing, smoking, and getting angry. To follow these practices is to be a "pure" (*chuya*) and powerful evangelical ("sinzhi ciric"). To be pure is to maximize God's flow of power into one's body as spiritual armor, good fortune, and the ability to heal.

Nonetheless, the notion that Runa evangelicals are shamans is contradictory, for one must reject "traditional" notions of shamanism to become an evangelical. To say that evangelicals "shamanize," however, is not a contradiction (Campbell 1989). For example, one "strong" evangelical told me that yachacs repeatedly threatened him with death. He fought many spiritual battles from which God (and he by association) emerged victorious: "These shamans publicly stated that they would kill me. They said, 'We will kill you. Never will I let an *evangelista* into our community.' What happened? Sometime later, this man who threatened me dropped dead all of a sudden. He was not an old man. Later, just as he perished, so too did the others. Do you not think now that God takes care of those who follow him?" Other evangelicals recounted similar stories of the power of their beliefs and practices for protecting them against shamanism and dangerous spirits.

Evangelicals in Napo constitute a small minority compared to the large and powerful Catholic presence there, but the evangelical movement resonates with indigenous notions of spiritual power, sociality, and opposition to domination (see Uzendoski 2003). Churches in indigenous communities, for example, are controlled by local indigenous leaders, not outsiders. The pattern of preaching copies Runa social structure, with heads-of-households taking turns delivering messages. In addition, indigenous evangelicals have recently formed their own federation. Many of these indigenous evangelicals were on the front lines, side by side with Catholic Runa and non-Christian Runa, during the 2001 uprising.

Predatory aspects of shamanism make shamanizing through evangelical Christianity attractive. The mythical world of Jesus (accessible through the Bible as well as experience), like those of many other alters in Napo Runa cosmology, is an important source of ushai and transformative power.[7] In Napo, as in other places in Amazonia, Christianity and shamanism are recognized as complementary forces within a unified field of cosmological power.

I am not the first to attempt to rethink shamanism in this way and to emphasize that there are many sides to shamanism, including both "dark" and more "angelic" sides. In his effort to understand shamanism in Guyana, Whitehead (2002:128) finds the need to analyze the term as including "both the alleluia prophets (iwepyatàsak) and the Christian evangelists." Christianity, he argues, manifests itself as a "light" or good form of shamanism, a force for combating dark forces and spirits that are constantly seeking victims. While it may be opposed to dark and other forms of shamanism, Christianity is conceptually reinforced and strengthened by them. In a world where every living thing is capable of both causing and receiving a violent spirit death, Christian discourses about desires, bodily control, and emotional states often resonate powerfully with native religiosities.

In Napo many Quichua songs used in evangelical services feature shape-shifting themes—namely, the process of becoming a sinzhi ciric, or strong evangelical. Such songs capture the experiences of coming into the "shape" of God's state, expressed, for example, through a phrase invoking spatial movement: "Diospacma ringaj," which means "to go to God's place." The image is one of movement from an old state of being to a new state inhabited by God. To reach this latter state one must defeat spirits associated with dark shamanism that evangelicals believe to be constantly stalking them. The term *supai* is used polysemously here, referring not only to the Christian devil but also to Amazonian spiritual forces that heal or cause sickness and misfortune. Christ is presented as spiritual armor, and service to him allows one to take on his form. The term *causai* (life force) is often used to indicate God's protective spiritual presence within a Christian. Songs also employ the concept of tucuna, or transformation. The message in these evangelical songs is that one must take on Christ's form, becoming a shape-shifter for the forces of God.

Humor and Shape-Shifting

Shape-shifting appears with the domain of humor, too. People who tell jokes and make life convivial are regarded as special. These are often people with shamanic qualities associated with power. As Joanna Overing writes of humor: "Good laughter is essential to the health of the community. . . . The Piaroa leader must be a master of laughter, and nowhere is this more evident than in the telling of myths. The absurdities of myth are good theatre" (2000:76). Indeed, the power to make another person laugh is a sign of one's strong will, one's ability to put a funny edge on the seriousness, fears, tragedies, and mundane challenges of daily life.

Humor and wit are intrinsic to the everyday life, speech acts, and narratives in Napo Runa communities. When I failed to understand a joke, a man from Pucara told me, "Quichua is a very figurative language. It allows us to make very creative and funny jokes. These kinds of jokes cannot be made in Spanish. What seems funny in Quichua doesn't translate into Spanish." The joke I did not understand was "Alcu iyacpi, rupaiyachiwangui," that is, "In thinking of the dog, make me warm." The humor lies in imagining the heat created by a dog's fur to be mimetically transferred to the human body of the speaker, who is feeling cold and asks the listener to warm him or her.[8] In addition, the joke shows an intimate connection between the body and the mind of the speaker. The body feels cold, but the mind thinks heat by reference to a dog. This particular joke, I learned, was repeated often among a specific group of people from Pucara, so that it had come to represent a human relationship among a group of kin.

Imagine that instead of saying "I am cold," one says to a friend, "Thinking of the dog, make me warm." This innovative and more humorous phrasing then becomes a memory and a symbol of a relationship among kin. To repeat it is to invoke a common history and the common somatic experience of feeling heat and cold. Such is a common usage of Quichua humor: jokes indicate shared experiences and memories of comfort, pain, and other bodily and emotional states. As does the aforementioned joke, Quichua humor often speaks of the body as a subject, something that perceives, feels, and acts in the world.

The Runa laugh at everything, from the most trivial to the most serious. They even laugh at death itself, as Lucas's account of the Izhu shows. Sumaco laughs boastfully at his rival only to meet his own demise in the ensuing flood. Lucas's forefathers stand atop Chiuta and laugh at the auca as they perish in the water, turning over and over. Laughing at the deaths of others might seem cruel, but keep in mind that the term *auca* refers to any enemy that kills the Runa. Lucas laughed at what he feared—and there is a serious and dangerous reality behind the Izhu myth: Amazonian floods are highly destructive events that destroy gardens and houses and kill people. In Napo many people have lost close relatives in the currents of flood waters.

Humor creates relations but also gives them an aesthetic patterning and affectivity that complements the substance forms and complexities of kinship. Once while attending a fiesta, I noticed a man who was going around telling jokes, singing songs, and entertaining people. He stopped by our area, and we began talking. I commented on his sense of humor. He responded, "I make a point of making people laugh so as to spread a sense of happiness [*cushi*] by conversing, singing, and telling jokes. This is our custom, and I am proud to be a Runa. That is why I want people to call me not by my Spanish name but by my nickname, Cushillu [the kinkajou, *Potos flavus*, a monkeylike animal]. I am like a cushillu in essence. I am not as crazy as the *machín* [a monkey of the genus *Cebus*], but I am funny and easy to be around."

Cushillu casts the funny person as a mimetic shape-shifter and a creator of emotion. These emotions are central to the way people conceptualize and live kinship. Like Lucas and Jacinta, Cushillu connects people to unai by showing them that they are linked to one another in destiny, substance, and laughter. Again, one body is many bodies.

Pierre Clastres (1989:150) characterizes Native Amazonian humor as a "gay science" that serves to further a special convivial and mimetic quality. Humor, he argues, is the "cathartic function of the myth, so to speak: in its narration it frees one of the . . . passions, the secret obsession to laugh at what one fears. It devalues on the plane of language a thing that cannot be taken lightly in reality, and, manifesting in laughter an equivalent of death, it instructs us that among the Indians, ridicule kills" (ibid., 146). I agree with the central idea of this statement: that humor is a form of interaction closely associated with transformations and qualities of life and death. If the connection of humor to shamanism is not yet clear, perhaps a description of a shamanic séance will help to focus the relations.

Whitten and Whitten (1988:34) note that in a séance, the shaman "figuratively appropriates the order of the universe, pastes together a montage of palpable images drawn from Canelos Quichua [Pastaza Runa] concepts of 'our culture,' and 'other cultures,' and repositions patient, audience, and agencies of illness in the new construct of 'our order.'" Shamans manipulate divergent and imposed realities through shape-shifting, transforming those realities into Runa symbols, tropes, and terms as they go. Humor, like shamanism, can eschew the fixed identities, hegemonies, and tragedies of death and illness and the conflicts of daily life. Both humor and shamanism are mimetic and highly aesthetic; they rely heavily on the transformations, symbolism, and subjectivities of emotional and bodily states.

The shaman controls and enters patients' bodies through mystical means; the joke teller does the same by making people laugh. Both can heal, resulting in happiness, but they can also create conflict, do harm (*waglichina*), or cause illness. Illnesses are more commonly associated with the yachac shamans, but people can do damage using jokes, especially when joking is accompanied by envy and a sentiment or intention of ill will. Like sorcery, the "evil joke" appears to be something it is not, with the appearance and reality differing in essence.

Consider the end of a myth that describes how the Avila Runa killed a Jesuit priest who kept making people get sick and die (Foletti-Castegnaro 1993:150–56). The priest was initially thought to be a good man, one who baptized and married people, but the Runa kept getting ill and dying after his visits. They finally got together and determined that the priest was killing them. They still did not do anything until an even worse epidemic occurred. They then killed the priest, but they did not do so simply. As the text says, "they killed him by making fun [*burlana*] of him in many ways." They mixed urine and feces in chicha and made the priest drink it. They beat him. They scolded him by saying that the recently dead would still be living if he had not come and that it was his fault that they were getting sick. The story later tells that those who killed the priest were unable to have children. The priest had the last joke in this one: they were cursed.[9]

Shape-Shifting in Making Kin

Shape-shifting and its aesthetic qualities are not only pertinent to narrative, music, joke telling, and shamanism but also fundamental to the processes of kinship. In living among the Napo Runa, I observed that people usually referred to others using direct terms of kinship. The basic terms of substance are *yaya* (father), *mama* (mother), *wauki* (brother with male ego), *turi* (brother with female ego), *pani* (sister with male ego), *ñaña* (sister with female ego), *churi* (son), and *ushushi* (daughter). Affines are referred to as *masha* (daughter's husband/sister's husband) or *cachun* (son's wife/brother's wife). A masha, however, must refer to his wife's parents using the substance terms (*yaya* and *mama*), and a cachun must also refer to her husband's parents in like fashion.

When describing their collective kinship networks, the Runa use the terms *ayllu* (kin group) or *muntun* (kindred). The upside-down shigra, discussed in the introduction, provides a visual representation of both, for all three involve a network of expansive relations (see fig. 1). *Muntun* can refer to groups of various scales, such as households, collections of households, villages, and entire communities. It is understood that the people living in a muntun are related through substance and affinal ties and share a common spiritual, material, historical, and political destiny. These people are also ayllu, or consanguineal relatives. At first I though that the terms *ayllu* and *muntun* conveyed fixed social groupings, much like the modern Western notion of a nation (see Wagner 1974). I later realized, however, that these notions are structured by shape-shifting and performative acts of affectivity, much as the aesthetic discourses of Lucas, Jacinta, and Cushillu were.

One day we went to the market in Tena and were interested in purchasing a medicinal remedy from the indigenous vendors who frequent the plaza on the weekends. There were many women selling all kinds of Runa products—crafts, herbs, medicine, and foods. We approached a line of women, all of whom were unfamiliar. After chatting with them for some time, we ended up buying from one woman because she had a distant uncle who had married someone from my host ayllu.

Sometime later Bancu said to me, "It is always better to buy from someone who is ayllu." He continued, "They don't cheat you and will often give you what you need on credit." I noticed that he returned to the same woman

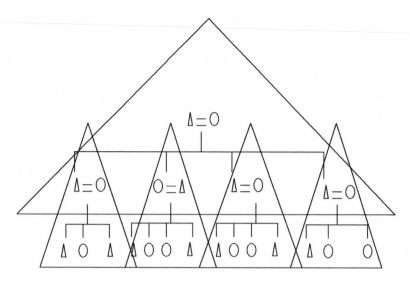

Figure 1. Kindred (adapted from Whitten 1985)

whenever he needed something. Furthermore, the relationship grew. Bancu and the woman often exchanged gifts of small food items and shared jokes, personal stories, and life experiences. They would talk often and became quite close. The category of ayllu was meaningful as the aesthetic expression of their increasingly intimate relation.

While living in Runa communities I was amazed at people's skill at remembering complicated kinship ties. Residents of one community always recognized those from others. Even if they did not know their names, they recognized their faces and associated the faces with specific communities and sets of relations. They also recognized the children of many of these people. Runa adults know the basic kinship affiliations of hundreds of people. More amazingly, this kinship knowledge often extends into other Amazonian regions, such as Lower Napo, Puyo, Ahuano, Lago Agrio, and beyond.

Indeed, as time went on I realized that my ayllu was more expansive than I had previously thought it to be. Not just limited to Yacu Llacta, it expanded to Tena and numerous other communities near Tena and then to Coca, Lower Napo, Puyo, and even into the Putumayo area of Colombia. I noticed that my host ayllu maintained relations with kin in these distant places. Family members would often visit siblings who lived in different places and exchange food, medicines, herbs, plants, and other things. They would also help each other in times of need, when someone was ill, or in preparing for the wedding of a son or godson. I was able to help and participate in one such wedding in the Lower Napo community of Santa Yacu.

The ayllu are powerful social and communication networks. My first experience with the communicative power of the ayllu was disconcerting. Early in my fieldwork I and several American friends from Quito decided to spend an evening dancing in the discos in Tena. I was hoping to forget about fieldwork for a while. We had a nice night, and nothing special happened.

Some days later, when I returned to my host ayllu, I was shocked to find out that they knew with whom I had gone, where I had gone, what discos I had visited, and even with whom I had danced. I was very surprised. They explained to me that a distant cousin had been passing the evening in the discos that same night. He had related to them my movements through the kin network, with the news arriving in Yacu Llacta before I did.

Using kinship as a means of communication is highly effective. People traveling from one region or community to the next often pass messages to and from ayllu within a chain of kin relations. As one person commented after the incident in the discos, "Our ayllu networks are better than television or even the Internet. We know what is going on everywhere." It is customary for the Runa to make small talk with those they do not know when arriving at a place, waiting for the bus, or standing in line. Conversation about one's life and the lives of others moves from place to place in this way. For example, one can have an idea of what is going on in the lives of relatives who live in different communities by talking to others who live nearer to them. A look to the past shows that these ayllu networks were used in organizing revolts against the Spanish in colonial times (see Oberem 1980; Muratorio 1991; Uzendoski 2004a) and, more recently, in the 2001 uprising.

The preceding examples highlight the shape-shifting nature of Napo Runa kinship. The polysemic terms *ayllu* and *muntun* can be applied widely to indicate a relationship of intimacy among people related in various ways (Whitten 1976, 1985). Speakers can express the strength versus weakness of a particular substance relation by qualifying these terms with an adjective, such as *my* ("ñuca ayllu"), *my own* ("kinkin ayllu"), or *distant* ("caru ayllu"). The terms *ayllu* and *muntun* cannot be divorced from feeling and the shifting dynamics of relationships. The notion of kinship carries with it the idea that people share not only a common substance but also a common destiny that requires sharing things and the experiences of life. At the same time, just as those who become close and share life become kin, those who lose their connections can become lost to one ayllu. The social logics of Runa kinship, however, always allow people to recombine into another ayllu, for the constituent relations shift to accommodate movement. Indeed, many people become connected to more than one ayllu, and sometimes several of them, over the courses of their lives. Moreover, because aylluguna flow into one another, it is difficult to see where one ayllu ends and another begins.

Seeing Their Faces

Willful beings, or "shamans," define and organize the relationships of kinship. To put the matter in Whitten and Whitten's words, they "provide mechanisms for unifying and separating, expanding and contracting *ayllu* space" (1984:217). I have already mentioned that one does not have to be a shaman to practice shamanism. Nonetheless, shamanic figures are those who, in transforming kinship relations, produce mature, high-value relationships of reciprocity and sharing. Directly connected to the life cycle itself, such processes of substance metamorphosis are integral to personhood. The social must be constantly nourished.

In Ambatu Yacu and other places in Napo, collective social maturation moves from an emphasis on parent-child relationships to networks of relationships among brothers and sisters, affines, and mutual godparents. One might say that social process begins with concerns of feeding (asymmetrical exchanges between parents and children) and turns into one of reciprocity (continued delayed exchanges between brothers and sisters and among affines). This metamorphosis entails the divestment of certain relationships so that new ones can be defined and transformed. These exchange and circulatory pathways are mediated by strong-willed ayllu heads—shape-shifters—who nourish their kin networks. The cycle of communal development conceptually mirrors the cycle of human maturation and strengthening, a point I will demonstrate more fully in later chapters. Like humans, ayllu and muntun forms must be reproduced through productive social action.

The Runa say they generally dislike living far away from their kin because doing so prevents them from regularly encountering siblings, seeing their children grow up, or sharing the day-to-day experiences of life with them. Siblings feel an emotional and spiritual bond often expressed in dreaming. Siblings make one another dream about future or current events in their individual and mutual lives. The idiom of substance defines these relations, even in mystical form. The Runa view siblingship as an ideal kind of relationship, using the idiom to express closeness to nonsiblings such as cousins and friends. By calling a friend or a cousin a "brother," or a "sister," they express the closeness of the bond and inclusion within a boundary of difference.

Siblingship is an ideal form of sociality elicited in negotiating relationships and boundaries within communities. Consider how people in Pucara wrote the history of their community:

> At the beginning there were few families in Pucara. Of the Andi group, there were Francisco, Sikli, and Bancu. On the Apayacu side the first inhabitants were Ushpa, Coto, and Sicu. The Calapucha group lived in Jatuncocha. The Shiguango group lived in Chimballacta, and the other group, of Samuel Grefa, lived below what is now the mission. Shicti Huarapu (father of Anga) lived in Dumbiqui. The family of Rafael Cerda lived in a part of Yacullacta where Jaimie Grefa is buried, and the other group lived in Pucara itself. ("Historia de la Escuela de Pucara")

Notice that the narrator does not trace the history of Pucara to one patriarchal figure but specifically names groups of fathers who implicitly formed the heads of ayllu networks. These networks are associated with specific places in the landscape. Some of these fathers are then linked to sets of their sons, who have fathered their own kindred groups. These different groups are not like idealized nations, for they are not bounded, essentialized designations of identity given a priori. Relations are focused around the father-figure, yet one ayllu flows into the next; one body is many bodies. It is impossible to ascertain the exact nature of these entities without knowing the specific kinship relations involved. The history's method of tracking relations over time through pathways of fathers, however, also mirrors the focus on origins found in Lucas's mythical account of Izhu. Both the history of Pucara and Lucas's account of Izhu highlight the predominance of fathers in creating and founding the kin networks of specific places in the Upper Napo landscape.

Conclusion

Overing and Passes argue that the poetics of the Amazonian world constitute that world's theory of the social: "It is a world at one with poetics and aesthetics, which contrasts with our modern Western sensibilities where the work of the poet and artist must be kept separate from (what is viewed as) the tedium of workaday, everyday life" (2000:8). These contrasting views of art, that of modern Westerners versus that of Native Amazonians, highlight the point that value and art cannot be divorced from each other. Modern Western views of art are dominated by the social relations and values of commodification (see Benjamin 1968).[10] By contrast, Amazonian cultures reveal the predominance of aesthetics in speech, cosmology, and daily social and ritual activities. For Amazonian peoples, beautiful expressions reflect a core social and cosmological principle by which people are created, related, and transformed through complex notions of the power of aesthetic form (Guss 1989).

Among the Napo Runa, I have argued, the forces of samai, substance, and affective life are configured by an aesthetics of shape-shifting and transformation. Shape-shifting, a notion often associated with predation (Whitehead 2002), is present in the social logics and transformations of kinship, too. Because people are viewed as beings defined by the presence and circulation of cosmic life forces, the Napo Runa see themselves as changing form and substance through mediating relationships with other Runa, spirits, cosmic forces, and nature. Especially powerful shape-shifters are those who practice shamanism. Shamanic beings have strong wills and direct not only social relations but also energy flows by organizing and translating various realities and power flows into "our order" (Whitten 1988:297–303).

Marriage itself is a social process of shape-shifting among the Runa, and marriage recombines mythical paternal and maternal substance lines into new forms. Århem (1981:315–19) has argued that Native Amazonians often hold distinct conceptual models of both descent and alliance in their social formations. The Runa mode of social action, however, cannot so easily be carved up by these two models, for the terms reify the more intersubjective processes of conviviality and shape-shifting. Among the Runa, descent does not create a bounded a priori social unit, nor does alliance exclusively relate such "units." As I will show, ritual marriage is a social process of substance transformation.

3

Ritual Marriage and Making Kin

Weddings are celebrated by three days' festivity, which consists
principally in chicha drinking, with singing, dancing, and music
kept up incessantly day and night.
—Alfred Simson (1883:24) on Napo Runa weddings

Before my wedding, during the "dry" months of 1994, I and those associated with my adoptive family in Yacu Llacta spent months preparing for the arrival of the warmi parti, or "woman's side." On the day the warmi parti was due, I was particularly exhausted from having stayed up all the previous night, participating in the fiesta for the cari parti, or "man's side." We had been preparing for weeks: fishing, harvesting manioc, preparing beverages and food, recruiting helpers and other ritual participants for the wedding ceremony, and providing the warmi parti with transportation from Pucara.

Galo and I were now waiting for the buses that were to bring the bride and her relatives, both near and distant, from Pucara. The river was clear, low, and slow moving under an unforgiving sun; we waited for hours on that incredibly hot day. At one point Galo said to me, "They aren't coming. They stood you up. Let's go home." Dejected and tired, I replied, "Let's wait just a few more minutes."

Suddenly we heard the rumble of a bus in the distance. In a few minutes three buses emerged from the trees and came to an abrupt stop amid a cloud of dust. People began exiting quickly. They were talking in an animated fashion, carrying many things, and shouting and laughing. A grandmother got off the bus and came right up to me. She greeted me as *masha* (son-in-law) and took my hand, stroking it gently. She said, "It is our custom to give the masha a name on his wedding day. I don't think I have ever seen such a hot summer day as this. Look how the sun burns." She looked up at the sun and then turned around, announcing, "This is our inti masha [sun masha]."

Liminality and Production

According to Van Gennep (1965:3), "The life of an individual in any society is a series of passages from one age to another." Van Gennep thus saw society as a series of transformations. His insight was to suggest that transitional rites exhibit a general logic of three essential phases. First there is separation. Next there is the "liminal" period, in which the person is symbolically outside society and "in-between" communities or cohorts. Last there is incorporation, which signals a new status of the postliminal person (Van Gennep 1965; Morris 1987). This schema has influenced many different anthropologists, but Victor Turner in particular has developed and refined this complex of ideas.

In "Betwixt and Between," from *The Forest of Symbols* (1967), Turner describes the characteristics of the liminal period. Liminality is an ambiguous condition in which all categories and classifications are ritually dissolved, with the dissolution often expressed through metaphors and role reversals. In addition, liminality often includes a period of seclusion or symbols thereof. Moreover, stress is put on the absolute authority of elders, who are the keepers of morality and ritual knowledge. Turner thus views liminality as a mode of ritual action linked to social process, a means of creating and transforming social relationships. Turner shows that explanations of liminality must rest not on structure but rather on its negation.

Ritual liminality produces real effects within society, for rituals create value by transforming relationships. Indeed, the rituals I will discuss employ antistructural processes to emphasize dissolving relationships and identities. The destructive aspect of ritual and public action, however, is internal to production itself (Damon 2002b:127). Ritual marriage among the Runa exhibits principles of destruction that allow for social recombination and the production of valued relationships that define adult personhood. Ritual involves the exchange and circulation not only of things but also of the relational parts of persons (Damon 2002b).

This view of ritual, however, becomes clear when framed in terms of the argument that marriage among the Runa is part of a total social process. Marriage processes unfold from the Napo Runa notion of persons "with relationship already implied" (Wagner 1991:163). As I will detail later, marriage not only transforms individual persons but also reproduces the whole of Napo Runa society. Napo Runa people say that their marriage rituals define their culture, their tradition. I think they say this because marriage rituals are essential to the reproduction of society itself.[1]

Runa Marriage

According to the anthropologist Theodore Macdonald, "The Runa's principal rituals surround marriage. Three formal events—*tapuna* (request), *pactachina* (fulfillment of agreements), and *bura* (wedding)—punctuate a lengthy process through which a group acquires a wife for one of its members. This ceremonial sequence dramatizes the efforts of the groom's family . . . to impress and demonstrate respect for the bride's family" (1999:21). Although Macdonald defines the essentials of the marriage process as ritualistic and public, marriage relations often begin more informally. Today marriages usually begin through flirting relationships. In this arena young people exchange low-value things such as candies, colas, and kisses. These exchanges occur outside the view of adults, but adults are sometimes aware of them. Until something serious happens in the way of public recognition, adults don't mind flirting among the young, for it is *yanga* (for nothing).

Many Runa told me that when a young man feels love for someone with whom he has been flirting, he goes to his father, makes his feelings known, and asks him to do something about the situation. If the father and other relatives agree that the person and timing are right, the ayllu will then plan a course of action. In past times parents arranged marriages and selected their children's mates when they were very little. This practice is followed less frequently today, but marriage still involves a heavy element of parental arrangement. Flirting relationships, for example, cannot become something more if parents do not formalize them. Indeed, this was my own experience.

Edith and I had been seeing each other for quite some time. Bancu knew of our relation and constantly made fun of me. He described our relationship as one of *wambrana*, or "fooling around." Over several months my host brothers and I often visited Edith's relatives in town and in Pucara, bringing them gifts of fish, meat, and other things. My host brothers were friends with a few of Edith's sisters and cousins, so we all enjoyed visiting. Through this process I became familiar with Edith's father and all her brothers, sisters, and other relatives. I acknowledged to all except her father that I was seeing Edith and asked permission to continue seeing her. Edith's brothers were distrustful and often asked about my intentions. Only after I had confessed to Edith's father did Bancu become convinced of my seriousness. One morning we had a conversation in which he told me that we would now move forward with formalizing the relationship. He stressed that the wedding process had to be done in strict accordance with established Runa custom and that it had to take place in Yacu Llacta.

In Runa marriage the young woman usually leaves her natal ayllu and becomes integrated into her husband's—a social idea evoked in the songs of women as birds I discussed in chapter 2. Daughters who "fly away" become other people's wives. Nevertheless, this custom can provoke dismay in the parents of young women, making it difficult for suitors to convince them to give up their daughters. In Runa society, where kinship and interpersonal relationships are intense, the prospect of losing a relative that marriage entails is a scary, tense, and emotionally charged affair. People are explicitly considered to be the highest form of value in Runa society, and the ritual processes of marriage reflect the explicit value of people as relational entities of circulation.

The Beginnings of Liminality: Tapuna, or the Request

The first step in contracting marriage is for the young man's ayllu to organize a *tapuna,* the ritual request for the woman's hand. During the tapuna the bride's ayllu is referred to as the "warmi muntun" (woman's group). The groom's ayllu is called the "cari muntun" (man's group). These bodies are ritually identified as the "warmi parti" (woman's party or side) and the "cari parti" (man's party or side), and they form the principal opposition on which the marriage process centers. Although the tapuna is a formal, public ritual, people usually speak informally with the young woman's father ("warmi yaya") beforehand to ensure that they will receive consent. Because a tapuna requires considerable labor, food, and money from the young man's ayllu, people do not feel it wise to execute tapuna rituals whose success is in doubt. To perform a tapuna, the young man's father must go to the prospective wife's house, accompanied by his ayllu-muntun and compadres, to make arrangements with the girl's father, mother, aunts, and uncles. This event features an assemblage of persons identifying with two different aylluguna. In some cases the two aylluguna do not know each other well. The ritual is a small but formal affair.

The young man's ayllu must play host in the girl's house, even though they are relative strangers. They must serve the woman's side ample food and drink. They must plead using humble and respectful words. The key actor in the tapuna is the young woman's father ("warmi yaya"), the final authority on whether to accept the agreement. By proposing to take his daughter, the young man's ayllu begins a relationship of extreme debt. This attitude—that the man's side owes the woman's side an extreme debt—manifests itself in the behavior of both parties. The woman's side acts in an angry or offended manner, while the man's side acts very humbly and graciously.

In the tapuna ritual the young woman's father, mother, brothers, sisters, compadres and any other close relatives line up in a long row, seated on benches and wearing serious expressions. The young man's ayllu must then go to each in turn, beginning with the father, asking permission for the young man to marry the young woman. As a sign of their humility, the young man and his relatives must kneel as they pass through the entire line. The prospective groom follows his father and mother, and the godparents follow him. Each exchange can last up to ten or fifteen minutes. Conversation on the part of the woman's ayllu revolves around establishing that the groom will take care of their daughter and treat her well. Wife beating is a concern in these negotiations, and often the bride's relatives will explicitly warn the groom not to beat her. The groom's father and others promise that the bride (whom they call "your daughter") will be treated well, and each exchange ends with the polite request, "Manzhu chaskinara ushapawangui [Can't you just accept me]?" A ritual handshake symbolizes that the agreement has been made an official pact.

The young woman is absent from these ritual happenings, and she will often hide while her fate is being negotiated. (In fact, some potential brides run away during the tapuna negotiations.) During these exchanges it is not uncommon for the women, especially the young woman's mother, to cry. Younger members of each household, children and adolescents, will stand in the corners and watch or accompany the young girl.

The men, and especially the young woman's father, are more stoic, and the warmi yaya is expected to show displeasure and annoyance but not open anger. It is up to the young man's father to offer him gifts that calm his irritation. The young man's father uses humble language and offers many chickens, bottles of liquor, and other gifts—all mainly prestige items. I heard of one tapuna where the woman's father would not agree until he was given thirty chickens and the young man's father swore that he would call the bride not *cachun* but *ushushi* (daughter). Such acts, which win the confidence of others through dramatic ritual conflict and resolution, become part of the histories of aylluguna and their relations.

After the negotiations are done and promises have been tendered and accepted, the fathers make speeches. These words seal the agreement and signal the beginning of the festive phase. During the negotiations people have been cooking and preparing a meal in the background. The helpers—men and women who are not part of the negotiations—have been brought by the groom's father for this purpose. Only certain foods are acceptable for a tapuna, all of them foods that the Runa view as having high value. Purchased items, such as soft drinks, beer, and good rum, are necessary, as are large quantities of hunted meat and fish and *asua,* or manioc brew.

The first course usually consists of a soup or broth of chickens (*atalba*). The main course consists of manioc and plantains, along with game and fish. People normally do not accept beef or any kind of tinned meat for a tapuna. Because they require game, the young man's ayllu will intensely hunt and fish before the tapuna. They will try to obtain some of the choicest kinds of game and fish as a sign of their "love" and respect for the young woman's father and his ayllu. If the woman's father or her relatives find the food unacceptable at the tapuna, they may reject the marriage proposal.

After eating, the men of both sides usually drink heavily. Each side begins to refer to the other as *auya* (allies; the term also means "alliance"). Drinking (*upina*) is the privilege of the woman's side, and the cari parti must keep the flow of asua and other alcoholic drinks going toward their auya. The man's side serves and drinks with the woman's side; cigarettes are provided and consumed in the same way. These drinking sessions often go into the morning.

Many elements that Victor Turner (1967) describes for liminality are represented in the tapuna. Ambiguity is represented in the uncertainly that the agreement will be fulfilled or that the tapuna will go well. Dissolution is expressed primarily through drinking and drunkenness and in the completion of an agreement. Role reversals occur mainly through representations of gender inversions of producer, consumer, and status level. The groom's ayllu takes on the feminine role in both words and exchange. They cook for and serve the woman's ayllu, just as a woman might serve a man. They also serve the bride's relatives, entertaining them, giving them respect, and making them happy. Seclusion is symbolized in the bride's absence from most of the activity and her separation from the groom. Lastly, the proceedings stress the elders' absolute authority based on their ritual knowledge. Elders emphasize that they know the ritual language and behavior of the tapuna and that young people should follow their leads. These aspects are further intensified in later fiestas.

Ongoing Liminality: Pactachina

The next phase in marriage is the performance of a pactachina, which is a higher-order tapuna. The pactachina also contains ritual elements of the bura, such as the *virsaru* (drummer and chanter), the *tocadur* (violinist), and dancing (see plate 1). It is common to invite relatives from other households of the ayllu, but like the tapuna, the pactachina is for close relatives. Because

Plate 1. A visaru and a tocadur making music at a wedding in 1994.

the pactachina is a scaled-up version of the tapuna and is nowadays often skipped, I do not detail it here.

Outcome: The Bura

At some point during the tapuna or pactachina the date is set for the bura. The bura is not only a ritual ceremony of increased scale but also one in which social actors "finish" the social and liminal transformations of marriage. The tapuna initiates liminality, and the pactachina continues it, but the separations necessary for the full liminal state are not achieved until the bura, which is the most encompassing and important of the three rituals (figure 2 illustrates the increasing scope of these ceremonies). The bura incorporates and encompasses the greatest magnitude of social relations, including relations between the communities of both the man's side and the woman's side.

The bura is a grueling endeavor, and during my wedding people repeatedly told me that young men often decide to break their promises while they are suffering the preparations. I, too, felt this pressure during some of the most stressful moments leading up to my bura in Yacu Llacta. The bura requires great quantities of game and fish to be served for an afternoon meal

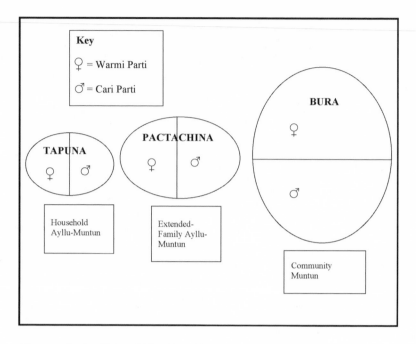

Figure 2. Scale of Ritual Marriage Fiestas

and as gifts to the woman's side. The appropriate kinds of game are those that confer prestige, such as peccary, agouti (*Dasyprocta fuliginosa*), paca (*Agouti paca*), and monkey. Fish are also acceptable, but it is necessary to catch large quantities. The Runa do not normally accept beef or any other kind of "city" meat for the wedding. Even though they like to eat beef, they do not consider it to be appropriate for a bura. The cosmological reasons for this preference of hunted meat and fish will be made clear in later chapters; for now, it suffices to mention that prestige food is associated with showing respect and love. I noticed that, in the context of weddings, people were constantly worried about being able to serve enough game and fish to the woman's side, for weddings are judged first and foremost by the quality and quantity of food and drink.

In wedding preparations the groom is meant to suffer, especially during hunting and fishing trips. He must perform all the auxiliary tasks, such as carrying supplies and fetching things. His father and elder relatives do most of the actual hunting, but he too will hunt. Marriage preparations themselves are considered a rite of passage in masculine productivity. Some people make trips to Lower Napo to visit their relatives and to hunt there, where game is more abundant. Others enlist the help of the Huaorani, whom they pay in cash for the meat they obtain. In the week preceding a bura people do not rely on any single source of game and fish, for hunting is a precarious business. They scramble to obtain as much help as they can, trading on prior relationships, and this physically and emotionally taxing work requires extreme humility and deference to those whose assistance is sought. Compadres are essential to this process.

In weddings goods from town are important as signs of prestige and respect. In the past the patron would provide all the goods that people needed, and they would run up debts to be paid back with labor (see Muratorio 1991). Today people may obtain what they need on credit or save enough money. Purchased beverages include soft drinks, beer, and hard liquor. Other small items needed are clothes, a bottle of perfume to spray on the bride, and new shoes for the bride. Flowers are not bought, for spectacular flowers can be gathered from the forest. People also procure a *discomóvil*, a music station with large speakers operated by a disc jockey. The discomóvil is used for the informal dancing that occurs after the ceremony. In the past people made their own music with drums, violin, and voice. Nowadays modern Runa music, called "Runa Paju," is expected. This music is usually played through the discomóvil, but sometimes a group will perform live at a wedding. Although this music uses electronic keyboards and other nontraditional elements, it retains the rhythmic structure and feel of Amazonian music. The lively and creative lyrics of this incredibly figurative music are always in Quichua and address themes present in Napo Runa culture.

People obtain money for weddings in various ways. Sometimes a young man will go to work for a petroleum company as a wage laborer for a number of months. Other people borrow money, sell cattle, or work in tourism. If the family has someone who is a teacher or other kind of professional, that person will often loan or give a large sum of money to the wedding cause. Cash crops such as cacao, maize, and coffee are sold. The amount of purchased goods depends on the relative economic status of an ayllu and the resources at hand.

The various beverages and other purchased things used for the bura are all linked closely to prestige. These items, which are initially bought as commodities, are transformed into gifts in the social context of the wedding, where they take on different symbolic and social meanings. These transformations reflect an important phenomenon that transcends essentialist divisions between gifts and commodities. Gregory, for example, describes this as a "commodity-gift" transformation where "the social form of a product undergoes a transformation but the crucial transformation is the final one . . . into a gift" (1997:55–56). Soft drinks, beer, rum, and other purchased products help to create the festive atmosphere of love and respect necessary for ritual transformation. This use of commodities and their subsequent transformation into gifts (and interpersonal relations) highlights the complementary rather than contradictory nature of gift and commodity exchange (Piot 1999)—although the complementarity is subordinated to the purposes of Runa sociality.

While men are busy with game and fish, the women are preoccupied with getting enough manioc and plantains and making various kinds of asua. Large vats for storing the asua mass are procured from a school or church, for the hosting ayllu usually does not have such large items. The amount of manioc needed for a bura is astounding. Manioc is used to make the asua and the *lugru* (a mixture of crushed manioc and meat) and as an accompaniment to the main meal. In the wedding itself the women from the man's side keep the asua flowing. Women work collectively, and young men may help them haul heavy loads and or pull out long manioc roots. Other relatives help by donating manioc (harvested or unharvested) and plantains. All in all, the atmosphere of preparing for a bura is one of communal helping (*yanapana*).

Time and Weddings

The bura requires people to be abnormally productive so that the woman's side can consume to an extraordinary degree, so it usually occurs during those seasons in which meat and fish are easiest to procure. The preferred time for a wedding is during the time of *chonta* (peach palm) abundance (approximately December through March), which coincides roughly with the dry season. This season sees relatively less rain, although showers are possible every day. Sometimes, though, this period will produce a series of hot, dry days, and the resulting low river levels make for easier fishing. (An overly wet and muddy bura would create bad memories of *turu,* or mud—and to dream about mud before a wedding is a bad omen.)

The peach palm is intimately intertwined with productive cycles. This abundant fruit is made into a delicious asua that adds yet more diversity to the drinks available. Weddings are times of special convivial kinds of asua not consumed every day. During the chonta season many animals will be found feeding on the peach-palm fruit. Hunters have easier kills of agouti, paca, peccary, and armadillo. In the expectation of a wedding, men set up *chapana* (hiding shelters) and regularly leave fruit on the ground to "teach" (*yachachina*) the animals to feed. The hunters thus prepare their potential kills for the wedding time. Again, summer's low river levels are conducive to fishing, for they leave the fish more exposed. The *challua,* or *bocachico,* swim upstream during the dry season, when they are more abundant. Other kinds of large fish, such as the *bagre, jandia,* and *pacu,* are easier to obtain during this time as well. The fish are smoked and kept in hanging baskets above cooking fires until the lugru is made.

Duality: Amazonia and the Andes

As I have mentioned, the wedding revolves around the duality of the cari parti and the warmi parti. This patterning of duality links the bura to the ritual forms of the adjacent Andean world, where dual forms (symmetrical and asymmetrical) are the essential deep structures by which social complementaries are created and symbolized. Isbell (1978:138), for example, argues that the cross represents a dominant symbol of Andean life: it corresponds to the ancestors, fertility and abundance, and sacredness and seriousness, as well as to the synthetic union of male and female elements. The cross represents in condensed form a procreative duality and "complementarity"—a patterning also mirrored in social relations and daily life (Isbell 1978:214). Catherine Allen makes a similar point with regard to the Andean concept of *yanatin* (a matched pair or helpmates). She writes, "Antagonists automatically paired themselves with their most equal counterpart. Rivals in battle, like lovers, are *yanatin.* . . . Any release of energy—whether constructive or destructive—calls for collaboration" (Allen 1988:187).

Duality in the Andean and Amazonian worlds is not a static principle but rather a pragmatic and dynamic classificatory aesthetic by which transformation, exchange, and energy flows are circulated. As I will show, a certain "unity of duality" emerges in the ritual forms of Napo Runa weddings.

The Elements of Runa Weddings

Principal Participants

The principal actors of the man's side are the groom's father, the groom (*cari*), his mother (*cari mama*), the godfather (*padrinu* or *marcayaya*), and godmother (*padrina* or *marcamama*), as well as the accompaniment (*compañac*)—an elder couple of secondary godparents, usually an uncle and aunt of the groom. Apart from these, a whole host of helpers contribute, in many little yet important ways, to the preparations for and execution of the wedding.

The man's side also contracts a virsaru and a tocadur; the former performs the ritual chanting and drumming that define the wedding activities, and the latter provides violin accompaniment. At first glance the Runa violin appears to be a copy of the Western instrument, but it is made from a single block of wood and has only three strings. It sounds very different from a Western violin because the Runa submit this instrument to the conventions of their own music. Although more research is required to describe this music in precise terms, the wedding music resembles shamanic music generally (see Belzner and Whitten [1979] for a recording and analysis of Amazonian Quichua music). The skills of the virsaru and tocadur are passed from father to son, and a few of these specialists remain in Upper Napo, traveling from community to community to perform at weddings. Bancu was one such specialist.

The principal actor of the woman's side is the father of the bride. He seats the guests according to their importance to his ayllu-muntun and designates the amount of food to be given to each person. Other principal actors on the woman's side include the mother, the godparents, aunts and uncles, brothers and sisters, and other close kin. The bride is the focal point of the wedding, for her movement from the woman's side to the man's side represents the transformation of all the relationships involved.

The invitations fall mainly to the woman's side, and most of the invited are ayllu from the bride's community. The man's side also invites certain people, but most of the relations on this side are already participants and helpers. The invitations are given verbally, so it is difficult to predict the exact number of people who will attend. Many uninvited guests accompany the invited; they are not given priority during serving but are usually fed. In any event, the woman's side is expected to tell the man's side how many people will come. The number of people for a bura is often open to negotiations during the tapuna and pactachina.

Phase One: Cari Parti

The bura begins the night before the actual wedding, for the man's side then holds its own formal fiesta to celebrate the completion of preparations and to reiterate the collective will in the bura. This fiesta inaugurates the long wait for the woman's side, which will arrive the next morning. It is a preview of the bura in which the man's side goes through the ritual phases of greetings (*salurana*), asking permission (*warmira mañana*) and dancing (*tushuna*), just as in the bura. Like the bura, which separates the bride from her ayllu, the groom-side fiesta is intended to separate the groom from his mother and father and to hand over "authority" to the godparents.

By executing this fiesta, people on the man's side gain valuable experience in coordinating dancing movements with the virsaru's signals and get a chance to polish the "beautiful words" they will employ the next day. The practice allows them to avoid embarrassment before the woman's side on the following day. The fiesta further allows those on the man's side to break the tension of waiting by enjoying themselves and celebrating. No one sleeps during this time of ample drink and festive behavior.

It is important not to make mistakes. During this phase in my wedding at Yacu Llacta, for example, my godfather repeated to me, "Mana pandana, mana pandana [No mistakes, no mistakes]." The first wedding I attended was in Urai Llacta, where I was a helper. My host father, Bancu, was the virsaru. The night before the bura he began with the following chanted greeting:

Man's father
Man's mother
ayllu
everyone here
the compañac
and just like that
here in front of all of you
"good afternoon" we came

Now we have begun the fiesta
Now we have begun just for that
now with this godfather
again
here now
the last fiesta
to make the bura
and to make the groom understand
to make the groom dance
to make him value our ways
to think about "elder" life
we were here

like this
my godfather
my compaña

my man's father
man's mother
man's brothers [and sisters]
cari parti ayllu
here they have given me [the task of]
the little drum
I am going to play
with your permission
just like that
with everyone's permission
my compañac
my godfather
with permission
I was going to play
being so
now we are going to start
with a little music
as in ancient times
our way of making a fiesta

Bancu's chanting identified the purpose of the reunion—to perform the last of the ritual fiestas, the bura—and he named the principal actors of the man's side. He equated the bura with "our way" "as in ancient times," stating that the elders intended to "make the groom understand." This rhetoric obviates the division of man's side and woman's side by reference to the unifying distinction of elders and young, a point I return to later. The bura had officially begun, for the groom's parents had given permission to go on with the fiesta.

While Bancu was chanting, the godfather and godmother knelt in front of the mother and father and engaged in ritual talk. The godparents asked the parents to permit their son to wed. The father and mother publicly revisited their decision to find a wife for their son and discussed why they chose Rafael and his wife to be their son's godparents. The godfather told the parents, "Ña cunan canba churi mama makimanda llushipichina [Now it is time to separate your son from the hand of his mother]." The godfather also says, "It is time to let your son out from under your wing." In this rhetoric of separation, which the godfather will use again the next day in asking for the bride, the words *llushpichina* (to separate) and *ishkindiyachina* (to make into two) are employed in complementary fashion. Here we have a liminal state being described as the precursor to the unity of duality. The discourse offers the clear image of severing relations to refashion them into the "unity of two." The specific entities are husband and wife and the nascent alliance that is to be formed between the two aylluguna. This imagery and rhetoric of separation conveys the idea that relations must be severed to create new ones.

The "asking permission" segment incorporates a mix of rhetoric, as in some of the phrases I just mentioned, and an open discourse about one's thoughts, feelings, and emotions surrounding the events of the bura. Among the Runa, stories are customarily told from beginning to end, and asking permission is no exception. For example, the godfather in the Urai Llacta wedding, Rafael, began his discourse with the events leading up to his becoming a godfather. The father, Vicente, began his discourse by saying that he was "getting old and felt the need to begin looking for a wife" for his son. In Bancu's discourse quoted previously, Bancu recounts how he was asked to play the drum for the wedding events. All social relations involved have a history, and this history must be told before one begins to transform them through ritual.

The chanting itself mixes ritual rhetoric and creative commentary. The virsaru drums while he chants, and the chanting corresponds to the drumming.

Many of the phrases draw on specialized forms of discourse not used in everyday speech. As events unfold, the virsaru not only describes events but also dictates them. He is both part of a story and the teller of that story. During the previously quoted chanting from Urai Llacta, for example, I observed the godfather ask the parents for permission to separate their son from them, so that he might be wed. The key words in Bancu's chanting resonate with or repeat the words used by the godfather in asking permission (*separating* and *obligating* and the figurative constructions of "separating from under your arm" and "separating from under your crown"). I saw that, when the godfather and father seemed to talk a bit too long, Bancu interjected the following into his chanting: "Pa-dri-nu-lla, ca-ri ya-ya, ya-nga ya-nga cue-nta-na-ra ya-nga ya-nga cue-nta-na-ra [Little godfather and the son's father are conversing over nothing, nothing, conversing over nothing, nothing]." This commentary constitutes a shining example of ritual chanting's innovative aspect, a mark of a good virsaru. The virsaru must stay alert, for he not only chants and plays the drum but must observe and listen to events around him with great care. As a kind of shamanic performer, his job is to create order, manage relations, and assist in their transformation.

Phase Two: Arrival and Greeting

The next day the woman's side begins to arrive amid a general atmosphere of festivity. The guests are seated according to their relative importance; the warmi yaya has the principal role. The virsaru and the tocadur begin to play, and the women of the man's side begin serving manioc brew to the guests. The groom and the principal actors of the man's side are visible and greet the guests by shaking hands with each person. The godfather and father give a speech to the woman's side, welcoming the guests and telling them to enjoy themselves.

Asua is consumed differently at a bura than at nonritual times. The women line up, each with her own vat of asua, and go down the rows of guests, one after the other. Each serving woman, called an "asua mama," controls the bowl and holds it to the guest's mouth, often while dancing. The consumers are expected to drink only a few mouthfuls, not the entire bowl, since they are faced with one server after the next.

In Urai Llacta I did not yet know this nuance and proceeded to gulp down entire bowl after bowl of asua in the fashion of nonritual drinking. This produced great laughter at my expense. At some point people begin to get drunk, but the asua mamas continue serving the brew and obligate people to keep drinking. Anyone who refuses to drink may well have the asua poured over his or her head. The trick to surviving a wedding is to consume constantly but in small quantities. It is appropriate to say, "Amushun" or "Ishkindi upishun" (both mean "Let's drink together"). If one of these phrases is used, custom dictates that the asua mama should drink a bowl with the guest. During this phase the asua mamas and the guests constantly exchange good-natured mockery. These joking episodes produce outbursts of laughter around the most mischievous guests. Men also flirt with the asua mamas and ask them to dance, drink with them, or simply come near them. Drinking asua itself is a sign of intimacy and a means of arousing masculine desire. The scene is one of anticipation and happiness where the circulation of greetings and asua symbolizes the guests' inclusion and initiation into the ritual theater.

The virsaru provides the greeting, which is addressed to the *auyaguna*, or affines. He implores them to have a good time and greets them with "much love" (aschca llakina), a phrase that expresses much conviviality and graciousness. After the greeting the virsaru takes a short break. He will next ask permission to begin the wedding, addressing the man's side, the bride's father, the woman's side, and all the guests.

Phase Three: Asking Permission

At this point the virsaru resumes chanting and drumming, accompanied by the tocadur. As the virsaru catches the rhythm, the principal actors of the man's side again ask permission for their "son" to marry the "daughter" of the woman's side. The virsaru will narrate these events as he chants. This phase repeats the tapuna and pactachina, but on a bigger scale; whereas these are spectacles created for close relatives, the bura, the most public of all rituals, is a spectacle designed for an entire community. The Runa emphasize that this process, wherein the man's side asks permission and the woman's side grants it, must be public to legitimize the proposed union.

The principals of the man's side go down the line, each kneeling in front of every principal of the woman's side. The latter are arranged in following order: the grandparents, the godparents, "close" aunts and uncles, elder brothers and sisters, and the parents. This is different from the tapuna, where the father is the first to be asked. Again, the bride is absent. As they make their way down this line, the principals of the cari parti will ask that their "son" be permitted to marry the warmi parti's "daughter"; at each interaction the history of that particular relationship must be related and appropriate emotions must be expressed. At this time the bride's mother, godmother, aunts, and sisters often cry, usually by ritually chanting their sadness. This is their chance to express public and dramatic sadness at the prospect of "losing" their daughter. The virsaru will narrate these events, talking about all the important relations of the woman's side and reactions to the permission-seeking requests from the man's side.

While talking to the bride's grandmother during the permission-asking phase at the Urai Llacta bura, Rafael, the godfather, said, "I come here today to ask something very big. Can't you let your daughter out from under your wing so that she can become two with her husband [ishki]?" During this discourse Bancu played in the background and chanted, using words that referred to the events taking place: *conversing, asking permission, thanking, obligating,* and *asking.* At the same time, he caricatured the principals of the woman's side. Suddenly, the grandmother of the bride began to wail by chanting. She sang to Rafael, saying, "I am sad, I am sad; even though I give permission, I still am sad." Bancu then altered his chanting to address this emotional outburst. He began to chant about sadness: "Grandmother mama will be sad, grandfather father will be sad, grandmother mama will be sad, aunts and uncles will be sad if permission is given." It is difficult to translate the poetics and emotion of these events. They are not simply "ceremonial" but also dramatic.

Such discourses on sadness are a major theme of the wedding and elucidate the intense affectivity that accompanies and defines the ritual severing of kinship relations. The grandmother sees marriage as a painful loss. Nonetheless, she understands that her loss is necessary if the process of fulfilling personhood as Napo Runa is to be completed not only for the daughter but also for her parents. Marriage transforms both.

Phase Three: Cari Parti Dancing

The next phase begins with the virsaru again taking a break while the man's side lines up to perform ritual dancing. The purpose of this phase is to make the groom attractive to the woman's side by having him dance before all the guests. The groom is flanked on one side by the godfather and on the other by the compaña; opposing them are the godmother, the compaña's wife, and a "substitute" wife for the groom (sometimes the wife of the virsaru or the groom's own mother). The two sides, masculine and feminine, face each other.

In this dance the two lines approach and retreat from each other, guided by the chanted commands of the virsaru, who says, "Come here" and "Come there" to indicate going back and forth. He says, "Meet in the middle" when the two lines meet in the center. After a certain number of passes, the lines perform a half-revolution. They then dance more passes and rotate once more. The men then pass their sombreros to the women, and the pattern repeats (see figure 3 for the basic alignment of the dancing, based on the wedding I witnessed at Urai Llacta).

Even though the dancing seems simple—merely a matter of walking back and forth—people are particular about the style, which is difficult to execute. One must bounce just right, looking fluid and relaxed, not nervous or lazy. Those in the woman's side are supposed to enjoy the dancing of the man's side, and it is not uncommon to hear them scream, whistle, and shout as each move is performed. People in the woman's side will remember anyone who danced poorly and make fun of that person for years to come.

Phase Four: Preparing the Bride

After the man's side has danced, the woman's side hands over the bride to the man's side. In a symbolic representation of her liminality, the man's side changes her clothes and shoes in front of everyone. She is then sprayed with perfume. Her new clothing has been arranged beforehand, purchased or sewn

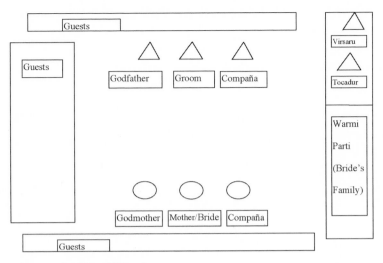

Figure 3. Cari Parti Dancing

by someone of the man's side. The man's side also places a shawl around the face of the bride, who must dance with her face covered.

Phase Five: The Bride's Dance

Next the bride is taken to the center of the dancing area so that those on the man's side can dance with her. This dance basically repeats the earlier one, with the bride assuming her place across from the groom. She is flanked by the compaña's wife and her godmother, while the groom is flanked by the compaña and his godfather. The virsaru continues chanting the commands and interjects confirmations of the beauty of the bride. He says she has lots of beautiful jewelry (munanaita sarsilluna). He refers to her as "ñucanchi señorita, ñucanchi señorara [our girl, our woman]." This statement reflects her ambiguous status of personhood, between a girl and woman. In the wedding in Urai Llacta Bancu inserted a joking line at this point:

ñau-pa-man-da	From the front
ri-cu-pi-ga	If you look
mu-na-nai-ta	A beautiful
se-ñor-i-ta	Girl
shay-a-wan-gui	You stand
wa-sha-ma-nda	From behind
ri-cu-pi-ga	Looking

u-shpa si-qui	Ashen rear
chu-li-ta-ra	"Cholita"
cha-ri-nga-wa	In order to have
ñu-can-chi-pa	Our
se-ño-ri-to	Boy

For a long time I considered why Bancu said that viewed from the front the bride was a beautiful girl but that from behind (*washamanda*) she was seen to have an "ashen rear." The hidden meanings of these phrases are structured by the qualities of duality—reflecting various aspects of femininity and its relationship within masculine-feminine complementarity.[2] In Quichua *washa* (behind) also means "later," and *ñaupa* (front) also means "before" or "beginning." The suggestion is thus that the bride is beautiful now, but age will turn her buttocks ashen. In addition, this reference to her buttocks evokes the productive activities of women, who often squat in the gardens while weeding and get their skirts dirty in the ashen soil of slash-and-burn agriculture. Bancu was making a commentary something akin to the idea that "youth is in its flower now, but all things age." He offered two representations of women, one glittery and flashy and the other associated with the earth.

The end of dancing signals that the bride has been severed from her natal ayllu and folded into the man's. The ritual transformation of her liminality is complete. Macdonald expresses this separation and transformation as an "absorption" filled with sexual symbolism that culminates in dance: "The bride, with all the hesitancy, tension, and excitement of a first encounter, moves onto the floor and dances opposite the groom. As she portrays a wife she becomes absorbed into her husband's group" (1979:122).

The social and aesthetic forms of the Napo Runa wedding ritual have persisted for a remarkably long time. In a description of a "Quixos," or Napo Runa, wedding in 1846–48, for example, Osculati relates many of the elements I observed in Napo when I was there. He writes:

They began dancing, and the two pairs advanced, accompanied by two godfathers and the two godmothers. . . . In finishing the first dance, the two pairs greeted the assistants, moving their hands close to their faces [ritual handshakes], at the same time pronouncing the word *licencia* or *permiso*. They retired to another *choza* [hut] not very far away. A group of men . . . made . . . noise with their instruments. Others, singing in the corners, were remembering all the activities and hunting successes of the grooms. At the same time, many women celebrated the beauty

of the bride and groom. . . . Everyone greeted each other . . . and they
made us drink, at much cost, many bowls of the . . . beer. (Osculati
2000:119)

Osculati mentions a number of features still in practice: dancing, music,
ritual handshakes, the rhetoric of permission, and the overwhelming presence of conviviality, storytelling, and asua. (Interestingly, Osculati refers to
these people not as "Runa" but rather as "Quijos," a now discarded ethnic
label; I will discuss this topic later.) Unfortunately, without the language or
interpretive skills to appreciate the aesthetic and social forms of the Napo
Runa wedding, Osculati views the ritual as a quaint and illogical custom. He
also describes the beer as "nauseating" (Osculati 2000:119). The Napo Runa
themselves, of course, see matter quite differently. Still, Osculati's 150-year-old
text clearly describes the same forms of sociality that manifest themselves in
Napo Runa weddings even today.

Phase Six: Eating

Even though the bride has been handed over, the bura is just beginning.
While the bura's main purpose is to unite a man and a woman in marriage,
the larger communities—the man's side and the woman's side—remain to
be unified. The man's side moves toward this through the monumental task
of feeding the guests, helpers, and participants with the prestigious foods
of Napo Runa culture. The eating part of the wedding becomes the theater
wherein those on the man's side can continue to perform their respect, love,
and commitment to those on the woman's side by giving them abundant
gifts of meat and fish.

The first course is a broth made from free-range chickens. This broth is
served with manioc, plantains, salt, and capsicum pepper sauce. After the soup
has been served and eaten, the next course is lugru, a dish typical of weddings
and usually eaten only for special occasions. Lugru, a delicious mixture of
manioc and game or fish, is *mishki,* or "sweet." It is made by cooking the
smoked meat and fish along with the manioc. The whole is then partially
mashed to combine the flavors. Lugru is defined by the flavor of game meat,
which the Runa love and which every wedding must include. Lugru will be
served to most of the less important guests.

Special guests, however, are given significant cuts of smoked meat in a
special area near the serving area. They are given nice tables and chairs, and
many helpers attend to their needs. The warmi yaya takes a primary role in
the distribution of the meat. He is expected to stand in the serving area and

tell the servers how much meat to give each person. Meat flows from the man's side to the woman's side freely and in large quantities. On the woman's side the father, mother, godparents, aunts, uncles, brothers, and sisters are given the choicest pieces. It is customary to give more food than guests can eat, and guests relish taking home leftovers more than they do eating at the wedding. Guests wrap the unconsumed meat in leaves to make a *wanlla*, a "take-home gift."

In all three weddings I witnessed, the bride's father was not overly aggressive in commanding the meat distribution. Although people say that the bride's father can be demanding in this regard (see Macdonald 1979:125–34), the men I witnessed in this role were more like gift consultants. In general, the bride's father helps the servers to calculate the cari parti's degree of intimacy to each of the many relatives who receive special portions of meat. Intimacy translates into more meat, and those who are close to the bride not only expect but demand that they be recognized. This ritual action demonstrates one of the defining characteristics of gifting: giving is defined by moral obligations, which the Runa calculate carefully (Mauss 1990). Giving gifts is a complex form of exchange, and the exchanges transform social relations.

By giving meat, the man's side increases the prestige of both the woman's side and, through their generosity, themselves. This generosity is key to leaving the guests with the general opinion that it was a good wedding. Close relatives of the bride are assured a bountiful meal; other guests are not, but feeding all who attend is crucial to a successful outcome. People say that they come to weddings in order to eat, and the eating is the highlight of the wedding. Mashaguna are often remembered by the kind of food they served at their weddings. People, especially elders, will tease the young of marriageable age by saying to them, "Why don't you get married? I want to eat lugru." Again, it is customary to assign the groom a nickname at the wedding, and this name is often derived from the kind of game that is most important during the consumption phase. I heard of one wedding where the man's side served a tapir head (sacha wagra) to the bride's mother in dramatic fashion. The heads of game animals are the choicest cuts, and it is customary to serve heads to important women on the woman's side. When the bride's mother received the head, she declared that her new "son" would from then on be referred to as wagra—as he is indeed now known. Countless similar stories, names, and performances define the identities and personal histories of men in Upper Napo.

Phase Seven: Finishing, the Unity of Duality

In the wedding's final phase the two sides dance together. This dance follows the same pattern as previous phases but occurs on a larger scale. The man's side and woman's side both form long lines of relatives, the two sides facing each other. The lines dance in and out, rotating and repeating as previously described. The virsaru, however, alters his discourse to highlight the "finishing" quality of this phase of dancing. Elders are more involved and relish showing their knowledge and well-practiced steps. They also greatly enjoy this validation of Napo Runa cultural knowledge and performance. The dancing goes on for hours, with people taking turns and briefly stopping to drink asua.

If those on the man's side are especially loving, they will perform a kind of playful trick on the bride's-side women to show them prestige and "make them happy." During the dance the man's side will have prepared special leaf packages of monkey meat with straps resembling those of a basket. When the women are in the middle of dancing and least expect it, boys run up from behind and slip the straps over the women's foreheads, hanging the packages off their backs. The women continue to dance with the monkey meat on their backs as a sign of the loving relationship between the man's side and the woman's side (see plate 2).

Typically the dancing and drinking continue until morning. Nowadays, however, people perform the traditional dance only for some hours, after which the festivities become organized around the more modern-sounding dance music of Runa Paju. Young people really like this time of the wedding, because it allows them to flirt and to drink. The principals of the man's side are expected to remain active and visible and to drink with all the guests. The bride and groom are expected to serve asua together to all the guests, drink with them, and in the early morning hours serve wayusa tea. They are not allowed privacy or individual space but must attend to the guests' enjoyment of their new public union.

The next morning the man's side is again expected to feed all the guests. A host of chickens will have been saved for this purpose; they will slaughtered in the early morning to make soup. There will still be plenty of manioc, plantains, and asua, for no one is allowed to go home hungry. The woman's side is sad, however, because the bride will stay with her new husband. But they are also happy, for those on the man's side are now true auya.

Plate 2. Warmi parti dancing with meat gifts during a wedding in 1994. The meat packages are hung on the backs of the guests in a way that resembles how women carry their children.

Conclusion

Ritual marriage among the Runa is based on a series of fiestas that increase in intensity and scale. The progression of these fiestas takes the form of a rite-of-passage ritual in which the actions of liminality transform social relations. Transformation is achieved through a system of exchange and circulation whose ultimate goal is the exchange of a person and the circulation of social relations and substance between two aylluguna. The two aylluguna become auya to each other as they combine substance through their children. *Auya*, a rich relational term, reflects this combining or crossing of substance lines. It refers to the unity of duality.

These arguments about marriage apply to the theory of value production. As Rivière (1971) has argued, marriage is relevant when studied in relationship to an array of other social relationships. Previous chapters have demonstrated the importance of marriage (and male-female complementarity) to the general process of personhood and maturity—and to the production of other kinds of relationships. Marriage rituals transform one set of relations into another by divestment and recombination. Liminality in marriage rituals reflects this "betwixt and between" aspect of such transformations.

The transformations of the ritual also reflect both the finite and open-ended aspects of social reproduction. Marriage not only exchanges social perspectives but also circulates them. Marriage transforms people into social persons of a more mature form that is socially recognizable and valued. I believe that people invest so much time, energy, and trouble into marrying ritually rather than individually because marriage is the key to producing the highest and widest values of Runa socioculture.

The day after my wedding, I was preparing to enter a motor-driven dugout canoe; the canoe and its mooring place were the same as those I mentioned in the introductory episode, which had occurred eleven months earlier. The river continued to flow, and the trees still bent downward. The insects still buzzed, and the birds continued their sorties overhead. Accompanying me on this journey, however, were my new spouse and my affinal relatives, to whom I now referred with different terms of address and sociality. As I tried to say good-bye to my host ayllu and the people of Yacu Llacta, I broke down in tears. Completely overwhelmed by the intense emotional and physical process I had been through, I remember struggling to find something to say. A grandmother from Yacu Llacta who had been my godmother in the wedding rituals came up to me and gave me a glass of aguardiente. She said, "This will warm you up as you go." It was January 10, 1994. My visa was to expire in three days.

In the summer of 2002, after two more trips back and forth between Ecuador and the United States, we once again returned to Ambatu Yacu, this time for our goddaughter's marriage. The wedding took place in Sisa Llacta, a community some distance from Ambatu Yacu. We boarded a bus, lugging our gifts and other things, and arrived in two hours' time. When we descended from the bus, we were immediately greeted with shouts by women dressed in *cushma* blouses and colorful skirts (*anacu* or *pacha*) with *chumbi* belts. Their faces were painted with the red *achiote,* and they danced in circles, holding decorated calabashes above their heads. They lowered the calabashes and served us the contents. I tasted a festive asua made with *inchic,* an Amazonian peanut with a wonderful flavor. We drank the bowls dry, swallowed the peanuts, and placed our gifts in the appropriate place.

The bride and groom were first married in the local evangelical church. This Western-style church wedding is called "misa bura" in Quichua, and the practice can be traced to "Jesuit times," when Runa people were required by law to be married by clergy. The Runa, however, have always felt that church weddings were incomplete without the Runa bura. The church activities usually last for an hour or two. The bura that follows lasts many hours, usually well into the next day.

In the later phases of the Runa bura that night, I was sitting around drinking manioc brew, bottled beer, rum, and soft drinks with the men and women of Ambatu Yacu. The men were joking about my role as the godfather, and one said that I should "get angry [as in the old days] and demand more beer and a big bottle of expensive rum." We recounted our experiences and reflections on marriage, life, and the changing times. Many stories and jokes were told, and the ambience was one of extreme conviviality. After the bura we all agreed with a senior uncle, who said, "They performed the ritual very nicely. It was very beautiful. We have been given much respect and love [*llakinawa*] and are very thankful."

4

The Transformation of Affinity into Consanguinity

In this chapter I move away from the ritual transformations of the bura to discuss various forms of affinal relationships: masha/cachun incorporation, *compadrazgo* (coparenthood), alliance, and adoption.[1] These kinship forms all exhibit a common theme: the transformation of affinity into consanguinity. They are modeled on the idea of consanguineal relations and the sharing of substance. In addition, I will discuss circuits of exchange (Bohannan 1955, 1959; Piot 1991; Damon 1980, 1983, 1990; Mayer 1977, 2002) that structure the metamorphosis of value and show that daily life is oriented along a continuum of giving and reciprocal relations in which exchange relates but substance defines.

Bride-Price and Personification

While living in Napo Runa communities, I heard many people talk about the difficulties of completing the marriage rituals described in the previous chapter. They often said that Runa women are very "valuable" ("yapa valinaun"), for marriage requires many gifts and labor that move from the groom's ayllu to the bride's. I sometimes heard people refer to this marriage system as "buying" or "selling" a wife ("warmira randina" or "warmira ca-tuna"). These statements were figurative, likening exchanges of marriage to commodity exchanges—a trope that shows how gift giving and commodity exchange form complementary structures in Runa thought. When people used such commercial terminology in conversation, however, their remarks were interpreted as humorous and not to be taken seriously. People did not consider marriage a form of true commerce, for they understood the market as a space defined by its lack of morality and human sociality (Mayer 2002). While it is acceptable for people to exchange things commercially, it is morally reprehensible to exchange persons in such a way.

I was surprised, however, that many people were interested in sister exchange as a viable and legitimate means of marriage. Before I was married, my sister came to visit me in Ecuador. People were constantly engaging in conversations about the possibilities of exchanging my sister for one of theirs, suggesting that I marry the sister of some man and he marry mine. Such conversations about sister exchange were common, I discovered, not just between the Runa and the ethnographer but also among the Runa themselves. Indeed, some of the people in the older generation of my host ayllu had exchanged sisters. They told me they exchanged sisters to tighten the auya bond between the aylluguna.

I later realized that there were important but not immediately obvious social principles behind this marriage talk. According to Runa morality, a person (here, a bride) should be exchanged for another person, not simply given. Although person exchange seemed to be fairly infrequent, it was conceptualized as an ideal solution to the value problem that weddings present: one ayllu "loses" a daughter and another "gains" a wife. This raises a fundamental anthropological problem, that of relating the exchange of things to the circulation of people.

The issue of bride-price versus the direct exchange of persons in Amazonia remains an active topic of debate (see Knauft 1997; Dean 1995, 1998). On the surface, Runa weddings appear as "commercial" transactions involving brides and their prices—in other terms, the commodification of women. The ritual marriage forms I have analyzed, however, are more appropriately understood as the process of converting things into people (and the relationships implied in them), which Gregory (1982) calls "personification." I think that the English term *bride-price* itself creates distortions in translating the social forms under consideration. As I showed in the previous chapter, the gift system by which persons are circulated in Napo Runa society has little to do with price or the commodification of women; commodities are central to the process of marriage, but they are transformed into gifts as they are converted into social relationships. Furthermore, these processes of personification do not end with marriage, as if marriage were a finished transaction. Personification continues after marriage and implies further substance transformations that put the dynamic and complex theory of Runa kinship into fuller view.

Conversion in Marriage Rituals

An adopted (apasha iñachischa) girl was to get married. Although she had been raised by her adoptive parents, she knew and visited her biological parents. I was present at a conversation with the suitor ayllu, whose members were discussing which set of parents they should approach to ask for the woman's hand. They decided that their greatest obligation was to the adoptive parents, who had "suffered" and worked the hardest in the girl's upbringing. Nonetheless, they also acknowledged that they should "recognize" the biological parents, who still interacted with and cared for their daughter. The conversation ended with the thought that they would have to talk with the girl to clarify how much her biological parents had contributed to her upbringing.

This story speaks directly to the problem of relating reproduction to value. The issue crucial to the Runa was not biology. They were interested in calculating who was most responsible for sustaining and loving the girl and how that value should be recognized in her marriage. This complex situation clearly shows that marriage among the Runa cannot be viewed as simple circulation without considering how value and people are produced. I will now more closely consider the processes of personification and the way value is converted into people.

In living and conversing with the Runa, I observed three main spheres of value; in descending order, they are that of persons, that of prestige foods (asua and meat), and that of basic foods (manioc and plantains). In the weddings beautiful words accompany prestige items to effect social transformations. These categories do not make a formal structure but roughly correspond to the amount of time and energy needed to produce the items that they encompass. Greater or lesser value reflects the degree to which someone had to sacrifice or suffer (tormintarina or jumbina) in production. For example, people talked about raising a son or a daughter as requiring much suffering and work. In addition, as the previous chapter showed, during weddings the Runa publicly display their suffering in bringing up a son or daughter through expressions of sadness and loss.

During weddings people follow a social logic resembling that of "conversion" (Bohannan 1955:65), an exchange of items from different categories of value. Conversions can be contrasted to conveyances, the exchange of items within the same value category. Conveyance usually does not "excite . . . moral judgments," but conversion does (Bohannan 1955:65). Conversions are usually morally charged because equivalency is impossible to achieve. A thing of a lesser category of value is exchanged for something of a greater category of value, so that one party is left in a "good" position and the other in a "bad" one. Bohannan is thus convinced that conversions are like "investments" (1955:66).

Bohannan's framework can help us understand the practical difficulties of achieving equivalency in ritual marriage among the Napo Runa. Because the direct exchange of sisters—a conveyance—is only an ideal form of "generalized exchange" (see Lévi-Strauss 1969:481), people must use conversion to obtain wives. Meat, manioc brew, and beautiful words are the stuff of these conversions. The bura follows a social logic of conversion by using things of prestige to obligate transformations of relationships in the kinship sphere.

Unfortunately, Bohannan's statement that conversion is an investment-like maximization behavior reads a commodity economics into the phenomenon. One can discard the capitalistic social schema, however, to search for more appropriate and ethnographically relevant principles. For example, when the Runa "convert" value in a wedding, they are not simply exchanging a woman from one ayllu to another. They are transforming all the relationships between the two aylluguna into a higher order of value. Although this alliance begins through the proposal that the daughter switch residence, that transference is really only the beginning of a host of relationship transformations. The real value of marriage lies in producing relationships. Moving from tapuna to pactachina and then to bura, people add value by intensifying relations in the ritual process. (This process is not unlike the creation and circulation of a kula valuable and its association with rites of passage [Damon 2002b].) Weddings do more than just combine people; they also build a sense of community and collective identity in which ritual's power to cut and tie the knots of ayllu relations becomes realized and affirmed.

Marriage without Permission and Bride Service

While marriage by bura is ideal, not everyone goes through the protocol of the ritual fiestas in obtaining a wife. Some men obtain their wives without asking the woman's ayllu for permission; in such cases, the couple will go into hiding. I refer to this practice as marriage without permission. The Runa call it "abducting" or "stealing" a woman (warmira shuwana).

Marriage without permission, categorically different from marriage by ritual, has its advantages for both parties. The two methods use different means, but if marriage without permission succeeds, the result will be the same: the two young people are married, and good relations are established between their aylluguna. The bura is a ritualistic way of achieving this end through moral obligations and gifting; marriage without permission is a more precarious but equally viable means toward this same end. Marriage without permission, too, can transform relationships and make a wife of someone else's daughter.

Marriage without permission is a social transgression in that the parents, especially those of the young woman, are left out of the decision-making process. Blame is always placed on the man, even though the woman typically participates in deciding to elope. That is, the women is "stolen" only socially, for she almost always chooses to elope. I cannot stress this point too much. Marriage without permission is not a physical abduction, and no force is involved. The transgression is moral, and often the young woman assists so that she can be "stolen."

The couple makes off to a distant relative's house, usually in a different region, where they will be far away from the woman's ayllu. The woman's father, brothers, and other ayllu members feel slighted, for the "theft" of a relative is a serious offense. Word spreads quickly around the community, and the woman's relatives, especially her mother, become worried. Shortly after the abduction, details of the events begin to circulate. People will speculate on the location of the couple, who remain secluded for some time—not less than two or three days and usually several weeks—before returning to the woman's house to fix up (*alichina*) things.

At this time the young man apologetically and humbly tries to make amends and show goodwill to his wife's ayllu. He will attempt to make them his relatives. There are multitudinous ways to achieve this tenuous agreement, but long-term arrangements must be made between fathers. The woman's ayllu usually demands a bura to legitimize the union. Of course, the man and his ayllu benefit from a marriage without permission because little or no money, labor, and time need be spent in the initial procurement of the wife. The benefits to the woman's ayllu are less obvious but become evident if we compare the living arrangements of marriage by ritual to those of marriage without permission.

Marriage by ritual often (but not always) occurs when the bride and groom are from distant or at least different communities. This relational distance does not always obtain, but where it does, it always implies a relational gap that can be filled only through ritual transformations. Marriage without permission, however, usually occurs when the young man and woman are from the same community and live in relative proximity to each other. Although the young man takes the young woman far away for a short while during the initial "abduction," the couple is likely to live closer to the young woman's parents thereafter, because the man's ayllu, too, lives in the same area. Because the bride usually lives with her husband's ayllu, people consider it a boon to have a masha who lives close to them.

What is lost in the initial ritual value can thus be gained in daily extractions of service, typically labor. The woman's ayllu can potentially gain much more influence over the new masha, and it is assured that the new bride will not go far. Moreover, the woman's parents will live close to their auyaguna, who are sometimes compadres as well. The ritual fiesta of the bura is not lost, only delayed, for it is requested after the fact. Even though it may take years for the man's ayllu to comply, the sense of an uncompleted bura allows for some leverage in making demands—especially initially—until the groom's ayllu completes at least a pactachina.

Brides who go far away are lost to their ayllu in the sense that they no longer participate in the daily conviviality, life, and labor that make up the preferred way of living among the Napo Runa. When a woman travels far away to her husband's family, it is more difficult to sustain a shared life apart from ritual theater. Exchanges involve greater distances and are potentially infrequent. In marriage without permission, however, much of this relational groundwork may already be present, and forcing the issue of marriage often proves successful.

Different communities sometimes emphasize one strategy or the other. The choice is influenced by a host of possible factors, such as ecology, population, economic wealth, individual preferences, individual character, and spousal availability. In particular, the density and semiurbanity spawned by processes of modernity and development influence the choices facing young men and their aylluguna when someone wants to get married. I noticed that the rural/urban distinction was salient in the contrasting marriage strategies of the young men from Yacu Llacta and those from Pucara. At the time of my fieldwork, Yacu Llacta was rural, and its inhabitants considered one another to be ayllu. Living in a social system governed by exogamy, the young men of Yacu Llacta had limited choices for potential spouses. Adjacent communities comprised colonist populations, so they had no real local alter in which to marry. Most young men sought wives from distant communities, and they tended toward ritual marriage. They had few chances to develop relationships that might lead to elopement.

Pucara, however, was a more "urbanized" indigenous community with various institutions, a commercial center, roads, bus service, schools, and a higher population density. Because people had easy access to potential spouses, marriage without permission was relatively easy. Young men and women had ample opportunities for flirting in various community institutions, recreational contexts, and places of communal congregation. They also had an easy escape route via the town's regular bus service. I heard of such elopements frequently during my stay in the Pucara area. When a Pucara man did perform a bura, it was usually after he and his wife had been living together for a number of years and had one or two children.

Although the Pucara Runa often get their wives without ritual permission, they almost always complete some form of a bura, even if it is on only a small scale, "like a pactachina." They do this to give the young woman's parents a sense of moral legitimacy for the union and to publicly finalize the relationship. I often heard parents of women in such situations haranguing their mashaguna to perform a bura. The masha is never allowed to forget that he has committed a moral transgression. His relationship is described as *yanga,* or "for nothing," implying it is not yet legitimized even if the couple has been married civilly. The lack of a completed bura is often a source of tension between relatives united by marriage, for it signals a lack of respect between them, the man's side not having recognized the moral debt of a person.

Marriage signals a host of productive and everyday exchanges not only within an ayllu but also among aylluguna. Once a couple marries, the excitement of ritual exchanges wavers in the face of everyday production and consumption relationships. This transformation reflects the gist of Bancu's previously discussed comment about the "beautiful girl" becoming transformed into someone with "ashen buttocks." Ritual exchanges and "theft" initiate the relationships of marriage, but service relationships and the pragmatics of everyday life in the ayllu complete them and transform them into substance forms. Issues central to the Runa theory of kinship surface here once again.

Notes on Muntun Maturation

The ayllu-muntun can be looked at as a kind of life cycle through which individuals pass in the courses of their lives. These muntunguna go through various kinds of separations and unions in which intimate personal kinship relations flow into various relations of community and compadres. These processes require transforming one set of relations into more mature relations. The dynamic is one of alternating separations and unions defined by certain life events, such as marriage, childbirth, maturation, and death. These life events also signal a progressive increase in the overall value of the social relations, as the productive capacities of persons increase along with their convivial attachment to others. In other words, increased value in ayllu relations requires increased production by a marital unit to the point where they provide for the consumption of others. In turn, the others provide for their consumption through exchange. Value lies in the spirit of giving and the notion that one passes on some of the substance of one's own life to others, an implicit proposition of the gift (Mauss 1990) that defines convivial life in Napo.

Although women are encouraged to follow the ideal of patrilocal residence, matrilocal residence is a viable option. The system's relational nature allows people to be fluid and pragmatic in their choices, and residence patterns reflect this flexibility to create productive relations in a variety of social and ecological contexts. Despite its flexibility, however, Runa modes of social action contain certain points of possible conflict, especially reflected in the tensions surrounding the newness of a masha or cachun. Most often these tensions surround the reputation of a cachun, but tensions emerge regarding the character of a masha as well. When a masha or cachun is integrated into an ayllu-muntun, his or her newness is reflected in a subordination and low status in relation to elder resident kin. Domination, subordination, and status are in turn reflected in the patterns of ayllu development.

The patterns of domination and subordination found in a relatively young muntun are easily discerned in the forms of address used for affines. When a cachun or masha first joins the new household, she or he must refer to the spouse's parents as "mother" or "father" (mama or yaya). People use these forms of address because one's spouse's parents are considered secondary parents. Married life begins with a second upbringing, a period of socialization by these secondary parents. The use of the substance term, however, is not reciprocal. The spouse's parents use the affinal terms *masha* and *cachun*.

This asymmetrical use of terms of address reinforces the idea that the parents are dominant and younger affines are subordinate. By referring to his or her spouse's father with the more intimate term of *yaya*, a masha or cachun is conveying the proper respect for his position of authority. But when the spouse's father invokes the terms *masha* or *cachun*, he is indicating his political authority and the fact that anyone in these categories bears obligations to him. These terms indicate a service relationship and the flow of labor from mashaguna and cachunguna to the senior members of an ayllu.

The father and mother are not the only ayllu members who refer to sons-

and daughters-in-law using *masha* and *cachun*. Elder brothers and sisters, too, use these terms, as do aunts, uncles, and grandparents. A masha or cachun, however, must refer to his or her spouse's siblings as "wife's brother" (warmi turi), "wife's sister" (warmi ñaña), "husband's brother" (cari wauki), or "husband's sister" (cari pani). Many mashaguna and cachunguna refer to their spouses' siblings either by their names or by the Spanish *cuñado* or *cuñada* (brother-in-law and sister-in-law, respectively).

A Runa man will often tease another man by calling him "warmi turi." The man thus implies that he is sleeping with, and will make a wife of, the other man's sister. While this joke is often also heard in Spanish using *cuñado*, it is a favorite of many Runa men, especially when dealing with people from far away. This joke also reflects the hostile and conflictive nature of affines, for the joker makes claims to the other's sister without fulfilling any obligations to her ayllu. In addition, the joke shows a complete lack of respect, the opposite of good affinal behavior.

Such a joke may seem innocent, but it highlights the idea that new affines are always a point of tension and concern. As "inside outsiders," affines are privy to the intimate happenings of daily life in the ayllu—and unscrupulous or careless in-laws may pass along information that later develops into rumors. It takes time for affines to feel and behave as ayllu. In the beginning phases of married life, a masha or cachun is of lower status than the more defined sons and daughters of the ayllu-muntun. Mashaguna and cachunguna are expected to prove themselves; they should contribute labor and services to the affairs of their secondary parents and help their spouses' siblings. Cachunguna are treated less well than consanguineal daughters are, and in domestic activities the mother and elder daughters have the right to assign chores to the cachun. A masha is expected to labor with the brothers of the muntun; both the elder brothers and the father have expectations of him. With respect to the categories of masha and cachun, both intergenerational and intragenerational terms of address and status relationships are asymmetrical. This social positioning reflects the affine's outsider status in the muntun, at least initially.

Reputations and Subversions

People say that there is nothing worse than having a lazy cachun. A lazy cachun is, among other evil things, a subversive element who feminizes the husband, for he must make up for her lack of domestic prowess with his own labor. People feel that a lazy cachun is "making fun" (*burlana*) of her husband's ayllu by not fulfilling the expectation of respect or meeting her obligations. The same is true of a masha who lives with his wife's muntun solely to enjoy their resources.

Most of the domestic problems I saw in Runa households were not simply husband-wife conflicts but also conflicts of the entire ayllu and between the aylluguna of the husband and wife. A husband may beat or neglect his wife, but there is not much done about such abuse unless her ayllu is advised. The entire ayllu of woman feels offended, as does the wife, and her brothers often will beat up a masha or threaten him with shamanic violence. In previous times the Runa reserved a special punishment for an abusive masha. The woman's ayllu would tie up the offender and put hot pepper in his eyes. The point of such violence is to alter behavior and instill in the masha a new sense of responsibility and respect, but these tactics do not always succeed. In Pucara I once saw a domestic dispute over the behavior of a masha that provoked members of the wife's ayllu to hurl rocks at him. His head was cut, and he had to go to the hospital.

Some men move into their wives' muntunguna. Ideally most young couples will live between the two ayllu-muntunguna for a while. A masha who lives in his wife's muntun is expected to get up early in the morning, fish, hunt, and contribute his labor to the designs of his wife's father. After a few years, when the masha begins to prove himself worthy within the household, the father and brothers begin to consider him as being "like a real son" or "like a real brother." They will often refer to him using the consanguineal rather than the affinal term, a point I revisit later.

Not every Runa woman becomes a good cachun. As Blanca Muratorio (1998) points out, some gain and keep bad reputations.[2] Moreover, just as a cachun may have a good or bad reputation, so too may a masha. In addition, a masha may acquire a reputation for being lazy or for physically abusing his wife. Many a masha finds that his wife's ayllu judges his character as suspect, at least at first. Mashaguna are often publicly shamed through criticism, and many men do change their ways because of this social pressure. The main provocations for such criticism are beating one's wife, drinking too much, or being a poor food producer.

The previously cited tensions surrounding affinal relationships of the categories of cachun and masha are typical and can be found in almost every ayllu. Such tensions reflect a general problem in Runa life: that of integrating affines into the ayllu-muntun and obligating them to fulfill their duties. In Runa social life the subordination of young people is reinforced by collective attitudes surrounding the character of mashaguna and cachunguna: they are always judged in relation to their giving behavior toward relatives of the elder class. No one wants to be thought of as *killa* (lazy), *shuwa* (thieving), *mitsa* (greedy), or *llulla* (untruthful) within the ayllu or larger community. Although these damaging terms can be used to describe any person, such character talk often focuses on a newer masha or cachun, for these relations are closely scrutinized. This scrutiny, however, usually disappears as the couple has children, matures, and rises in status: the cachun becomes an *apamama* (strong woman), and the masha becomes an *apayaya* (strong man).

The Transformation of Affinity

I observed that when a new spouse has proven him- or herself to his or her secondary parents, the latter begin to use intimate terms of address when referring to their masha or cachun. The parents refer to a masha as "son" (*churi*) and a cachun as "daughter" (*ushushi*). By dropping the subordinating sense of the terms *masha* and *cachun*, the parents start to eliminate the sense of outsider status represented by the asymmetrical terms of address. While they do not use these forms of address all the time, the occasional use signifies a transformation of the relationship to one of same substance, the metaphoric association of the affine with a true son or daughter.

One day my warmi turi said to me, "Michael, you are no longer just a masha. Now you are a real brother, a true brother [kikin wauki]." This use of kin terminology to describe the relationship between a masha and his spouse's brother expresses the general idea of a same-substance relationship, that is, a relationship analogous to, or the same as, one of substance. A cachun is sometimes addressed as "ñaña," or sister, by her spouse's sisters. The same-substance labeling of affines is an expression of their status in the muntun structure and their shared destiny. They further share food, living quarters, work, and play. As the muntun matures, the forms of address for affines change to reflect a more intimate relation. Whereas asymmetry was reinforced in the early phases, affines will later be considered as being of the same substance and ayllu. This transformation of status takes time and is intimately tied into the practices of production and circulation.

As I discussed in chapter 1, the couvade signals the combination and transformation of substance through the production of children. This convivial transformation is enhanced as the cachunguna and mashaguna contribute materially and pragmatically to the growth and health of the muntun through gifts of meat, labor, and loyalty. These transformations relate to the strength- and life-giving character of the masha or cachun and the relational quality of the marriage between the masha or cachun and the household's daughter or son (see figure 4).

Compadrazgo and Ritual Kinship

The transformation of substance forms in Runa communities cannot be understood without considering the institution of compadrazgo, or ritual kinship. All Runa have compadres, an institution conceptualized as Runa kinship rather than Christian or Hispanic religious practice. The relationship of compadrazgo and Runa social forms presents a complex historical and sociological question deserving more detailed research. In *Sacha Runa* Whitten stresses compadrazgo among the Canelos Quichua. He describes the *gumba* system (*gumba* is a diminutive for *compadre*) as a system of the same order as the ayllu. Whitten writes, "The *gumba* network is fundamentally an address system out of which some kin class terminologies may be transformed. Polysemy, extension, connotation, and metaphor . . . are crucial processes in such transformations" (1976:110). Compadrazgo forms are associated with both coparenthood and ceremonial friendship, both of which are established institutions in Native Amazonian cultures (Whitten 1976;

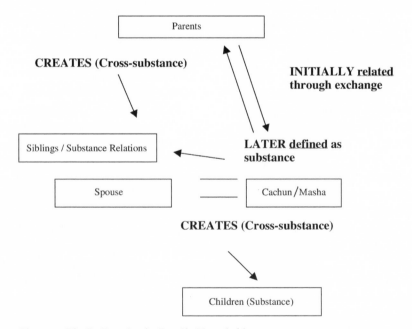

Figure 4. The In-Law in the Family Household

Descola 1996b). I, however, will emphasize compadrazgo as a furthering and intensification of substance. Among the Runa, compadrazgo cannot be divorced from ayllu-muntun networks and their symbolic associations with parenthood and affinal flows.[3]

The literature on compadrazgo revisits some of the issues discussed earlier regarding the couvade. For example, Rivière (1974:432) ties the couvade ritual to compadrazgo as phenomena that concern spiritual links between physical and divine aspects of personhood and being.[4] Similarly, compadrazgo is for the Runa an important part of the process of creating social persons and the relations that define them. Like other rites of passage, compadrazgo reflects both the exchange and the circulation of relationships. I agree with Pitt-River's (1957, 1977) general point that compadrazgo must be studied in ethnographic context and in relation to the sociocultural systems of a particular peoples, without assuming it to be the same in all societies and cultures. Among the Runa, compadrazgo is defined by its relation to other relations—namely, substance relations and affinal relations. I will now examine these relations in more detail.

Godparenthood carries with it a special terminology in Quichua. The Runa call the godfather "marcayaya"; the godmother, "marcamama"; the godson, "marcachuri"; and the goddaughter, "marcaushushi." These categories are the normal parent-child kinship designations of *yaya, mama, churi,* and *ushushi* attached to the prefix *marca-*, a derivative of the Quichua term *marcana* (to hold or lift). When people ask someone to become a godparent to one of their children, they say, "Cai wawara marcai," which means "Please hold my child." The use of *marcana* is both a figurative and metonymic gloss. It is figurative because the context of becoming godparents is linked to the imagery of a parent cradling a child in his or her arms. It is metonymic because the relevant kinship designations (*marcayaya, marcamama, marcachuri,* and *marcaushushi*) are built on the previously discussed system of values related to substance categories between parents and children.

When one set of parents chooses another to become the godparents of their children, the child's parents become compadres to the child's godparents. Godfathers in general are sometimes referred to by the Quichua diminutive *cumpa,* which is short for *compadre* in the Napo vernacular. Whereas the kinship categories preceded by the prefix *marca-* connote a hierarchical parent-child relationship, compadre relations imply symmetry, mutual respect, and caring. The Runa say that compadres are permanent relations by which one must live *llakisha,* or "lovingly." Because people collapse the notion of love with material and social exchanges, compadres are linked by reciprocal exchange relationships, in contrast to the exchange patterns of parental conviviality, which are necessarily giving and asymmetrical.

When a child reaches two to four years of age, the parents seek an appropriate couple to become the godparents of their child and act as compadres to them. When choosing compadres, people seek a relation of mature status that will be capable of fulfilling obligations to their child. As secondary parents, godparents are expected to foster the child's development by, among other things, contributing to its material welfare. Godparents provide food, clothing, and other necessary items for their godchildren. Today schoolbooks and clothing are important. Godparents also give advice and take an active part in making decisions regarding the child's future and, especially, in marriage rituals and negotiations. As discussed in chapter 3, godparents play a special role in wedding festivals.

When choosing godparents, parents seek individuals with whom they expect to have a continuous and beneficial relationship of friendship, caring, exchange, mutual invitations to visit, and mutual help. Compadres, who form sets of parents, send gifts to each other and drink, celebrate, and work together. Choosing compadres allows people to expand and intensify their kin networks. One may use this domain of kinship to extend links outward to persons of a different ayllu or muntun. Alternatively, one may use compadrazgo to intensify existing ayllu relations. For example, siblings make ideal compadres, a development that intensifies an already existing relation. Siblings who become compadres generally refer to each other as "cumpa" or "comadre." To call someone "compadre" or "comadre" carries more intimacy and value than does using a sibling term.

Sometimes people choose compadres from the mestizo/white class, although I observed that this practice is rare. Runa from Lower Napo (Coca and below) often choose compadres from Upper Napo. The Upper Napo Runa say that the Lower Napo Runa do this because they want to be closer to the larger towns' educational and health-care facilities and job opportunities and to have easier access to manufactured commodities brought from Quito. People occasionally supplement geographically distant compadres with local ones for the same child, especially if the distant compadres seem uninvolved in the child's life. For the Runa, being a compadre means cultivating a pragmatic as well as socially symbolic relationship of caring and ritual friendship. The Runa explicitly state that compadre relationships are material as well as social. Exchange cannot be separated from the process of creating persons.

The Wawa Marcana Ritual

The ritual of becoming godparents is called "wawa marcana," or "holding the child." First, the child's parents talk to the prospective godparents informally to see whether they are interested in becoming godparents to the child. If they express interest, the parents must invite the prospective godparents to their house for a meal. This meal must include special food, such as might be served at a wedding (e.g., game meat). The meal must further include plenty of asua, and this is often accompanied by purchased liquor. One cannot become compadres in Runa society without first eating at the house of the godchild's parents. The social action of eating is emphasized, and people often gloss the whole ritual event as eating. If the context is understood, people say, "When are you coming over to eat?"

The ritual is simple yet elegant. The two sets of parents stand on each side of the child, they say a short prayer, the godparents choose a "godname," and water is poured over the child's head. The compadres then profess loyalty and vow to share labor and things with each other. They finish the ritual by eating and drinking. It is common for men to further emphasize bonding by getting drunk together. In the communities where I worked, compadrazgo rituals were conspicuously separated from the structures of the Christian churches and were affairs of the home (*wasi*).

The child's parents use gifts to "recruit" compadres. These gifts include food, drink, and beautiful words—the same spheres of exchange discussed in the context of weddings. Although compadrazgo rituals are similar to bura fiestas in both structure and function—both use gifts to create a separation and recombination of a person—compadrazgo differs from marriage because it explicitly deals with the "primary" socialization of children up to the point of marriage rather than the "secondary" socialization of young people into adulthood, a task left to their future spouses' parents. Most people remember the role their godparents played in the periods of childhood and premarriage and during the marriage ritual. Compadres, however, exist within symmetrical relations that last the rest of their lifetimes.

The compadrazgo and auya relationships are much the same in that both involve exchange and reciprocity. Compadrazgo is modeled on the idea of substance relations and their intensification through action. It can be viewed as a form of "marriage" between two sets of parents effected through the circulation of a child. As with the bride and groom in marriage, the focus is the circulation of relations. Compadrazgo is thus another form of same-substance relation constructed on the Runa notions of relationality, circulation, and personhood.

Adoption, or Apasha Iñachina

Earlier chapters have covered the ayllu and the substance relations of intimacy that define it, but nothing has yet been said of adoption, a practice quite common among the Runa of Upper Napo. Adoption follows the same relational logic of compadrazgo. In fact, sometimes godparents will adopt their godchildren, but this is by no means the only kind of adoptive relation. People are generally favorable toward adoption and often raise other people's children as their own.

In fact, I knew many people for several years before I realized that they had been raised by adoptive parents. These relations are not easily discerned without getting to know people in an intimate manner, because people talk about adoptive parents just as they do consanguineal parents. Similarly, people talk about their adoptive children using consanguineal terms. While there are special terms for adoptive kin, people generally do not use them often. The most common way to refer to an adopted child is to use the adjective *iñachishca* (reared) as in "iñachishca churi" (reared son). This way of describing the relationship emphasizes what adoption is rather than what it is not. The lack of biological connection is not an issue in the way it is in Western societies. The Runa focus on activity: the action and process of raising a child, which in the Runa theory of kinship creates substance. Adoptive kin become substance kin in both a symbolic and a material sense; in the process, adoptive kin are made into consanguines.

Weismantel has developed the idea that feeding creates kin in the context of highland Ecuador. She writes, "Those who eat together in the same household share the same flesh in a quite literal sense: they are made of the same stuff. It is when young Iza's boy has eaten so many meals with the family that his whole body is made of the same flesh as theirs that the bond will be unquestioned and real to the boy and his family" (Weismantel 1995:695). Feeding and its related practices, which constitute a powerful social value, transform an adoptive relationship into one of substance in a real way.

Weismantel's idea helps explain how, by sharing work and food, affines become ayllu—that is, related by substance. I mentioned the association of growth and substance relations in the ritual of the couvade, which rests on a similar logic, that of spiritual feeding. In Runa culture love, too, is a kind of feeding. These ideas all relate to the circulatory nature of soul substance, which can be transferred through healing and shamanic practices, through dreaming, or when "breath" is passed through the top of a child's head using tobacco or aguardiente. Within the symbolic associations of shared substance, adoptive children and other kinds of affinal kin come to share substance as they share life with others in the context of the ayllu.

There is another sense in which adoption takes on characteristics of marriage and compadrazgo in Runa culture. Like these other practices, adoption creates symmetrical relationships modeled on the auya relation; adoption functions as a social analogue to marriage in which the movement of a person from one group to another creates a social relationship between aylluguna, formally similar to the way that godparents become other kinds of parents to their godchildren. Paralleling compadrazgo and marriage, adoption often continues even after adopted sons and daughters have become "real" sons and daughters. Parents remember which children are adopted, and they often know and interact with the biological parents. Although adoption takes its essence from the substance relationships of the immediate ayllu, it, too, is metonymically related to affinal and all other "circulatory" relationships in Runa society. Salomon (1986:137) has expressed a similar idea in suggesting adoption as a possible form of alliance relationship in the pre-Columbian northern Andes. Weismantel (1995) argues that global economic forces affecting parents' ability to feed children are a big factor in Andean adoption, just as is "personal fulfillment" for those who may not be able to have children. Adoption is both an old and new form of affinal transformation and contributes a viable and crucial dimension to Napo Runa substance relations. While many researchers consider adoption to be a "contradiction" of kinship, the Runa take it to reflect their most basic kinship principles of substance transformation.

Alliance Relationships: Auya

A few clarifications on the alliance relationships of auya are now in order, for this relation is the primary form linking muntun as webs of value relations. Again, newlyweds do not have auya relations; only the newlyweds' aylluguna have them. Auya is a relation between two aylluguna connected by marriage. In the Runa world, to call one's spouse's father or mother "auya" is a strict contradiction of social logic. One's spouse's father is yaya, and one's spouse's mother is mama.

People from two aylluguna related through marriage use the term *auya* to refer to their alliance relationship. Auya relations, like compadre relations, are an intensifying kind of affinal relation. Like compadre relations, auya relations confer a mature adult status as they circulate relationships of maturity. Auya relations are high-status elder relationships that occupy a higher order of complexity in life-cycle development than compadre relations do. Only mature ayllu-muntunguna and parents with married children have auya; people gain compadres first and then auyaguna.

Conceptually compadre relations stand between substance and affinal relations. People say that, like compadre relations, auya relations should be marked by symmetry and caring. In addition, compadres and auyaguna are the principal recipients of high-status gifts, such as meat and fish. These are also the relations on which one calls when one needs labor help. A person calls on compadres and auyaguna to form a minga, or collective work party, for such things as cutting a garden, planting or harvesting maize, or building a house. Like compadre relations, auya relations are reciprocal and long-term.

Auya relations are quite complicated, for the relation's health depends on the married couple's ability to build a good reputation. Most cachunguna live with their husband's muntun, and the Runa say that people care well for their auya if they "love their cachun." That is, if one has a good relationship with one's cachun (which usually requires that the cachun have a good reputation), one extends this positive feeling toward one's auya. If one has a problem with a cachun (or a masha), then by extension one has problems with one's auya. Auya relations flow into one's own ayllu via the intermediary masha or cachun. They are an intimate and intense—and thus potentially dangerous—kind of cross-substance relation that connects the goings on of one's home to other ayllu. Ideally, however, people have good relationships with their auya and for the most part find them dependable. It is not uncommon for auya relations that get along really well to reinforce the relationship through a second marriage between the two aylluguna.

As time goes on, those who consider themselves auya to one another die. Their children and their grandchildren are what remain. Time creates an important transformation of perspective in this regard. What remains is the concept of one ayllu, for auya ceases to be a meaningful category. The current generation remembers their deceased relatives only as ayllu. The flow of substance, not affinity, remains, a principle revealed in the previously discussed myth narratives.

The Theory of Value among the Runa: Giving and Reciprocity

I have been moving toward the proposition that value in Runa society is not economic but social and specifically located in social relationships of reciprocal desire (Gow 1989; Piot 1999:76). During the first months of my stay in Yacu

Llacta, I constantly asked people whether I could buy them something they needed. The first gifts I purchased for my adoptive ayllu were a kerosene lantern and a radio. At first it was easy to pick up whatever was requested, and people did not ask for much. Later, as my network and intimacy with many people increased over the months and years, I found it more difficult to fulfill all their requests for things. Nevertheless, I gave as much as I could, for I in turn desired things from my hosts, and I depended on them for food and manioc brew. I also asked them for help with my research, which I received in abundance. What I learned through these exchanges was that need, desires, and conviviality are all involved in exchange. Mutual desires structure value, and it was always better to meet someone else's need than to address one's own. To meet the desires of the others with whom one shares life is to live convivially, to realize intersubjectivity as a socially meaningful being. This complex of ideas and practices constitutes the cultural forms of the value process.

In Napo socioculture value is closely linked to specific social pathways and socialities with specific forms of circulation. One form of circulation is giving and sharing, modes of exchange in which things are expected to be given freely. Bird-David explains this social logic aptly: "X wants something, say, a *biddi* (a type of cigarette), and he asks Y to give him one. If Y were to refuse, he would be criticized for being stingy, so he gives X a biddi. Some time later, Y notices that X has some biddies. Wanting one, he does not remind X that he gave him a biddi a few days ago, nor does he ask X for a biddi in return. He merely asks X to give him a biddi because X has biddies and he does not" (1990:191). This example shows both actors, X and Y, following a moral obligation to give, not an obligation to reciprocate. Reciprocity, by contrast, entails the moral obligation to give a return gift, although the actual exchange is usually delayed. One can and often does remind people of their debts to reciprocate a gift; those who shirk their responsibilities to reciprocate become known as people of suspect character, for they receive more than they give. These connotations are not present in mere giving. For example, in the context of the intimate relations of the household muntun, the Runa view giving and sharing as primary (Bird-David 1990, 1992; Rival 2002). People often talk about such relationships as loving (llakina). Parental love constitutes the clearest case, a kind of unconditional "feeding" of desires that moves mainly in the direction of parents to child. Fathers and mothers freely give the stuff of life (food and both spiritual and physical substance) to their children.

Husbands and wives, too, demand giving and unconditional sharing between them. In this form of giving, however, each party constantly demands things from the other, and their different gender roles complement each other. Men give meat, but the meat is then controlled by women. Women give manioc brew, which realizes its value in consumption by men. At the same time, senior men tend to dominate a muntun because they stand for the whole and are ultimately responsible for giving life and protection to all its inhabitants. They must order and fulfill desire, giving unconditionally and "sacrificing" (*tormintarina*) for all (Mosko 1995)—another asymmetrical relationship. Men who do not keep their houses in order or leave their households lacking in "love" are seen as bad husbands and fathers. Status requires living a convivial responsibility and bondage to the desires of others.

In the sphere of relationships outside the local muntun, however, people do not give on such unconditional terms. Life is still convivial, but somewhat less so than in the local muntun. People value reciprocity and relationships of mutual respect and caring. People expect those in reciprocal relations to maintain status equality, at least in the long term. This equality operates in many spheres, including the loaning and borrowing of things, money, and labor and the flow of gifts. When I loan or give something to someone, it is expected that this person will reciprocate with something of roughly equal value at a later date. This kind of give-and-take behavior is the basis of inter-muntun relations of alliance, friendship, and compadre links.

We can conceptualize the differences in these two spheres—within a domestic muntun and among muntunguna—as a difference of value weighting. The two kinds of values are not absolutes; rather, they lie on a continuum that forms a single conceptual system. Within the substance forms of the ayllu-muntun, relations of life giving are emphasized and their consequence is hierarchy. As the relations of the ayllu-muntun flow outward, reciprocity is emphasized more. These reciprocal forms are the relations that link people to one another as apayaya and apamama, strong beings of symmetrical status.

Giving and reciprocity are present in both domains (see figure 5). Giving behavior is expected to be mutual, but not equivalent, and reciprocal behavior is giving in spirit, but mutual giving lacks the moral obligation that one reciprocate equally. Reciprocity, however, demands an ultimate equality of value when one gives and receives. In reciprocity, status must be kept symmetrical. The two kinds of exchange thus produce differences of status. Giving makes sense to the Runa within the muntun substance context, because much of social life focuses on hierarchical relationships such as those between parents and their children. Hierarchy and subordination are the social results of giving; those that give usually dominate because they are

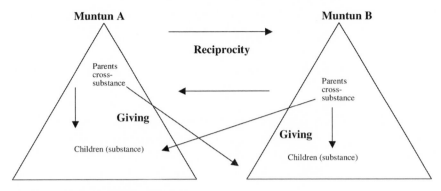

Figure 5. The Runa Theory of Value

providers of life.[5] Giving moves through and among different muntunguna as well, mainly through the relational networks of godparenthood.

Reciprocal behavior structures relations among muntunguna and within the community. These relationships are ideally symmetrical and occur among mature persons. They are blanketed with overtones, feelings, and discourses of convivial "respect" and reciprocity. Such respect relationships obtain among apayaya, apamama, auyaguna, compadres, and mature siblings.

Exchange Relates while Substance Defines

In Runa society social principles of both substance relations and affinal relations emerge as salient and important (Århem 1981). While notions of bilateral and patrilineal substance flows are vital to the conceptualization of ayllu family relations, affinal links are equally vital to the production of networks among ayllu flows. The two kinds of social relationships (ayllu versus auya) combine and separate in complicated ways. The muntun comprises both.

Substance relations are the beginning point of the life cycle and originate in and around the immediate ayllu-muntun. These relations, however, both produce and are produced by the cross-substance relation of masculine-feminine complementarity. Affinal relations are a result of the cross-substance relation, but over time affines come to be classified as being like brothers. Cross-substance relations produce both substance relations and same-substance relations, for they are modeled on the *idea* and material sociality of the substance relation. Same-substance relations are created through exchange and ritual.

The Runa notion of substance and substance relations is similar to that of the Daribi, a people from Papua New Guinea, who view consanguinity as linked to exchange. Among the Daribi consanguinity is "extensive" and *relates,* whereas exchange is "restrictive" and *defines* social relations (Wagner 1967:143). Blood ties may bind people in relationships for the rest of their lives, but exchange is needed to define those relations as meaningful, as in the case of the Daribi's special kin category of *pagebidi* (see Wagner 1967, 1977). Exchange, in other words, creates relationships of the highest value for the Daribi. While exchange relations are of a higher order, both exchange and substance are dynamically related as a circulatory system. The difference is in the weighting of the relations. Wagner, for example, writes that "exchange, as a principle of definition, is restrictive: it draws distinctions among people according to whether they share or exchange wealth; consanguinity is extensive: it relates people through substance regardless of the exchanges that are made" (1967:232).

This distinction of substance versus exchange in many ways works for explaining Runa kinship forms, too—but in the opposite direction. For the Runa, substance relationships are of higher value and must be elicited from affinity using exchange. For example, auya relations are created by ceding a daughter in exchange for gifts, but the exchange process combines substance differences ideally to create more productive, convivial, and lasting ayllu relations. These come to be conceptualized as highly valued relations of substance that define mature people (apayaya and apamama) who are at the fore of kin networks.

Both the Daribi and the Runa, however, conceptualize exchange as transformative; differences are brought into focus, combined, and "made" into other relations. Among the Runa, difference is the first step toward creating newer relations of consanguinity, the cross-substance relation of masculine-feminine complementarity, which in turn produces same-substance relations, the quasi-substance relations that have been the focus of this chapter. These relations are not fictive substance forms but real ones in the Runa view of things. The Runa theory of kinship itself, as I have discussed, is one of such substance transformations.

Conclusion

As I have shown, various categories of Runa affinal relationships, such as masha and cachun, compadrazgo, alliance, and adoption, are defined by and modeled on substance relations, allowing unrelated individuals to become "same substance." Affinity is thus transformed into consanguinity through various aspects of ritual and daily life. These observations in turn suggested a general Runa theory of value wherein value is social and contained in social relationships. This theory of value has a dual perspective; giving dominates within the intimate sphere of the muntun, while reciprocity dominates among muntunguna. Although giving and reciprocity are similar in spirit, they differ in that the former produces asymmetries, moving from parents to children (or from adult children to elderly parents). People who are unable to produce, or who produce less, have fewer reciprocal obligations; they are socially obligated to receive more than they give. Value is thus linked to the productive capabilities of persons as they mature and give more of the things of life to others.

Recent studies of Amazonian sociality have come to argue that consanguinity and affinity "mean very different things in Amazonian and modern Western kinship ideologies" (Viveiros de Castro 2001:19), but little research has explored these differences from the perspective of Amazonian notions of social action. Amazonian modes of relationship carry with them deeply complex philosophies of the way people and the relations they entail circulate. Ontologically there is no "relation without differentiation," to borrow a phrase from Viveiros de Castro (2001:25). Both affinity and consanguinity combine difference, although to different degrees of intensity, with affines being good to relate to and substance ties defining who one is. Kinship is never a finished process, however, and affinity is the means by which consanguinity is produced and reproduced. I have shown this dynamic relation of affinity becoming consanguinity throughout this chapter—the clearest examples being the incorporation of a masha or cachun and adoption. Future research in Napo may focus more on the dynamics and poetics of such transformative processes among people, as well as among people and natural and mythical beings.[6]

Meat, Manioc Brew, and Desire

The Runa say that people must become food producers before they can become life producers. This chapter addresses the relation between these two practices, food production and life production. Discussing this issue requires returning to issues covered in earlier chapters, but doing so in relation to a larger discussion about personhood, marriage, and value. I will therefore now examine how desire, gender complementarity, and cosmology are structured from the perspective of circulation and the general process of value production.

A Work Party

One day some men were loading a canoe with sacks of maize they planned to sell at the market, and I helped them with a few sacks. When we were done, they invited me to the market with them. We climbed in the motor canoe and went upriver. After selling the maize, the owners then bought a bottle of cachiwa, or aguardiente, and some cigarettes. They offered me the cachiwa and said that since I had helped with the sacks, I should drink with them. They used only one glass. The man who had bought the bottle filled the glass and offered it to each person. This went on until the bottle was empty. Someone else then bought another bottle, and the process repeated. Other men bought cigarettes and distributed them freely among the group until they were all gone.

Another day I had been at a fiesta in the community to celebrate a house building. Soft drinks, bottled beer, hard liquor, manioc brew, and various other consumables were available. People were dancing to the music of an Amazonian Quichua band, Los Playeros Quichua. The celebration lasted until the morning, and like almost everyone there, I spent the night drinking and talking with people from the community, visitors, and the band members. By the early morning I realized that I had experienced a unique social patterning of desire and desire regulation. While I had purchased several bottles of beer over the course of the night, I had not drunk any of them. Each time I followed the Runa custom of serving others and sharing the bottle. I, too, drank, but only what others had given me. By the end of the night almost everyone had gotten more or less drunk, but this physiological and psychological state was culturally realized in a specifically social way. Drunkenness was achieved though the mediation of one's desires by others, not by individual means. The Runa express this idea as *upichina,* or "to make drink." This phrase was expressed in various ways during the night, as one person told another with a bottle to make his friend drink: "Upichi." People sometimes say "Upichiway" (Make me drink) or mention *upinaya* (the urge to drink). People also say "Upi!" (Drink!), "Upishun" (Let's drink), or "Amushun" (Let's drink together). Most of this terminology refers to the social patterning of sharing and conviviality rather than the individual satisfaction of desire.

The Invention of Desire

In a now classic article, "The Perverse Child: Desire in a Native Amazonian Subsistence Economy," Peter Gow (1989) discusses the hunting-sex hypothesis of Siskind (1973). Gow's critique concerns Siskind's assumption that the hunting economy revolves around the scarcity of both game and women. Game is scarce, but feminine products (garden foods) are plentiful. At the same time, women are scarce in relation to men, for men are allowed to have more than one wife. This model suggests that women give sex in return for game and that men in turn give game in return for sex (Siskind 1973); that is, it involves the exchange of one scarce product for another.

Gow takes Siskind to task for imposing an alien commodity framework on Amazonian exchange. To posit the exchange of game for sex, argues Gow, is to assume a "logic of proprietorship" rather than address the fundamental issue, which is how people satisfy "hunger and sexual desire, and the satisfaction of these desires by other people" (1989:568). Gow's piece, which is the inspiration for this chapter, demonstrates the inappropriateness of assuming a Western subjectivity of commodity values when examining Native Amazonian exchanges and sociality (see also Dean 1995:90).[1] I do not merely follow Gow, however; I build on his insights to show that a value approach can yield further insights into thinking about the social and cultural logics of production, consumption, and circulation in Amazonia.

Gow's piece raises a larger question, too: how should anthropologists understand the concept of desire? Like Gow, I use the term *desire* to frame how individuals perceive other people and things and act in relation to them. The term can be misleading, however, mainly because it can be substituted for terms denoting the social forms by which desires are created, managed, and realized. Desire, like conviviality, can become too theoretically axiomatic. For example, Gow writes, "Desires link people inevitably to certain other people" (1989:568). While this statement makes sense, and is justified by the author, there is a potential ambiguity in treating desire as if it were a social form rather than a lived category of experience.

By positing desire as a social form, one not only makes it seem too important but also possibly confuses a biological urge with social and cultural relations. Speaking of food and sex in terms of desire suggests a general complex that exists among all people everywhere.[2] To further complicate things, Sahlins (1988:44) has argued that "human bondage to bodily desires" is a specifically Western historical product reflecting the bourgeois view of human freedom, especially as characterized in the work of St. Augustine.[3] Urban Western cultures, for example, might be characterized as social milieus where desires are rendered more problematic because they are managed through the social concept of the individual, as one person versus his or her desires. No one can deny, for example, that desires are a key feature of modern individualism and the consumer culture that thrives in it.

I go on about desire to highlight the point that, although the Runa certainly desire things, they desire them differently, which is the point of my stories about drinking. Desire understood as an isolated abstraction explains little. Rather, desires should be construed through larger relational complexes of cultural ideas, actions, and value forms from the native point of view. The crucial point is not the desires themselves but how they are perceived, discussed, mediated, and satiated through sociocultural forms.

Eating and Drinking

Like many Native Amazonian peoples, the Runa focus on food as the basis of life and constantly engage in activities that surround the production, consumption, and circulation of food. In addition, they continually talk about food and states of desire in relation to food. When visitors arrive, or when a member of the household returns from work or travel, people are invited to drink manioc brew and share food. In Napo Runa culture people almost never eat and drink alone, for these are quintessentially convivial actions.

When people ask, "Micucanguichu?" (Have you eaten?), they mean, Have you eaten a meal? A meal is usually defined as boiled manioc and some kind of meat, but boiled plantain or a plantain soup (*catu*) will often supplement the manioc. Meals are never complete without drink, or *upina,* and most meals are customarily punctuated with some kind of brew, or *asua.* After eating, the host will ask the guest to drink and will fill the guest's bowl a number of times. In addition, meals are incomplete without capsicum pepper, always available on the side.

The morning meal consists of upina, either asua or *chucula,* a sweet drink made by mashing ripe plantains in boiling water. The afternoon meal is the most important and usually includes meat. People eat again in the evening. Generally, people eat well when there is food available, whatever the time of day. In the morning drinking is considered a full meal. Chucula and asua, both customarily consumed in the morning, are satisfying, and one feels no hunger after drinking them. In the morning people do not ask, "Have you eaten?" Rather, they ask, "Do you come drinking?" (Upisha shamunguichu?).

Amazonian Quichua includes special words for giving. The verb *carana* refers uniquely to the action of giving food. As I mentioned earlier, people use *upichina* to refer specifically to the giving of drink. Whereas the verb *cuna* (to give) could be used to convey an unadorned act of giving someone some kind of food, usually raw, for later consumption, *carana* conveys giving someone cooked food. *Carana* conveys intimacy.[4] These terms and their meanings focus on nourishing other's bodies and on sharing in the realization of desires. Desire itself reflects a social perspectivism and intersubjectivity of seeing oneself through the desires of others (Viveiros de Castro 1998).

Labor and Gender Perspectives

Labor among the Runa is personified as a somatic quality. For example, they use the word *jumbi* (sweat) to indicate that they have been working. The Runa do not say, "I come from working in the field"; rather, they say, "I come sweating" (Jumbisha shamuni). Labor is regarded as essentially transformative and tied to the notion that people work to produce life. Gender cannot be divorced from acts of production and consumption, since both production and consumption connote a gendered essence of being. Gender too should be a cornerstone of Viveiros de Castro's (1998:476) notion of Amerindian ontological perspectivist relations, for "the point of view creates the subject," not the "object" (of an abstract humanity of which gender is only one aspect). Gendering is difference that creates a *subjective* point of reference, a separation necessary for the creation of social relations.

Labor is gendered as the spatial division of the natural world, of which humans form an integral part, and it too is perceived as gendered. For example, the forest (*sacha*) and river (*yacu*) are masculine and feminine, while gardens (*chagra*) are a feminine space (see Whitten and Whitten 1988:32–33). The house (*wasi*), especially its cooking area (*yanuna wasi*), is a space under strict feminine control. As separate kinds of human subjects, men and women fit into the division of labor as opposed but complementary productive beings. The Runa recognize that the essence of life is the coming together of complementary, opposing forces such as masculine and feminine, death and life, and this world and the other world. Opposites stand in a constant transformative and dynamic relationship (Crocker 1986) as energies and forces that humans use in reproducing society and the world.[5] For an illustration of this dynamic, consider the following example—a tale of hunting and food preparation that shows how complementary masculine and feminine labors transform death into the production of things of life.

Ricardo has returned to his *chapana,* or hunting blind, near the *chonta,* or peach-palm trees. Since it is the season when the chonta bears its fruit, many animals come to eat near this small hinterland grove. Ricardo has been spending a few hours now and then at dusk in the chapana, staking out a *sicu* (agouti). Although it is less than a kilometer from his home, the chapana is considered to be far away, mainly because it is located in dense forest and mountainous terrain. It is considered dangerous, too, principally because of the various kinds of forest-dwelling supai spirits, which the Runa say can make the hunter ill or even kill him. There is also the constant danger of poisonous snakes and other, human predators. As an ecological and social niche, the sacha differs from the secondary forest, around which homes and gardens are constructed. Because it is the outlying and most dangerous social-ecological sphere of being, it is the most appropriate for hunting activities. It is associated with the productive capacities of the masculine gender.

Ricardo waits in his chapana with his muzzle-loading shotgun ready. All of a sudden the sicu glides silently and quickly from under the forest growth, moving toward the coveted peach-palm fruit. Ricardo has only a few seconds, for the sicu's technique is to swiftly grab the globes of fruit and take them into cover for safe consumption.

Ricardo, however, knows the tricks of the agouti and has a few of his own. He knows that the sicu is very intelligent and swift, so he must fire when its head is down as it grabs the fruit. He must also not move or stick the barrel of the gun too far out of the blind, for the agouti would notice. Ricardo waits for the right moment. He does not squander his opportunity. The gun sounds, and the agouti is dead. Ricardo takes it home in his net carrying bag after covering it in a protective wrapping of leaves.

Upon returning home he hands his kill to Lorena, his wife. Up to this moment the agouti has been a masculine object in that it is raw meat procured through hunting. Killing is conceptualized as something necessary for the continuance of life, so neither remorse nor joy attends the practice in significant measure. At this time people do not speak much or ask many questions about the hunt. That would be considered bad manners. The women begin to prepare the kill for cooking, since fresh meat is always cooked immediately. While the women are busy making preparations for the meal, the men will often sit and watch in the kitchen.

Lorena takes the agouti down to the river and cleans it. She dresses out the carcass and carves it into pieces to make catu. No part of the agouti is wasted, and Lorena goes about her task with expertise. She then washes the pieces again, puts them in the pot she has brought from the house, and returns. She peels and grates about two pounds of the many plantains laying on the floor. Lorena's sister, her husband, and her brothers and their spouses arrive from the gardens. The other women help Lorena grate the plantains. They use an empty sardine can with holes punched into the metal for grating. They could employ a special palm root with knobs on it, but nowadays the sardine can is preferred. Few things are wasted in the forest.

Someone tends the fire, and Lorena burns the hair from the agouti, producing a crackling noise and filling the air with a strong odor (see plate 3; this procedure gives the meat a delicious and distinctive roasted flavor). Lorena then puts the plantain pulp and water in a pot on the fire and adds the agouti meat and a fistful of salt. Boiling is the preferred way of preparing game, but people also reserve pieces for roasting; they will eat some roasted pieces immediately and store others for a future meal.

The favorite method to preserve meat is to make a *maitu*, which involves using leaves to wrap meat that has been roasted on a fire. The maitu leaves (llaki panga) not only give the meat a delicious flavor but also protect it and facilitate its storage and transportation. The maitu is used for, among other things, sending gifts of meat to relatives, such as siblings, affines, or compadres.

Plate 3. A woman preparing a paca in 2002. The fur is being burned off as the first step in preparing the meat for consumption. The author is standing in the background.

While Lorena is busy with the catu, other women prepare the manioc and the uchu, or capsicum pepper sauce, that is present at almost all meals. The manioc is usually stored on the floor next to the plantains, and the household supply is restocked every two days or so. The roots are peeled with great skill and speed. Each root is then washed and split lengthwise to create spears that will fit into a medium-sized pot. Manioc is usually boiled, and it is a necessary ingredient for all meals. Plantains often accompany the manioc, but they are not an adequate substitute for it. People describe manioc as tender and delicious, but they often make jokes about plantains, saying they are hard and not as tasty as manioc. The Runa feel that manioc gives life and use it as their staple food. People see corn, plantains, and other nutrient-rich crops as important but subordinate to manioc and manioc products, which occupy an absolutely central place in their diets.

The ayllu then sits down to eat, and everyone is hungry for the fresh meat. The elder members are given slightly larger pieces. Lorena herself eats the head, the most prized cut for a woman. Ricardo then begins to recount the details of his kill, and the various brothers joke about many subjects, making fun of people and various situations. Although there is a table, the women prefer to eat sitting on the kitchen floor along with the children. The table is left mainly for the men (and visitors).

At some point during the preparation of the meal, Lorena decided how much agouti meat to put aside to make the maitu. Women typically prepare one or more maitu in addition to the catu, setting the former aside to eat at a later date and, more important, to send to other relatives. Lorena has her son bring a maitu to her children's godparents. Children often deliver maitu, and little or no fanfare is involved. The child will say simply, "My mother sent this." Sometimes he or she will not say anything.

Lorena has performed various domestic tasks that are quintessentially feminine. The way she grates plantains, for example, looks very Amazonian—squatting on the floor, her skirt hanging over her knees, with her hands performing the task in front of her lap, which is a typically feminine position. Most women prefer to wear long, light skirts that cover their legs when they squat to perform domestic tasks. In peeling manioc they keep their hands in front of their skirts and bodies so that the peels fall to the floor without soiling their clothes or bodies. The domestic tasks require strong and agile hands, as well as endurance in repetitive motion. Women perform domestic tasks together, and the copreparation of food is the foremost sign of female intimacy in the household. Catu is rarely prepared alone; asua almost never is.

By cooking the agouti Lorena has transformed it into a feminine object ready for consumption. But she has done more than this. She has combined various raw objects into finished ones, thus increasing their value for consumption and making the finished product feminine. The result represents the objectification of both masculine and feminine labor, but meat typically begins as a masculine object and finishes as a feminine one. Meat is never complete without other feminine products and feminine labors, and it is circulated through women, not men (Gow 1989). A discussion of gardens and production will further illuminate how the Runa transform desire into value.

Gardens and Manioc

The culinary system of Runa households is structured as a circuit of production, consumption, exchange, and circulation. Production centers on their gardens, or chagra, which are primarily manioc gardens. Women form the backbone of manioc production in Runa communities, for they are primarily responsible for creating and maintaining gardens and harvesting crops. Manioc is the main crop, but bananas, plantains, beans, and numerous other cultigens are grown as complements.

The myths of the Pastaza Runa show a clear association of the feminine body with gardening and manioc. Foletti-Castegnaro (1993:39–41) recounts the tale of a woman who is given a "manioc child" by Nunguli, the mother of the gardens. The child magically makes gardens and asua by singing. By the end of the myth, the manioc child sinks back into the earth, but the child has taught the secrets of manioc gardening to the woman, although now the woman is forced to produce. The implication is that the child becomes the manioc and that manioc roots are children (see Descola 1996b). Admittedly, this is not a Napo Runa myth, but when I told it to Napo women, they all made the association between manioc and children and understood the myth as one of their own. Indeed, there is other evidence that manioc cultivation and procreation are equated in Napo. People say that gardens must be kept tidy and neat, "just like one grooms the bodies of one's children." Harvested manioc roots, as well, must be carefully cleaned and handled, as if they were llullu—the same language used to deal with the care of children. As well, people say that one must not place harvested manioc roots sideways or upside down in the carrying basket, or else the woman's next child will be a breech birth (the image of crooked roots here transfers to the idea of a crooked birth, a clear example of a mimetic association [Taussig 1993]). Gardens and the gardening process are mimetically associated with the feminine body and the substance of her children (see Uzendoski 2004b).

Manioc and plantains are harvested every couple of days, and no household lacks them. Underlying this consumption-oriented economy is a philosophical commitment to a sense of freedom and flexibility in the social and cultural spheres built on this particular mode of production (Descola 1996b). For people concerned with maintaining a sense of freedom from time-consuming production, pursuing a manioc-based economy is a good strategy. As Lathrap (1970:49) has indicated, manioc is one of the most efficient food crops developed by humankind. Heckenberger (1998), for example, has commented that there are various ways of processing manioc and that processed manioc foods in tandem with aquatic resources allows for high population densities. Given that Amazonians have constructed their cultures and civilizations on manioc and manioc products, today's archaeologists are having to rethink prior assumptions about Amazonia as a limiting domain of human occupation.

Amazonians themselves contradict arguments about Amazonian environments as limiting. In response to my queries about the poorness of Amazonian soils, the Runa always asserted that their soil is good and that "manioc gives strength" (lumu urzara cun). From their perspective, Amazonian ecology gives all that one needs to live. Indeed, one can live off the forest if one knows how to do it, but centuries of "development" projects have unfortunately ignored indigenous knowledge and patterns of practice. Indigenous people often repeat the adage that if one knows the forest (sachara yachacpi), it gives life (causaira cun).

Hunting

While women are primarily responsible for manioc, men are expected to procure meat and fish. Meat and fish are relatively scarce and seasonal. During the chonta season men spend more time hunting. During the hotter and less-rainy months, when the rivers are low and fish easier to see, more time is spent in fishing. Men hunt and fish throughout the year, however; both are central to masculine identity and production.

Game does not exist randomly in the Runa universe. Each species of game has a *dueño*, or owner, who is the spirit master of the species. For a hunt to be successful, the dueño must release the animals for the hunter to kill. Hunting is akin to wooing women, for the hunter's primary concern is to get the dueño to release the animal. The hunter is thought of as attracting animals to him, a power associated with a man's accumulated supernatural or "soul" strength, his *ushai* (power) or *yachai* (knowledge). This power can be enhanced through magical objects such as anaconda teeth or power stones (yachai rumi).

Rivers are inhabited by the *amarun* (anaconda), a water snake known to "hunt" humans at night. The amarun owns the river, which it causes to flood, and maintains the various fish populations. Associated with unborn children, the amarun is further conceptualized as the primary source of all animal life, including humans. As Whitten and Whitten (1988:33) write, "Most, if not all, Andean and Amazonian peoples conceive of the anaconda as a source of ultimate inner power—chthonian power—collective and individual power from 'within.'" As discussed earlier, this internal power is a defining characteristic of Napo Runa personhood.

Two other spirit beings have "owner" status over the forest and water areas. These beings are of a higher order than the species dueños. The Sacha Warmi, or "forest woman," controls all the animals of the forest and is a teacher of shamans. The Yacu Warmi, or "water woman," is also a teacher of shamans, but she controls the domain of the water. She is the daughter of the anaconda. Although men are the unique procurers of game and fish, they ultimately receive it from feminine sources, the Sacha Warmi and the Yacu Warmi. These spiritual owners not only oversee game in the spirit world but also hand it over by way of the implicit affinity between masculine hunters and their spirit women. In this affinal relationship of spirits and men, men are the receivers rather than the producers of game. This circulatory arrangement is a mirror image of masculine and feminine relationships in everyday social life.

The Runa talk about the spirit world as a place where these powerful feminine beings desire men and woo hunters with their special power over animals and men. Men often talk about dreams where the spirit women attempt to seduce them or actually engage in sexual relations with them. Hunters occupy a subordinate position in this relation, and they are in no position to demand things of the spirit women. At the same time, hunters are viewed as "predators" of Runa women in this world. Men are dependent on the spirit women just as wives are dependent on husbands.

Meat, too, is intimately tied to feminine desire. Almost all women desire specific kinds of meat and fish, and they often talk about them. Men do not engage in such elaborate discourses about their desires for meat. Men will often act in the opposite way, expressing little or no desire to eat game, especially when it involves their own kill. Game and fish are produced by men for women, and women intensely enjoy eating game and fish. The mental model of meat production is marriage. By becoming kin to spirit beings, hunters gain access to the prey the spirits share, the fruit of their unions with the spirit women.

A Hunting Story

One day during the summer months of 2001 I went hunting with César. We had spent the morning weaving a thatch roof for a house in Ambatu Yacu, and he suggested we try hunting in the afternoon. We hiked through the forest for slightly over an hour before reaching his house, where we got his gun and drank some asua. We then hiked through the forest to some hunting blinds prepared near a stand of chonta trees. César positioned me in one of the blinds and went to another some distance away. I entered my leaf-house, which was so small that I could only stand upright and wait. I poked the gun through a space in the leaves and began scanning the forest. Standing in a chapana is uncomfortable; one notices every drop and gush, every bird and even insect that crosses one's visual path. Leaves often fall, shake, and move. Each movement is an event. As many people recounted to me, a hunter must never relax. One moment of inattention can result in a lost opportunity, a fact that I had experienced times before when hunting agouti. Spirits, they say, do things to distract the hunter, especially when animals are near. Soon the desire to sleep began to overcome me. I fought to stay upright. The shotgun weighed heavily on my arms.

Suddenly I heard a shot, which sounded deafening compared to the serene silence that had engulfed my invisible presence. César whistled, but I remained silent more out of shock than anything else. The sound of a herd was soon upon me. A Quichua speaker would repeat the noises of this moment using onomatopoeia, as in "turun, turun, turun, turun" (the sound of hoofs hitting the earth) or "tsaras, tsaras, tsaras, tsaras" (the sound of rasping against leaves and branches). A peccary, or sacha cuchi, moved toward me and froze in front of my chapana. To my unaccustomed eye, it appeared as a monster—large, strong, and bearing a bristling mane. My hands were trembling, but I managed to fire my one shot. I was engulfed with smoke, and only the noise of grunting and thrashing pierced the black cloud. Afraid I would be attacked, I reloaded before the smoke dissipated. I then exited the chapana to find César waiting for me. Each of us had brought down a peccary.

The hunting trip had taken us an entire afternoon, and now we had to walk a long way through the forest carrying a large load of meat. When I asked César if we could take only one of the peccaries and come back for the other, he said, "No, we must take them both back to the house. Otherwise, the jaguar will eat what we leave." Because this was my first large kill, he was also adamant that I carry the peccary I had downed. We made carrying straps out of vines and tied them around the feet of the peccaries. We then hung the loads off our backs and started for home. César led me to a point in the trail I recognized and then returned to his house. He said, "Don't get lost."

My muscles ached as I walked back to the house with blood running down my back and numerous flies biting and buzzing around my neck and head. Peccaries have a gland that emits a distinctive and rather unpleasant odor, and they also attract numerous flies that bite and harass humans. The familiar trail sometimes seemed unfamiliar, and all in all, the trek back to the community was tiring, arduous, and unpleasant. After I returned and all those present got over their surprise that I had killed my quarry, the peccary became an object of feminine labor. I lost all interest in touching the meat and was relieved to be rid of it. That night when I was sleeping, the smell remained in my nostrils, something that no one else detected. I was almost sorry that I had gone hunting and decided that I had learned enough about the activity from this one experience.

Some days later I went to visit Bancu in Yacu Llacta. I recounted my experiences to him in Quichua, doing the best I could to use the appropriate sound symbols and re-create a more aesthetic rendering of my experience. He laughed. While my recounting was good, I had used the wrong sounds to convey one of the events. I then asked him why, when I fired, the peccary appeared to me as a monster. He commented that the dueño of the animal had made me feel sleepy and that the power of the animal owner can affect one's body in this way. The owner can also make itself visible to the hunter and scare him in a powerful way. The owners can even make the ground shake and kill the hunter. "Hunting is dangerous because of the spirits and the dangers they pose. You are lucky to be alive," he said. I then told Bancu that this strong experience with the peccary had left me with absolutely no desire to eat the meat obtained in the hunt. I usually liked peccary meat and had eaten it many times, but this time I was ambivalent. He affirmed that he, too, felt the same way about the meat from animals that he had killed. He took this opportunity to teach me a social principle of hunting common throughout Amazonia. He said, "The hunter has little or no desire to eat the game he kills. It is better to eat the meat someone else offers."

While the women in Ambatu Yacu were cutting and smoking the meat in the kitchen, a young child tried to touch some of it. He was immediately reproached for his actions. I asked his mother why he shouldn't touch the meat, and she responded, "Raw meat from strong forest animals makes children ill. It has a spiritual energy that will do the child harm." The meat was more dangerous in its raw form, but even cooked meat could make the child sick.

In reflecting on these experiences, I came to realize that the Runa's attitudes toward the presence of spiritual beings and forces are not well explained by the notion of a so-called belief system. For the Runa, the presence of spirits is linked strongly to a particular mode of seeing the world that cannot be divorced from material reality. In their socioculture spirits transcend mere "belief," a term that creates the impression of falsity or superficiality, for they form an integral part of experience and empirical reality (E. Turner 1997).

Food and Kinship and Marriage

In Upper Napo the practices of food production cannot be separated from the relationships of marriage (Gow 1989). It is within the context of marriage that a couple begin to be productive and have gardens. The newly joined couple typically begin to live together within the house of the man's father, building an attachment to the main structure.

Although the parents and the new couple have separate sleeping rooms, they share a kitchen and are defined as a single productive, consuming unit. A newlywed couple's first garden is usually small. The pair spend more time helping the senior members of the household with their gardens. A subtle but crucial point is that, although both masha and cachun are part of the muntun, they are not initially part of the ayllu, a term that conveys a relation of shared substance. In the previous chapter I discussed the transformation of affinity into consanguinity as part of the processes of ayllu maturation and also analyzed the terms used to signal this transformation. The production of children is central to this process of converting affinity into consanguinity and incorporating cachun and masha into the substance flow of the ayllu. The couvade, for example, signals the crossing of different ayllu lines into one and marks the production of a new life. The essential point here is that production is centered in marriage, and there is little local production outside it.[6]

Clastres (1989) has discussed how Native Amazonians distrust power in the Western sense and do not respond to people who command or demand obedience. I have noticed that among the Runa, this ethic dominates production, too. Within the sociomoral context of a Runa community, no one can coerce someone to produce or to contribute labor. They must be asked politely, and they often refuse. Nonetheless, Gow has pointed out that spouses constitute the unique category whereby people "can and do make demands upon each other" (1989:572). The social universe is thus split into two categories: those who are in a position to demand things from each other and those who are not. The former relationships (of demand) congeal around marriage. The latter are termed relationships of respect and follow other kin pathways (ibid.).

As the last chapter showed, analogous concepts are present in Upper Napo. Relations within the muntun are characterized by giving. These are contrasted to relations among people from linked muntun, which are defined by symmetry and reciprocity. As I have shown, the basic principle of shared living is unconditional giving. People who continually give to their dependents are said to "give [them] life" (causaira cun). This logic governs parent-child relationships and represents hierarchy. Giving legitimizes hierarchy; those who give more of the essential things of life have a higher status and authority than those who are dependent. Parents are givers par excellence (see Santos-Granero 1986).

By contrast, relationships among muntun constitute respectful relations where it would be rude to ask for things and favors without at some point giving back to an equal degree. Relatives sharing a hearth often demand things of each other, whereas compadres, auya, and adult siblings who have built their own homes approach one another with more care. People in this latter category might be said to "share convivial life" (pareju llakinusha causana). A person who often takes more than he or she receives can be referred to as unbalanced, or a "chulla runa." Another subtle but important distinction is that, even though siblings are considered to be of the same ayllu, once they are established as separate muntun—that is, separate units of production—they treat each other with more respect and care. Substance relations are both hierarchical and symmetrical, and the reciprocal intimacy associated with respectful sibling relations makes these a model for other relations, such as compadres, affinal relations, and friendship.

In daily social life the Napo phrase respectful requests with special language, sometimes including the Spanish word *favor*, as in "Shuc favorta raway" (Do me a favor), or "Manzhu ushapangui shuc favorta ranara?" (Can't you just do a favor?). Quichua offers many ways of conveying respectful conviviality when asking for help. The suffix -*pa* adds respect; the use of *ushana* (to be able) avoids the use of command forms and makes clear that a refusal is not a breach of conduct. By requesting things using this special convivial terminology, one conveys a sense of moral responsibility to symmetry in regard to the other party.

When dealing with relationships of demand, however, people are more direct and less concerned with symmetry. They say "Cuyaway" (Give it to me) or "Upichiway" (Make me drink). The Napo Runa are not shy in asking for things (indeed, some acquire reputations as people who "ask too much"), nor are they hesitant to return a favor. Nevertheless, they are careful about whom they ask for favors. When they ask for them, they think ahead to what that person will ask of them later. People prefer to ask kin for favors because these are relations with whom they already have established sustained exchange relations and a sense of moral trust.

In short, the Runa sense of value demands that people get what they want and need by sharing and reciprocating rather than by individually producing and consuming. These value forms are not the systems' ends, however, but only its means. As I will argue, these principles of food production and consumption are intimately tied to sexuality and the production of people.

Sexuality

The relationship between giving and reciprocity is found within the production, consumption, and circulation of food, but it is intimately linked to sexuality and reproduction, too. Strong substance and cross-substance relationships result in demanding and giving behaviors, mainly between spouses and between children and their parents. Outside the circuit of the muntun, reciprocity and respect are emphasized. To understand how these relations are constituted and transformed, we must first consider the symbolism of sexuality and substance.

Talk about sexual relationships always involves the productive imagery and symbolism of the genders. Men are associated with killing and origins. They are said to "cut," "pierce," and "sever" women during sex. Women are said to drain the vital energy out of men. Both are analogous to the productive capacities of each gender. Men are hunters in sex, while women "cook" the semen of men and transform it into a new life. Men complain of being tired for days after a sexual encounter, a way of speaking about energy that was drained and recirculated during sex. I have heard men make similar complaints after they have been hunting.

The penis (*ullu*) is not figuratively associated with any particular food, but it is associated with the anaconda, which, as I mentioned earlier, is the "primary procreator" (Whitten and Whitten 1988:33). People do not eat anaconda, but they say that it controls all the fish that people catch and eat.

One myth I recorded speaks of the transformative powers of the penis and associates it with the powers of life. The myth concerns the twins. During their adventures, one twin had his penis pierced by a fowl, which flew away and stretched it to a considerable length. The other twin could not catch up to the fowl, so he cut the penis into sections. The sections fell into the rivers and became anacondas.

This myth ties into others about the yacu runaguna, a mythical anaconda people who inhabit rivers. As one story goes, a very young yacu runa was abandoned in human form on the edge of a river. Humans passing by took pity on the abandoned child and adopted him, raising him as their own. The woman breast-fed the child, and he grew quickly. As he grew, he developed an affection and passion for the water. He could fish very well and constantly brought fish to his mother. After a few years his mother came down to the river one afternoon and startled the boy. He had just transformed into his anaconda form and disappeared into the water on being discovered, never to return.

There are a number of interesting patterns in these two myths. First, the myth explicitly states that anacondas and humans share substance (through breast-feeding), just as the twins are thought to have shared jaguar substance (Uzendoski 1999). The combination of the myths creates a circular set of transformations: the human penis (twins) becomes the anacondas, which become human beings through adoption, which then return to anaconda state. The cycle is one of anaconda-human transformations, with the origins of water and water life being associated with the original "human" penises of the twins.

As I mentioned in chapter 1, using a chumbi to wrap babies so that they "look like the anaconda" is a mimetic practice evocative of this complex. Sexual energy, however, is linked to spiritual feeding, and spiritual feeding does not stop after conception or birth itself. It is continued with the couvade (Rivière 1974; Rival 1998) and in associations of the wrappings. Men, as hunters and fisherman, gain their powers from associations with the daughters of the yacu runaguna and sacha runaguna. By becoming masha to these entities, men are able to feed their own families.

Female genitalia, however, are associated with food. Most often the Runa refer to female genitalia as *churu* (snail), a favorite comestible. They also call female genitalia *muyu*, which can be translated as "fruit" or "seed." These figurative references connote both to the nutritive aspect of feminine nature and women's reproductive capability. At the same time, there is a direct analogy between hunting and sex in that men are understood to "hunt" women in much the same way they stalk game. A popular modern Quichua song by Patricio Alvarado talks about how a man waits for his woman just as a jaguar waits for his prey. Magical items associated with shamans, such as yachai rumi (knowledge stones), the teeth of the anaconda, and the genitalia of river dolphins, also function in hunting and sexual prowess. When a man obtains such an item, he must decide whether he wants its power to be channeled into hunting, fishing, or attracting women. A magical object will not function in more than one these domains. Women, too, use magic to attract men. This magic uses a substance made of a plant called *simayuca*, which the woman must rub on the hand of the person whom she desires. In addition, women's songs attract men (Harrison 1989). To better conceptualize feminine sexuality and attraction, I will now examine manioc brew in more detail.

The Fermentation of Life: Manioc Brew, or Asua

Asua exists within a fascinating circuit of knowledge, labor, and experience. In conversations about manioc brew, people from the United States and Europe, as well as nonindigenous Ecuadorians, frequently ask me how asua is made. When I explain the process, some people express disgust regarding the fermentation practices of Amazonian cultures.

One of the steps to making asua involves human saliva. Human saliva provides the enzyme ptyalin, which converts starch into sugar (see Buhner 1998:94). Nonindigenous people often comment that such methods of fermentation are unhygienic and reflect a "savage" or "barbaric" custom. In numerous movies where Amazonians appear, their fermented beverages are always presented as a marker of their apparent savagery. There is scene, for example, in Werner Herzog's film *Fitzcarraldo* where the colonialist Fitzcarraldo must drink manioc brew that the natives offer him. As it is served to him, someone comments that the beverage is manioc with "fermented human saliva." Fitzcarraldo drinks from the bowl but appears horror-struck and sickened after taking a small sip.

From the Amazonian perspective, however, manioc brew is very desirable and is thought of as very healthy. Indeed, many Westerners who learn to drink manioc beer come to cherish it and appreciate its distinctive flavors and convivial associations. The more crucial point, however, which goes beyond taste, is that the focal cultural values of Napo Runa society congeal within the processes of manioc-brew production, circulation, and consumption. From the Amazonian perspective, to live without manioc brew would be to lead a lowly existence. Manioc brew has a nice balance of fruity sweetness, acidity, alcohol, and texture. There are also infinite varieties and variations. I have never witnessed or heard of a bad batch of manioc brew. Beyond that, native fermentation processes are rich in symbolic meaning and associated with life and reproduction (Uzendoski 2004b).

Making asua is a developed art in Upper Napo, although the materials involved are simple: vegetable products, a large pot, a knife for peeling the manioc, a mashing board (*batan*), and a pounding instrument (*mucu*). The harvested manioc is peeled, boiled in a large pot, and then mashed in a large wooden basin. The women chew some of the mass, an activity known as *mucuna,* and then spit the mouthfuls back into the basin with the rest. The finished mass, called *asua capi,* is stored in a covered pot for anywhere from two days to a few weeks as it ferments, although it is generally ready in about a week. The fermenting agent is wild yeast.

To serve the asua the hostess takes out handfuls of the mash and dissolves it in a bowl or pot of water. This process is called *llapina* (squeezing) or *capina* (grabbing). The stems and hard particles of manioc that do not dissolve into the milky liquid are thrown out. This discarded part is called *ansi.* Most of the time "grabbing" is done in the same serving bowl from which the consumer will drink, and the server will graciously wipe off any excess ansi that might stick to the bowl.

There are many variations and varieties of asua. The main types I experienced during fieldwork were *yuramaba* (common manioc asua, white and milky in color), *allu* (cream-colored asua), *vinillu* (a sweet and strong form of allu asua wine), and *warapu* (a manioc-banana mixture, often red and more typical in Lower Napo river communities). These versions all contain manioc as their main source of fermenting starch. Allu and vinillu, however, are made with a special yeast (allu) that forms on a roasted plantain and is mixed in with the mash. Vinillu is made by collecting the sweet drippings of an allu mash.

Pucara is a dense, nutritious red asua made from peach-palm fruit. This variety is the staple beverage during the plant's fruit-bearing season. Whenever asua is not around, people replace it with a nonfermented drink made out of boiled and mashed *guineo,* a small plantain, which is never lacking. Unlike the banana or plantain, the guineo never needs to be planted, fertilized, or weeded. Nonetheless, the Runa desire guineo products less than true plantain or manioc products, and the guineo drink is not considered asua. In the household where I lived, my hosts would laugh whenever we had the guineo drink, calling it "pig's food."

In making asua women convert raw products into doubly finished, highly desirable ones. They produce different types with a variety of tastes, textures, and alcoholic contents. Asua can be fermented to different strengths to suit the taste of the drinkers, and most drinkers have personal favorites. Moreover, asua is specially tailored to suit the tastes and desires of men, not women. The Runa talk of asua as an "energy drink" that curbs both thirst and hunger. Asua, they say, is the staple of life, work, and happiness.

While serving asua is a feminine occupation, it is the husband who demands that his wife make it, and he invites his friends and relatives to his house to share in its consumption. Asua allows men to be convivial in transforming desire into sociality. A husband may tell his wife to make a lot of asua to mobilize labor for a minga or for a celebration. One rarely consumes asua by oneself, and it is customarily served by a woman, usually its owner, her daughter, or her cachun. The customary way to drink asua is to take it in a large bowl by one hand only (children drink with two hands) and make conversation while consuming the liquid. When the drinker finishes, the host will immediately refill the bowl. Women will often joke about their ability to get visiting men drunk from their asua. It is a sign of being a good host to have good asua that can intoxicate drinkers.

Asua and Meat: Gendered Spheres of Exchange

Although women produce and consume asua, it circulates throughout the community through the thoughts, stomachs, and even the names of men. This is the inverse of game, which is produced by men but circulates through the community in the names and thoughts of women. Gifts of both asua and game are transformational forms of exchange that circulate among aylluguna and muntunguna. These differ from "raw" products, which are mostly exchanged within them. Interestingly, the prestige spheres of meat and manioc brew are gendered and complementary—a typically Amazonian means of organizing production and consumption. Neither sphere is superior to the other, and ritual events would not be complete without both. Both are crucial in effecting the social transformations of personification. In addition, both meat and asua are thought to contain more samai than other foods.

The Hau, or Spirit, of Asua

Asua and game carry more prestige than other items do and are favored in ritual transformations. They carry more "love" (*llakinawa*) than other foods, too, and are ideal substances for personifying relationships. In a vague way, meat and asua are gifts that carry a life force similar to *hau*, or "spirit," as Mauss (1990) construes that notion. For the Runa, however, the life force or power of these gifts reflects their embodied energy and power of personification: they contain substance that defines the circulation of "breath" among nature and people. I have often heard people say that "asua is life" and that it gives people strength. Manioc, like meat, is anthropomorphized and viewed as part of the "human condition." Although plant and animal

beings are objectified in the process of making them gifts, their vitality is
not lost. Vitality is embodied within the gift itself (see Mauss 1990:8–10;
Jackson 1996:27–28).

The power of asua is linked to desire, too. In ritual and special contexts,
women serve asua to men while singing and dancing. People told me that in
"the old days" (rucu timpu), such practices were quite common, especially
after the man had come back from hunting or a long strenuous journey.
They would sing, "What do you want? Do you want vinillu? Do you want
yanamba? Do you want yuramba? Do you want vinillu? Little husband, what
do you want? Little husband, little husband."

The content of such asua songs makes explicit the analogy between asua
and female sexuality. The woman sings of having three kinds of asua from
which her husband can choose. The song is erotic in the way that the singer
concerns herself with the satisfaction of her man's desires. She refers to him as
"little husband" and "little man" (using the suffix -lla) as a means of endear-
ment; she repeats the phrase "do you want?" many times; and waiting and
"ready" for her husband, she pulls him up to make him drink asua. In these
feminine performances, the consumption of asua and sexuality are collapsed
in a ritual discourse about desire.

The notion that asua is life emerges when one looks at the symbolism of its
production.[7] The process of fermentation is described by the word *pucuna*
(to blow or mature), and fermented asua is described as *pucushca* (blown or
mature). Asua is also said to have samai. When making the final mash, one
leaves a hole so that the asua can breath. In addition, the large pot (*manga*)
in which the mash ferments has connotations of the female womb. It is a
container for transformation. In the twins myths, two unborn children, forc-
ibly taken from their mother's womb by man-eating jaguars, develop inside
an upside-down manga (see Uzendoski 1999). It is not the pot by itself that
symbolizes the womb but rather the image of containment, which mirrors
both the form and process of asua production.

Pucuna means "to blow," a notion synonymous with the vital energy of life,
but it also conveys processes of maturation. Fruits are described as pucushca,
or matured, when they are ripening. Although *iñana* (to grow) is the word
people most commonly use to describe how children, plants, and animals
grow, I have heard some employ the word *pucushca* to describe children in
the womb or still very tender (*llullu*). The word *iñana* appears to refer mainly
to external characteristics of growth, whereas *pucuna* refers to internal, less-
visible processes associated with the soul or samai; again, both hunted meat
and asua are thought to have more samai than other foods do.

The word *pucuna* connotes the energy of sexuality as well and is used for the blowgun, which is crafted from chonta wood. People say that chonta is the hardest wood in the Amazon. Like the blowgun itself, the chonta is often used as a trope for the male penis and the strength of masculine power. Another tie between asua and both sexuality and power stems from the notion that shamans blow invisible *biruti* (darts), which lodge in the bodies of victims to cause sickness and death. Curative magic revolves around the removal of biruti and other piercing pathogens. Sucking is a means of healing, just as blowing is power. The continued "sexual feeding" of the child after birth and couvade behavior by the parents are manifestations of breath. In short, the central trope of breath as power is the basis of the couvade, shamanism, hunting, and sexuality.

Women contribute breath to their children as they mature. Like breast milk, asua is a central substance of feminine nourishment. Both breast milk and asua are white, and both are contained by shapes of or associated with the female body. As babies are weaned off maternal milk, their mothers begin to give them soft, sweet asua. Asua replaces breast milk as the substance of nourishment at a very young age. Asua thus contains within it a condensed symbolism of feminine nourishment, production, substance formation, and life force itself. To view the full range of transformation elicited by the production and consumption of asua, however, we must examine how it circulates and is linked to reproduction.

Circulation of Asua and Cachiwa

Again, although women primarily produce asua, men consume it, and husbands get prestige from inviting others to partake of their wives' asua. Asua is consumed in a variety of contexts, and its consumption is linked to *communitas* (V. Turner 1969:96–97) and strong conviviality. Meals provide one context of asua consumption. This form of drinking provides sustenance and ayllu conversation. Another common context occurs when kinpersons, compadres, auya members, neighbors, or others come to visit. Asua is served, people converse, and the visitors stay a while. People usually do not get drunk as they would during a fiesta or wedding. Visitation and household forms of drinking are not a disruption but occur within the normal rhythms of daily life. Such drinking takes place, for example, when visitors stop by on their way home from their gardens.

In fiesta and wedding contexts, however, drinking asua leads to drunkenness and disruption of rhythms (Gow 1989). Sometimes men spontaneously decide to drink heavily without a special occasion, but this kind of drinking (if done regularly) can lead to social problems. This kind of consumption puts stress not only on feminine production but also on feminine circulation, for men are not productive when they are drinking and must depend on feminine labor. Fiestas and drinking parties usually last for two and sometimes three days.

Drinking creates a special kind of social space for everyone during ceremonial fiestas, but especially for men, who drink far more copiously and frequently than women do. Drinking is thought to characterize a sinzhi runa, or strong man. Masculine labor is limited during drunken fiestas, but women must continue to be attentive to their men, children, and guests. In addition, the women generally must watch the drunken men to make sure they do not do something harmful, such as falling into the river or fighting.

This dangerous space of drunkenness allows for social transformations that could not normally occur, as in the coming together of two different aylluguna in a wedding. In heavy drinking people are said to lose their inhibitions, and many state outright that this is the goal of heavy drinking at a fiesta. I have heard men say during heavy drinking, "We will expose our hearts to each other," or "I will not abandon you, and you cannot abandon me."

Most outsiders, going all the way back to the sixteenth century, have commented on the Napo Runa's extreme fondness for alcoholic drinks and drunken states (see Osculati 2000 [1846–47] and Ortegón 1989 [1577]). Outsiders associate these behaviors with a predilection for "vice" and lack of civilization, but the Runa themselves see such states through their religious view of the human condition as defined by samai. As José Sánchez-Parga (1997) has shown, by Ecuador's colonial period aguardiente and *trago* had already replaced coca as a sacred "social object" of communication with the spirit world.

Sánchez-Parga's association of aguardiente with coca and communication with the divine is supported by its ritual and symbolic uses in Napo. Shamans use cachiwa when performing a cleansing, and it is viewed as a medicinal substance that cures a variety of ailments on its own. It is thought to give strength and is commonly consumed in small quantities before sporting events or other strenuous activities. Some men claim to have shamanic visions and revelations when drinking. Indeed, the Quichua word for the altered state created by the hallucinogenic substances of wanduc and ayahuasca, *machashca* (drunken), is the same term used to describe the effects of drinking asua or cachiwa. Becoming machashca is said to open one's body to the spirit world so that one's "essence" is manifest. One friend of mine would claim to see

anacondas when he was drunk; he would further claim that the anacondas
became the muscles and sinews of his body.

In Runa society drunken states, although often leading to destructive
consequences, are generally seen as positive, a means of attaining knowledge
(see Abercrombie 1998:317–67). Evangelicals, however, have a more complex
relationship to drinking. I have addressed these elsewhere (Uzendoski 2003),
so I will not discuss the evangelicals here. My main point is simply that, like
asua, cachiwa is thought to contain life force and cosmic energy. Furthermore,
like coca as it is used in Peru and Bolivia, cachiwa is thought to be spiritually
powerful, and it constitutes a central part of Runa healing culture.

Personification and the Metamorphosis of Value

I have argued that the complex of asua production, consumption, and circulation is symbolically analogous to the production of children and reproduction
itself, an insight I take from Gow (1989). In Napo, festive asua drinking and
child production are both disruptive. These actions alter not only relationships among people but also the production and circulation of things. Both
drinking and the production of a child represent separations and recombina-
tions in the normal pattern of social life (Gow 1989:577).

From a circulatory view, one might follow Gow's proposition that the
production of children is linked to asua in that both are focal points of flow
in their respective domains, sexuality and food production. Asua production
and circulation begins with women, but it circulates through men's desires.
Men are the primary agents of the social transformations that occur in asua
consumption (Gow 1989). While I agree with Gow's insight that circulation of asua is intimately linked to the circulation of people, I think that
this proposition needs to be rephrased in terms of the local theory of value:
desire is the "urge," but value and value transformations are the form. As I
have discussed throughout this book, the Runa produce things that become
metamorphosed into persons. Manioc brew and children are social forms
of production by which value is made, but they operate at different levels
of value metamorphosis. There is more value contained in the relations surrounding a child than in the relations surrounding things.[8]

While drinking is mainly a male desire that brings out the sociality of
men (and often is the impetus for sexual relations), children are born into
the world as new subjects of desire. The birth of the child initiates a host
of transformations. Fathers become grandfathers, sisters and brothers be-

come "aunts" and "uncles," and the child's parents will soon be looking for compadres, or ritual coparents. The production of a child begins a social transformation where parents enter into higher value relationships and gain status. Compadre relations become possible, and later, when a child marries, one gains auya, or alliance relations. Through the maturation of children, one becomes a giver of life as well as a producer. As I showed in the previous chapter, after the birth and continued feeding of one or more children, people treat mashaguna and cachunguna as substance kin. Substance defines what exchange began.

Conclusion

Gow's (1989) observation that production, consumption, and circulation are configured within specific social relationships in Native Amazonian communities proves essential to understanding how sexual and alimentary desires are inextricably linked within the consciousness and social idioms associated with the indigenous culture. Native Amazonians do not exchange food products directly for sexual favors, nor do women offer their sexuality in return for meat products. This scarce-resource model ignores the fact that people in Amazonian societies exchange and circulate goods for prestige and value as well as reproduction. As Frederick Damon used to say in his economic anthropology seminar, scarce resource models pretend that "people are only producing use-values and not exchange-values." Sexual and alimentary desires are an important *idiom* by which people conceptualize and mediate social relationships within and beyond the ayllu and larger community. These desires are combined conceptually in the production of children, for feeding produces "flesh." Reproduction and feeding are both creative processes that transform social relations.

Male desires are realized primarily through the idiom of drinking asua, which on the one hand leads to the kind of disruptive behavior that is needed to initiate sexual relations and the transformations they require and on the other hand provides opportunities to behave convivially and respectfully by inviting compadres and others to drink. Female desire for game is realized by the productive activities of the husband, whose metaphoric marital liaison with forest and water women signifies his power and attractiveness. This power allows his wife to be convivial in giving presents of game and fish to those she respects and loves. A neat symbolic scheme emerges here: asua and its production are associated with ideas of feminine substance and the female body, whereas hunting draws on notions of marriage and alliance (see Descola 1996b). Value becomes articulated through a complementarity of masculine and feminine flows, the proper moral context for the mediation of desire in Runa society.

The production of children, however, creates a new subjectivity of desire and entails high status transformations in Runa social life, giving rise to compadre and auya relations. Because desire is increased, consumption, production, and circulation must intensify as well. This productive intensification for purposes of others' consumption is the key to prestige in Runa social spheres. The production of children allows a husband and wife to add new relationships of status and to acquire the highly valued relationships of reciprocity and respect in Runa communities. Such is the normal course of collective relations. The birth of children is the key event in this process: it forces one to become a life giver and not just a food producer.

There are, however, certain contradictions and negative potentialities within this economic and social system for managing masculine and feminine desires; I cannot discuss these at length for reasons of space. At the most basic level, improper food consumption is viewed as a perversion of collective values, a central feature of Gow's (1989) piece.[9] If children eat dirt, feces, or soap, which they sometimes do when hungry, their parents see such acts not as existing in a value-free realm but as putting the sociality at risk. Perhaps it is because the morality of desire is a focal aspect of food behavior that Native Amazonians display a remarkable self-control, or an absolute disregard for it, that typifies their dignified way of approaching material things. This kind of self-control is foreign to many modern Europeans and North Americans, nor is it something easily understood in the context of the free market. Little do we realize that modern Western economies of rational commodity desires produce the chain smoker, the drug addict, the obese, and the alcoholic. The modern Westerner who finds desire problematic is usually faced with the individual or group regulation of it.

6

The Return of Jumandy:
Value and the Indigenous Uprising
of 2001

> *The audience of Quito proceeded with its case against the three*
> *Pendes [shamans], who, with Jumandy, were the most guilty rebels.*
> *. . . The Pendes and Jumandy were found so guilty that . . . they*
> *were brought through the public streets of the city . . . , where they*
> *were injured with red-hot pliers. From there . . . they were hanged*
> *[and] cut into quarters. . . . All the indigenous justices and the*
> *majority of indigenous leaders of Avila, Baeza, and Archidona,*
> *and those of Quito, were forced to watch the punishment. The*
> *Spanish said that the same would be done to any similar offenders*
> *in the future and that this lesson should be sounded from generation*
> *to generation for all memory.*
> —Toribio de Ortiguera (1581–85)

In this chapter I will discuss how the ritual and kinship forms presented in earlier chapters structure views of past and future epochs and events. Instead of looking at the ethnographic present, I turn to the millennial nature of the Runa system of value (see Whitten 2003; Brown and Fernández 1991; Wright 1998; Hill 1988, 1996) to show more broadly why systems of value matter. Drawing on earlier themes in the book, I discuss how cultural defense, memory, and historical consciousness, too, are inhabited by the philosophy of the circulation of substances and symbols (see Rival and Whitehead 2001:10; Whitehead 2003). As I will show, an intensity of conviviality infuses the political actions of the 2001 indigenous uprising in Napo and its remembrance.

In studying the uprising of 2001, I will explore the proposition that the Napo Quichua concept of *pachacutic*—the transformation of space-time for a better life (Whitten 2003:x)—cannot be divorced from ushai (power) and unai (mythical space-time). As I will show, the poetics of kinship, myth, history, value, and power coalesce in the way that the Napo Runa have remembered and conceptualized their relationship to the great warrior Jumandy in the events following the 2001 uprising (for more on Amazonian historical consciousness, see Whitten 1988, 1996, 2003; T. Turner 1988; Basso 1995; Hendricks 1993; Graham 1995; Whitehead 2002). This remembrance, however, reveals a more general pattern. In connecting to their ancestors, the Runa subordinate ethnic and historical realities to the millennial purposes and affective flow of kinship.[1]

Who Was Jumandy?

As one enters the city of Tena from the west, the first thing one sees is a large, magnificent painted statue of an indigenous warrior, his chest bare and his musculature impeccable (see plate 4). The warrior holds a raised spear and is poised for battle. The inscription on the statue, put there by the region's indigenous federations, notes that this warrior is Jumandy, the great cacique of Napo and one of the principal leaders of the 1578 assault against the Spanish.[2] People's attitudes toward Jumandy resonate with the statue's imagery. His history is known by almost all the residents of Tena. He is the subject of poems by local poets and regarded as a defender of freedom. The Napo Runa, and many mestizos as well, recognize him as one of their great ancestors, even though anthropologists know Jumandy to have been Quijos rather than Runa. Indeed, he is synonymous with the uprising of 1578, the greatest indigenous revolution of Upper Napo.

Although it failed, the revolt of 1578 was marked by a great geographical scope. The plans for ousting the Spanish spanned the Andes and the Amazon. It involved caciques from the highlands and Tupian peoples of Lower Napo (Oberem 1980:89–90). It was the first great action of colonial resistance taken by the indigenous peoples of Upper Napo, and despite its failure, its consequences were monumental. The revolt led to a severe repression by the Spanish—so severe that some Quijos were reported to have strangled their children so that they would not have to pay tribute (ibid.). People fled the high forests around Baeza—the cultural hearth of the Quijos—for more remote parts of Amazonia. Over the next two centuries the ethnic category and language of Quijos died out entirely. What was once a vibrant region of trade connecting the Andes and the Amazonian regions became a frontier.

The Quijos people were not simply "lost," however, as many people have assumed. As many of them transculturated (into the Napo Runa), much

Plate 4. The statue of Jumandy in Tena; photo taken in 2003, after the statue was refurbished.

of their culture has persisted in new forms through ethnogenesis (Oberem 1980; Uzendoski 2004a). This proposition is supported by the way that the Napo Runa tell their own origins and view their history. They see the Quijos as their kin and "remember" Jumandy as achieving the first great victory of indigenous resistance. To them, these events signify the failure of conquest, a set of relations that have yet to be resolved (Todorov 1982).

The Levantamiento of 2001

The events of 2001 in Napo were part a pan-Ecuadorian indigenous *levantamiento*, or uprising, that several scholars have analyzed (see, e.g., García 2001, 2002; Chiriboga 2001; Barrera 2001; Kingman 2001). No one has specifically dealt with the uprising in Napo, however, nor has anyone studied this event in the larger historical and social context of Napo Runa culture and history. The uprising in question took place in Napo in February 2001. In the United States I followed the events closely through news reports and by phone. Four months after these events I returned to Napo for a summer of fieldwork and had the opportunity to follow up with questions and interviews of the participants themselves.

It was not hard to find people willing to talk, for everyone was thinking about and discussing the uprising. While the people of Napo had participated in various strikes (*paros*) in recent years, the 2001 uprising was distinctive because of the military repression faced by the protesters, the high level of violence, and the loss of life. The intense events were something of a collective trauma, for the people of Napo considered their protest to have been peaceful, yet they were attacked by the military. In addition, the stakes were high. This uprising was not merely a fight for indigenous cultural rights but a direct challenge to the sweeping neoliberal economic reforms created by "dollarization."

Behind the specific economic demands lay the sentiment, common among the Napo Runa and many other Ecuadorians, that Ecuador was becoming ever more dependent on the United States and therefore powerless in relation to it. Dollarization at this time signified much more than just converting the national money from the sucre to the dollar. Like the Melanesian notion of cargo, the notion of dollarization was rife with associations of a changing materiality (Wagner 1981:32). As one person stated to me: "You see this money—it has a gringo on it with white hair. This money does not belong to us. That we use this money now means that Ecuador is no longer a country. It is a province of the gringos now." Unlike the Melanesian notion of cargo, however, dollarization was understood by the Runa as a process of losing value, not gaining it. Many people, for example, commented to me that the sucre "lasted longer." After a couple of years of using the dollar, Runa people kept asking me how Americans could live with a form of money that "disappears so quickly" and makes other things, like cash crops, disappear more rapidly as well.

Unlike the 1578 rebellion, which had military objectives, the region's recent indigenous uprisings (which began in 1990) have focused on the achievement of political goals, referred to as "points," with the idea being "to resume transformed relationships between indigenous Ecuadorians and other Ecuadorians" (Whitten 1996:197). Fitting this general model, the 2001 indigenous uprising employed nonviolent tactics in pursuing its aims, blocking transportation in the rural sectors (mainly dominated by indigenous populations) so that political demands would be heard and, it was hoped, implemented.

The various communities around Tena were in charge of holding the long and narrow bridge that spans the Napo River. This bridge, which connects Puerto Napo to Tena, constitutes a lifeline for people wanting to get to Puyo, Ambato, and the highlands. Without an open bridge all commerce would stop. In particular, petroleum companies' trucks, people, and equipment needed to pass over this bridge.

The Runa set up a blockade on and around this bridge, and the military attempted to break it from the South. The bridge blockade was later attacked from the North by air force troops from Tena. Despite the military attacks, including barrages of tear gas and rubber bullets, the people holding the bridge fought with whatever weapons they had. People told me of a terrible scene that transpired after one person had been shot to death; the soldiers shouted at them, "Do you want to die, too? Now get out of here." These people made a point of saying that they did not run after the threat. They stood their ground and fought. After this episode another group of demonstrators moved to blockade the airport, fearing that the government would fly in more troops to kill them. A young boy was shot in this scuffle, and the people took revenge by destroying the airport. They burned the control tower, took soldiers prisoner, and confiscated their weapons.

The uprising was viewed as a victory by the Runa, although the two deaths and numerous injuries sustained left people in a kind of collective shock. The Runa had the support of almost all the mestizos living in Tena; indeed, the boy killed at the airport was a mestizo, and all the mestizos of Tena considered the government to have been the aggressor. No more soldiers were sent, and the uprising was resolved through political negotiations with the government. Peace was restored.

Four months after these events I came to Tena to watch an interschool competition of dance, culture, and speech. The competition was sponsored by the Directive of Intercultural Bilingual Education in Tena and was held outside that agency's offices. One of the competitions involved performing an oratory, in the "unified" dialect of Ecuadorian Quichua, dealing with the events of the 2001 uprising. A young woman whom I will call Dina spoke as the representative of the bilingual school in Pucara.

Dina was noticeably nervous as she stood alone on the scaffold. She struggled to articulate the highland pronunciations of the unified dialect of Quichua but spoke eloquently. She was tall, confident, and strong, and her presence and words captured the attention of all the Quichua speakers lining the streets. Dina spoke of the courage displayed by the demonstrators, their will to fight, and the way in which they overcame their fear of death. She framed her words in terms of sacrifice; the dead and wounded had sacrificed their well-being for the benefit of the living and future generations. Dina repeatedly stated that the wounded had sacrificed themselves for the "Runa causai," or "the Runa way of life," an interesting and condensed gloss.

The concept of causai is analogous to that of culture, and the Runa use the former much as anthropologists use the latter. Indeed, people often told me that my research focused on Runa causai. Causai goes beyond culture, however, for the term also connotes the vital energy or power that circulates through all people and other natural living beings. In short, the term *causai* means "life force" and as such is interchangeable with *samai* (breath). It can refer to the internal spirit of a power stone, a plant, or a person. There is then a double sense in which the demonstrators who had died had sacrificed themselves for Runa causai. Not only had they sacrificed themselves in challenging new economic and social policies that would damage their way of life; in addition, they had passed on their internal life force, their power, to the living. Their causai was still among those they had left behind.

Dina then invoked history, developing the idea that the demonstrators rose up to defend their territory just as the great revolutionary cacique Jumandy had done in 1578. Dina drew some analogies between the two uprisings. She said that the samai of Jumandy, who died fighting the Spanish, had inhabited the demonstrators and was still with them. Dina's thoughts and words were quite moving. I noticed that she spoke of Jumandy in the same way that people would speak of their elder loved ones, their parents or deceased grandparents. Dina was creating cultural memories of the great warrior Jumandy, eliciting kinship between the current generation and the great revolutionaries of the past.

Dina is not the only person to have remembered Jumandy in public. Luis Carlos Shiguango Dahua (2002), an indigenous anthropology student of Napo, similarly draws on Jumandy and other past revolutionaries of the region in his analysis of the uprising. In preparation for the 2002 Latin American Studies Association meetings in Quito, he wrote:

> The spirit of the struggle by our ancient heroes like Wituk, Wami, Jumandy, persists in each native and is transmitted from generation to generation. This power strengthens us when one has to endure the pain and suffering of the mobilizations and uprisings. As one grandfather said, "Our ancestors walked great distances day and night crossing rivers and mountains in continual wars with other groups of the region. They were strong and unbending, for they were always in contact with Mother Nature, which gave them many powers. Today we are weaker because we eat food of the white-*mestizo* people. One should bathe in the early morning in a cold river (beating oneself with black stones in the joints) so that one is resistant to pain and fatigue." (Shiguango Dahua 2002:4)

Shiguango Dahua "remembers" not only Jumandy but also other famed revolutionaries of the region, whose spirit, he affirms, circulates from generation to generation and gives strength to those living today. He cites a "grandfather" who criticizes his fellow Runa for weakening themselves by eating food from stores rather than from the Runa circuit of production and consumption. This grandfather further criticizes those Runa who do not practice traditional strengthening practices (*sinzhiyachina*), such as bathing in cold rivers. Shiguango Dahua affirms the power and wisdom of the elder generation. He highlights the notion that they are the source of strength and knowledge and, through their "love," connect people to the power of past natural, mythical, and historical beings.

After thinking a great deal about Dina's speech and Shiguango Dahua's analysis, I realized that there was an underlying cultural patterning to the political rhetoric. Both Dina and Shiguango Dahua elicited the native philosophy of kinship as a way of mediating historical reality. Dina and Shiguango Dahua were not conceptualizing time along the lines of space, with events moving into an increasingly distant past. Rather, they were affirming that time does not escape kinship, convivial thoughts, or the power of the ancestors. They were capturing a moment of negative emotion and bringing the past into the present. They highlighted the pain, death, suffering, and repression experienced both by the protesters and by past revolutionaries, transforming this negativity into a powerful set of positive emotions that transcended temporal boundaries. Dina's speech drew on feelings of kinship and collective suffering elicited through the conviviality her auditors felt in understanding themselves as descendants of the great warrior Jumandy. Shiguango Dahua did the same and further drew on the wisdom of elder generations. Both drew on an implicit notion of what I call the convivial person—a "warrior" who does not fear death and relies on ancestors in times of need. I take this concept, which I develop later, from Arguedas. First, however, I must put the indigenous uprising in its larger social and political context.

Uprisings in Ecuador and Indigenous Demands

The events of the indigenous uprising in 2001 must be understood in relation to the many indigenous uprisings that have occurred in Ecuador since 1990. These uprisings (which have occurred in 1990, 1992, 1996, 1999, 2000, and 2001) have provided indigenous people a means for pursuing dialogue with the Ecuadorian government (García 2002:2; Macas, Belote, and Belote 2003:224–225; Whitten 1996). These events underscore the growing indigenous movement in Ecuador, in which various individuals (indigenous leaders, scholars, and other professionals) promote social, economic, and cultural justice for indigenous people and peasants. Basically these groups have undertaken their uprisings and other political tactics to force the government into negotiations over their demands and to transform Ecuadorian society. The demands are practical aspects of policy and law that indigenous people see as fundamental to their continued survival and self-determination.

Before I discuss these demands in more detail, I should point out that the uprisings have not been small events led by powerless and desperate people. In 2000 the leaders of the indigenous movement, in cooperation with the general population, allied themselves with the military to seize the government. As Fernando García (2002:3) reports, "In the unfolding of the events of the 21st of January [2000], the military hierarchy played the final role as a mediator between the indigenous movement and the rest of the social sectors of the country. Power was handed over to Vice-President Noboa until January of 2003" (see also Whitten 2003:1–45). Rarely are indigenous movements comparable to state power structures, such as the military and the "government," but they enjoy that status in Ecuador. The Ecuadorian indigenous movement can form alliances, negotiate, and exert political pressure to a remarkable extent; while it cannot survive without cooperation from other sectors of society, its presence is felt by all.

Whitten has developed the concept of "millennial Ecuador" to convey the transformative power of the indigenous movement. According to Whitten, the transformations effected by such movements highlight "emerging and enduring nationalities with millennial agendas within a framework of a globalizing and localizing country—Ecuador—which, from time to time, has forced others in the Americas, in the American diasporas, and beyond, to take a careful look at alternatives to the modernities of Euro-American developmentalism and neoliberalism" (2003:xi). In other words, millennial Ecuador is an alternative modernity, a contested terrain where the present is questioned, "precisely because the present announces itself as the modern at every national and cultural site today" (Parameshwar Gaonkar 2001:14). As the Napo Runa case shows, political acts of contestation often derive from local, cultural bases and structures of value as well as myth. As Terence Turner has shown, "myth includes alternative modalities" that reflect specific cultural ethnotheories of productive and reproductive processes. These ethnotheories represent "profoundly different conceptions of social order" and materiality that define indigenous consciousnesses (Turner 1988:255). Indeed, the concept of alternative modernity has also been used by Whitten, Whitten, and Chango (1997:378) as a means of thinking through a protest march by Native Amazonians who marched to Quito seeking to transform the economic, national, and territorial realities left as a legacy of modernist colonialism.

Communitarianism and Conflicts of Value

That fact that the motivations for the indigenous uprising of 2001 were mainly economic may seem somewhat paradoxical given that the Napo system of value is based on personification and the transformation of things into people and social relationships. But no real contradiction is involved. Like most others, indigenous people depend on commodities for reproduction and enjoy having things that make life more enjoyable or entertaining. But there is a more complex answer to this apparent paradox. In rural contexts native people often domesticate and transform the meaning of commodities into gifts, which they use to produce their own identities and relationships. For example, in chapter 3 I showed how Napo Runa marriage rituals draw on many things coming from the larger commodity market, yet these things are transformed into gifts and converted into people in the social context of marriage. Indigenous people are not antithetical to the idea of the market, but they know that if the market is left to define them, it will subvert what they hold sacred.

In its fourth congress, held in December 1993, the Confederation of Indigenous Nationalities of Ecuador (CONAIE) proposed "communitarianism" as value in the sense that it informs how indigenous peoples view the organization of economic life. The document from this congress states:

> Communitarianism is the form of life of the indigenous peoples and nationalities, based on reciprocity, solidarity and equality; that is, a socio-economic political system of a collective character in which all its members actively participate. The communitarianism of the indigenous peoples and nationalities has been adapting to external economic and political processes, has been modified but has not disappeared, and lives and is practiced among the indigenous peoples and nationalities. The model of the society we propose is a communitarian society. The bases for the construction of the new multinational nation will be family-personal property, communitarian self-managed property, multinational state property and mixed forms. (Confederation of Indigenous Nationalities of Ecuador 1993)

While the notion of communitarianism is a politicized abstraction of a more complex social reality, such notions are too often dismissed as utopian idealism or political clichés when they are pronounced by indigenous peoples. Communitarianism should be interpreted through the ethnography of chapters 4 and 5, where I showed the specific social mechanisms by which native exchange is centered on persons and the social actions of giving and reciprocity—the complexity of which cannot be expressed in political documents. The CONAIE document, however, has a greater vision. It proposes to transform *all* society by way of indigenous notions of value: "the model of society we propose is a communitarian society," a system of indigenous value writ large.

Such notions of indigenous value writ large, which have a long tradition within indigenous political movements in Ecuador (see Whitten and Torres 1998; Whitten 2003), remind me of Sahlins's points regarding capitalism and native transformations of its ethos. For example, Sahlins develops the idea that many indigenous peoples seek to transform "development" from their own cultural sense of value, "from the perspective of the people concerned: their own culture on a bigger and better scale" (1993:17). As promoted by its leadership, the indigenous movement offers an social and economic vision that I think extends beyond the rural areas of the Amazon and the high Andean plains. It invites people everywhere to assist in reshaping the world order using indigenous value perspectives. These perspectives clearly have analogs in "developed" Western nations (gift modes, for example) but are repressed and subordinated to the subjectivities of commodity values, which orient human lives around market forces and alienation (Amariglio and Callari 1993; Godelier 1999, 2000).

Conflicts of value are central to the concerns of the global indigenous social movement. For example, recent (August 2002) demands by indigenous leaders presented in the Kimberly Declaration (International Indigenous Peoples Summit on Sustainable Development, held at Kimberley, South Africa) reflect concerns over globalization and the recognition of the viability of indigenous economic systems. Consider the following statement:

> Economic globalization constitutes one of the main obstacles for the recognition of the rights of Indigenous Peoples. . . . We are determined to ensure the equal participation of all Indigenous Peoples throughout the world in all aspects of planning for a sustainable future with the inclusion of women, men, elders and youth. Equal access to resources is required to achieve this participation. . . . Recognizing the vital role that pastoralism and hunting-gathering play in the livelihoods of many Indigenous Peoples, we urge governments to recognize, accept, support and invest in pastoralism and hunting-gathering as viable and sustainable economic systems. (International Indigenous Peoples Summit on Sustainable Development 2002)

One challenge for anthropologists has been to cultivate healthy collaborative relationships not only with local research consultants but also with the global indigenous social movement. In the future, anthropologists will no doubt find themselves under increased scrutiny from global indigenous bodies regarding the way they study and write about indigenous people. The Kimberly Declaration, for example, addresses the issue of knowledge appropriation. It states, "Our traditional knowledge systems must be respected, promoted and protected; our collective intellectual property rights must be guaranteed and ensured. . . . Unauthorized use and misappropriation of traditional knowledge is theft" (International Indigenous Peoples Summit on Sustainable Development 2002).

This statement presents a serious charge to those who write about native cultures, especially anthropologists, most of whom are expected to use indigenous knowledge as mere "data" to advance their professional careers. Consciously or not, anthropologists use what they learn primarily to further their departmental rankings, citation counts, and anthropological reputations. In trying to make my own career, for example, I have felt pangs of conscience in putting my individual name in the space for author. While there is no easy way to promote indigenous knowledge systems without also appropriating them, I find it refreshing that the authors of the Kimberly Declaration do not simply apply a Westernized notion of proprietary rights, nor do they seek to simply commodify indigenous knowledge. As the document states, indigenous knowledge is "collective."

Anthropologists, however, can become part of indigenous collectives, as many have, through such diverse modes of relation as friendship, adoption, ritual processes, activism, shamanism, reciprocal interdependence, and other forms of kinship. Many native peoples appreciate that Westerners can become "changed" (Goulet 1993), especially as the subjects of indigenous knowledge. It has been my experience, however, that indigenous people expect and demand a lifetime of loyalty and promotion in return for their knowledge, a rather daunting proposition. Scholars who are willing to become the subjects of the people and knowledge they study practice something similar to what Wagner proposes by the "anthropology of the subject," an approach in which "the very means of knowing were already appropriated by the people being studied" (Wagner 2001:xvii). Similarly, Gregory (1997:311) urges anthropologists to take on intellectual and political perspectives appropriate to the "subaltern" status of the peoples they study. Studying other cultures can be powerfully transformative. It allows one to take on multiple and conflicting points of view, to reconstruct the world and oneself from alternative viewpoints.

One potent way to support indigenous peoples is to write ethnography. Whereas anthropologists themselves experience alternative knowledge systems while conducting fieldwork, their published works allow others to experience those systems as well. There is a complicated responsibility here, one predicated on the complexities of knowledge commodification and the role that knowledge plays in socioeconomic domination. Anthropologists, however, are professionally trained experts in the techniques of fieldwork, cultural analysis, and anthropological writing. Today most graduate students receive instruction dealing with the complexities of representing other cultures. Indeed, I think that anthropologists are those most qualified to carry out translations of other cultures. Not only must they master the science of culture and techniques of fieldwork; in addition, they receive more intensive training in the art of writing. Popular accounts of other cultures that do not successfully convey the humanity, beauty, and political struggles of the people they describe sometimes end up making those people appear less human, exotic, or completely unknowable. I have already mentioned Werner Herzog's film *Fitzcarraldo*. Such accounts can also romanticize native peoples, however. As Taussig (1993) has shown, such representations reinforce and "naturalize" the inequalities and social hierarchies of national and global orders.

I disagree with those who prefer tropes of self-criticism and loathing when speaking of anthropology's current state. I agree with Maurice Godelier, a preeminent French scholar, who writes, "We need more and more anthropology and anthropologists in the world we are living in or are entering into. And we have to break the relative isolation of anthropology within our societies and . . . direct our work more outwards" (1997:5). Indeed, one of the most exciting transformations of our discipline is the expansion of anthropologists into a variety of career paths in addition to the traditional ones of teaching and research.

A few scholars, although not representative of the majority of anthropologists, seek to deconstruct and delegitimize indigenous claims to self-determination as mere political "rhetoric" or power grabbing. For example, Adam Kuper (2003) has recently argued that the rhetoric of the indigenous peoples movement resonates with the mission of many "right-wing parties in Europe," the link being a so-called essentialistic politics against immigrants. Kuper's argument suffers from extreme short-sightedness, however, for it completely ignores the complexities of Ecuador, one of the world's centers of indigenous activism. The Ecuadorian indigenous movement is not simply for "indigenous peoples"; indeed, it actively promotes the inclusion of others into indigenous ways of thinking, forms of identity, and lifeways.

In the literature on Ecuador, Selverston-Sher has found it problematic that many mestizo people claim indigenous status for reasons of power. She writes, "An apparent increase in the number of people who identify themselves as indigenous suggests that the concept is indeed fluid. . . . indigenous identity can be seen as a 'resource' mobilized for political objectives" (2001:67). There is some truth to this statement, but, like Kuper's analysis, it reduces indigenous identities to mere power grabbing. I have argued that the fluidity of indigenous identities derives more from the nature of native social philosophy itself. For example, I have shown a relational system in which differences are combined and mediated by symbolic and material configurations of value and network making; in this system the most salient and valued identities are not racial or ethnic but those of kinship.[3] These patterns of sociality resonate powerfully with the indigenous movement's political goals to transform society, and the world, by making it more "indigenous." Indeed, mediating differences across cultural, so-called ethnic, and national boundaries has been a marked feature of indigenous political sociality in Ecuador from the beginning.

Affectivity and Power

Throughout this book I have referred to Runa notions of llakina, or "love," not as a defining paradigm of Amazonian culture in general but as a lived and powerful feature of Napo Runa culture in particular. I have also argued that there are two sides to Napo Runa sociality: the positive and the negative, or in simplistic terms, love and hate (Santos-Granero 2000). In Napo the extreme closeness of ayllu relatives and their emotional attachment to one another creates situations of great anger and conflict when one side or person feels wronged. Just as the people of Napo express positive feelings openly and unabashedly, they do the same with anger. As one Napo Runa person stated on observing a conflict between two cousins, "This is our custom. When we are angry we do not hide it. We get in the person's face and let them know that we are angry with them."

Among the Runa, as among many other Amazonian peoples, predation has great conceptual presence; the flow of life is a delicate balance between conviviality and predation (Fausto 2000). Previous chapters have shown that much of the Runa reproductive complex focuses on making people sinzhi (strong), the term connoting a warrior-like ethic of being and a mimetic attachment to the qualities of the predator (see Uzendoski 1999). To be a "loving" person is to possess or have access to powers that allow for fighting off enemies, spirits, and other predatory forces.

As chapter 2's discussion of feminine shape-shifting showed, women, too, are "warriors" and considered sinzhi. Motivated by love and knowledge, they fend off and transform not only the predatory nature of masculinity but other destructive forces as well. Napo Runa women have for centuries battled powers and forces causing illness and death, including the social processes of colonialism. As many people mentioned to me, women stood with men on the front lines during the 2001 uprising and were a crucial part of the uprising's moral and physical strength.

The notion that a convivial person is sinzhi has been expressed in a literary way by José María Arguedas (1978:80). As Arguedas shows, many native persons view themselves as spiritual-cosmic beings who are connected to the world and not isolated from any aspect of it, especially not nature (which is a living being). These people do not fear death, for they feel themselves to be connected to a greater presence. To draw power, one sings to mountain lords in times of danger, as does the character Ernesto in *Deep Rivers* (Arguedas 1978:80). I take from Arguedas the idea that many native peoples would rather die than live without feeling and that general well-being is connected to healthy doses of intense affectivity. As Arguedas writes in a letter in defiance to his critics: "Let death walk towards us, let these unknown people come. . . . We will await them; we are the sons of the father of all the lord mountains; sons of the father of all the rivers" (1978:xiv–xv). I have noticed that many native peoples do not fear death in the way that many modern Western persons do. Native cosmologies articulate death and dying as integral to the poetics and flow of life itself. By contrast, the normative Western self, being located and focused "in the world," is shielded from the affective forms and poetics of an Arguedas-like "deep river."

Pierre Clastres, in *Chronicle of the Guayaki Indians* (1998), develops the similar idea that death is integral to the Native Amazonian philosophy of life and that native people's greatest fear is ceasing to exist, not death. The Atchei, he shows, are close to death in practical and ritual life: "Ritual actions of the Indians lead to the discovery—repeated again and again—that men are not eternal, that one must resign oneself to finitude, and that one cannot be himself and someone else at the same time. . . . the Indian and the philosopher share a way of thinking because, in the end, the obstacle to their efforts lies in the sheer impossibility of thinking of life without thinking of death" (Clastres 1998:41).

Clastres's tragic story describes encroachment by whites, slave raiding, and a number of terrible events leading to the demise of the Atchei during the 1960s. The Atchei women, realizing that they and their children are doomed by the advent of the whites, decided to stop having children. "It was too hard for the women," writes Clastres, so "finding out they were pregnant, [they] would ask their husbands to perform *ykwa,* to give them an abortion" (1998:143). This difficult-to-read book documents in painful detail the dignity by which the Atchei confronted a hopeless situation. They chose to die out rather than live without conviviality (see Clastres 1998:13).

In contrast to the Atchei situation of self-elimination, the 2001 Napo uprising can be interpreted as an event in which a defining aspect of the movement was a collective sentiment of anger and repression against the newest form of colonialism to reach Napo, dollarization. I have shown that, through memory, kinship, and mythical reality, these experiences of anger and negative feelings were transformed into a state of positive, collective conviviality. Clearly the participants in these events experienced powerful and complex positive and negative emotions: anger, grief, apprehension, hunger, pain, happiness, and love. Nonetheless, like certain characters in Arguedas's (1978:102) chapter "The Insurrection"—dancers who use song to make fun of the soldier's rifle and his will to fight—the Napo Runa were able to subordinate death to conviviality through the power of kinship.[4]

The Circulation of Substances and Memory among the Napo Runa

Again, the social theory of kinship in Napo is based on the idea of shared physical and spiritual substance. The circulation of this substance through time and space represents a complex cosmology that is perhaps common throughout Amazonia as well as the Andes. Among the Runa, kinship constitutes more than just a theory of the social person or the self. It is a complex social and cosmological philosophical system in its own right (Vivieros de Castro 2001; Overing and Passes 2000). Indeed, the volumes of literature on kinship in Amazonia and its importance suggests that kinship provides the principal means to creating the dominant values in these places. To use an analogy, kinship for Amazonia is akin to capital in neoliberal societies. It is the set of relations around which all other relations are not only organized but also produced.

The discussion of kinship in this book relates directly to the proposition that no human experience of kinship is given a priori. Human reality must be produced and created as given. Kinship, like history, is constructed through human action and organized by symbols. As I have argued, among the Napo Runa exchange relates but substance defines. Consanguinity, the ideal of becoming ayllu, must be created. These ideas resonate with Vivieros de Castro's (2001:19) point that Native Amazonians view affinity as a given relation while consanguinity falls within the domain of human action and intentionality.[5] In previous chapters I have shown how Napo Runa social process involves both separation and recombination; chapter 3, for example, outlined the processes whereby marriage separates and combines the person relations of two aylluguna into one. The affinal giveness of human sociality is indeed the basis of the creation of kinship. I showed, for example, that adopted children become full substance kin within the muntun and that mashaguna and cachunguna become insiders to the substance relations of the ayllu. In addition, I have mentioned myths about Runa parents adopting anaconda babies in human form and raising them as their own. These sets of relations show that affinity is the elementary form of relationship that, through human action, becomes consanguinity.

One work that might help to explain such transformations of affinity is Whorf's (1941) study of Hopi thought. According to Whorf, Hopi people believe that, in thinking about another being, such as a rose bush, they transfer their energy to it and can make it grow or die. Whorf provides evidence that Hopi thought does not exist in an imaginary space apart from social action. In other words, Whorf shows Hopi thought to be affinal. He writes: "A Hopi would naturally suppose that his thought (or he himself) traffics with the actual rose bush—or more likely, corn plant—that he is thinking about. The thought then should leave some trace of itself with the plant in the field. If it is a good thought, one about health and growth, it is good for the plant; if a bad thought, the reverse" (Whorf 1941:86).

This passage speaks to the relational basis of Hopi thought, where thinking is taken to create substance relations between the thinker and the object of thought. Good thoughts lead to health, while negative thoughts (e.g., anger) lead to illness. Thinking about someone or something cannot be divorced from one's "kinship" to it. Although there are important differences between Amazonian cultures and the Hopi, one can see a similarity in that people relate to the actual living or human entities about which they think, not just to imagined images of them. The Hopi concept of energy transfer, it could be argued, resembles the Napo Runa concept of vital energy, or samai (breath), as circulating among all living beings. In the cases of the Hopi and the Napo Runa, thought itself is productive or destructive power; it is a type of exchange. Even if the comparison fails, the point I wish to convey is that, among the Napo Runa, thought itself can and often does create some kind of affinity between the thinker and the "recipient" of the thoughts.

In Upper Napo and elsewhere in Amazonia, the power of thought is intimately related to conviviality and mimesis. *The Power of Love* is a clear and well-known example of a complex Amazonian ethnotheory of love in which forms of love generate knowledge and social power (Santos-Granero 1991:296–97). As Santos-Granero writes, "The Amuesha . . . conceive of genesis and the giving of life as a primordial act of love. . . . They see love as permeating every aspect of human interaction—whether between humans, or between human-kind and the world of sacred beings" (200–201). The opposite pole of love is anger. In Amazonia anger is a power just as love is. It causes damage to another person; people who are the objects of anger are thought to get ill or die. As Luisa Elvira Belaunde (2000:19) highlights, the significations and feelings associated with anger are conceptualized as transformative of social reality. Anger severs people from social relations and alters their status as cosmological-social beings. In Napo, too, anger is supposed to make people sick, cause tragedies, and even burn down houses. As Bancu once explained to me, "If the shaman is angry, his anger emanates from his flesh and can make people ill, even if he does not consciously exert himself. If I get angry, others might die." Shamans should thus have gentle dispositions. Angry shamans cause sickness and kill.

It is perhaps underappreciated that positive thoughts and emotions are linked to the way people view legitimate power in many Amazonian societies. Notions of power are connected to the ability to create relations of convivial-ity, life giving, and life sharing among kin. As Joanna Overing has argued, the Amazonian leader is a "specialist in fertility" as well as in conviviality: "They [leaders] must protect and enable the fertility of their people, as they also do for the land and the rivers people use" (2000:78). In Napo, too, the love of parents, grandparents, great-grandparents, and other ancestors is viewed as manifest within the social person as spiritual power and knowledge. This "conviviality-as-power" is represented in the ritual and general symbolism by which the spiritual substance of past beings is articulated as residing and living within the current generation.

Love as power is expressed nicely in Muratorio's (1991) monograph on the Napo Runa. The power passed on from elders is thought to be able to "concentrate that strength, knowledge, experience, and skill, signifying excellence in a given practice; for example that of being a good cargo bearer or a good hunter" (Muratorio 1991:205). Similarly, as Muratorio points out, thought (iyai) and breath (samai) are power. The power of someone's internal state—what I have termed the will—can supposedly make others dream (Mu-ratorio 1991:205). While a powerful inner soul circulates among the people sharing substance relations, the power of breath is seen to have real effects: powerful persons make others dream, have thoughts about them, and bend social actions to their wills.

People in Napo often link their personal power (ushai) or strength (their being sinzhi) to the love (llakina) of parents, grandparents, aunts, uncles, and other ancestors or ancestor beings. Thoughts of conviviality express the flow of power. As Bancu stated in relation to his personal power, "My granduncle was a powerful shaman. He had an army of jaguars at his disposal. When I was little he treated me as his son. He loved me very much." By drawing a link of llakina to his granduncle, Bancu was performing the convivial ge-nealogy of his power. I noticed that others, women as well as men, did the same. In an earlier discussion I showed how Grandmother Jacinta and Lucas referred to creator mountains, birds, and their ancestors to draw genealogies of power through the aesthetics of shape-shifting. I will now discuss how such genealogies of power relate to history and historical consciousness.

History and Thought Conviviality Forms of Kinship

Amazonians are often referred to as people who lack history (see Rival and Whitehead 2001:9; Taylor 1999:237). As my analysis of Dina's speech should show, however, Amazonian peoples are not ahistorical. They think of history differently, but this does not mean that they lack history. I have found that Whorf's hypothesis, even if it does not directly apply, helps in conceptualizing such differences between Western and Napo Runa historical forms. The Western theory of history is that the past exists in an imaginary or abstract space marked off from the present. History is conceptualized as the linear progression of events that move into an increasingly distant past. As my examples have demonstrated, by contrast, people in Napo do not see history as such an imaginary space, or mere mental image, standing apart from the present. History as it is told and remembered is filled with structures of thought conviviality, the power to, among other things, influence and transform the present. Historical thought creates affinity.

We can observe this principle of thought conviviality and history within a myth, collected by Warvin in the 1920s, that deals with the 1578 Jumandy uprising. While the content of the story is historical, its structure is that of a well-known myth in Napo. I will first summarize the primordial myth and then discuss the historical account in question.

The myth is one of those about the Cuillurguna, or twins. In this story the primordial jaguar and his sons "feed" on humans. To save humankind, the twins must trap the primordial jaguar. They decide to lure him into the mountain Galeras and trap him there. They make the inside of the mountain seem like a nice resting place, lure the jaguar inside, and trap him by sealing the entrance with a large boulder. The myth states that the primordial jaguar, still living, remains trapped inside Galeras and is sure to escape again when the world comes to an end (the Izhu Punzha).

The historical account collected by Warvin has essentially the same structure as this primordial jaguar myth. The account is historical because the narrator is "remembering" events involving the Spanish.

> When the Spanish came, they made slaves of and tormented the indigenous people. The shamans got together to talk. They decided that they

all would retreat to the farthest corners of the forest, where, to evade those who were pursuing them, they would turn into enormous jaguars of various colors. [As a result] those who went into the forest to hunt were devoured. The towns were also being devastated. The fierce ones [i.e., the jaguars] did so many bad things that the population decided to put an end to this carnage. . . . They were able to discover the beasts' hiding place. They penetrated into a great subterranean room where they saw numerous and variously colored jaguar hides. Intrigued, they hid. Soon they saw the men [i.e., the shamans], each of whom took a jaguar hide and covered himself with it. Cleverly they led the jaguars to the mountain Galeras. When all the jaguars were inside the great cavern, they closed the opening with a huge rock and covered the exit, which one can see from far away. (Warvin 1927:328–29; also in Muratorio 1987:342)

Both the myth and the history refer to trapping human-eating jaguars inside the mountain Galeras. The "history," however, while having a mythi-cal structure, deals with features of the colonial period—the Spanish, towns, and fleeing pursuit. This story thus relates to the 1578 Jumandy uprising, a point elaborated in Muratorio's (1991) book. The details of the uprising are significant, as Muratorio (1991) shows. After the indigenous fighters de-stroyed the cities of Avila and Archidona, the rebellion failed in Baeza. The shamans, the instigators of the resistance, fled to hide in the forest and were pursued by Spanish troops. With the help of other indigenous people, they were finally caught and taken to Quito, where they and Jumandy were finally put to death in a public spectacle. Muratorio (1991) states that in this story history and myth come together within a tradition of cultural resistance. I agree, but I think that the myth demonstrates further relations.

For example, in the second account the role of the twins is taken over by the shamans who live in, or are affiliated with, the towns. The role of the primordial jaguars is taken over by the fleeing shamans who instigated the rebellion. Like the primordial jaguars, these are beings who are devouring the current population of people. Like the twins, the urban shamans trap their prey (the rebellious shamans) in the mountain Galeras. In addition, and like the culture heroes Cuillur and Dociru (the previously discussed mythic twins), they make life possible again. The urban shamans rid the region of the rebel shamans and create a new time-space epoch where people can once again construct convivial communities and towns. The urban shamans save not only the indigenous people but also the Spanish. They make colonial society possible and establish a relation of conviviality to colonial time and space. In other words, one feature of this history is the idea that the love and concern of the urban shamans permitted life to continue into the present. Their love ushers in a new age of time and space, a pachacutic, "the world again."

One feature of this account is that it fails to specify the narrator's relation to the shamans and the events. Most Napo Runa explicitly or implicitly identify the teller's relationships to the historical and mythical figures. In addition, narrators often indicate a specific kinship relation to the mythical or histori- cal figures in the telling, as Lucas did in his account of the primordial flood. When Lucas recounted to me yet another version of the Galeras myth, he told me that his "fathers" knew the twins personally. This structure is essentially the same message as we find in Warvin's account; it is a story in which the conviviality and suffering of the ancestors give life to the community.

Narrators affirm their personal power by using the rhetoric and aesthetics of shape-shifting. They connect their inner essences to the mythical beings and primordial time of unai. While the narrator of Warvin's story does not specify his link to the urban or loving shamans, a shape-shifting relation is implicit. The loving shamans take on the role of the ancestor who gives the things necessary for descendants to thrive. Just as, within Runa kin forms, giving defines parent-child relations, this value form dominates historical and mythical thought about the relations among generations as well. People use the notion of shape-shifting to "jump" generations, and one set of ancestors is collapsed into others, for substance transmission defines them. In this way, as I have argued earlier, mythical and historical time form part of the current system of kinship relations. Like myth, kinship and memory are shaped by pachacutic, shape-shifting and conviviality.

The Psychological Politics of History and Anthropology

Various anthropologists and other scholars have predicted that the Napo Runa would "assimilate" and eventually disappear (see, e.g., Oberem 1980; Hudleson 1981), yet the Napo Runa continue to reinvent themselves as people defined through the presence of unai. Insensitivity to Napo Runa notions of historicity and sociality has produced a wide gap between the way the Napo Runa see themselves and the ways others have viewed them. For example, Udo Oberem's (1980) book on Upper Napo underestimates the power of native historicity and ethnogenesis. Oberem, an insightful ethnographer and ethnohistorian, comments on the failure of the 1892 uprising, in which the Napo Runa took action against the Jesuits. I am most interested in Oberem's comments on the psychological state of the Napo Runa facing blanco-mestizo society. He writes:

The Indians retire fearfully into the forest and in a short time peace reigns over the region of Quijos [Upper Napo]. With this ends the last intent of rebellion by the Quijos [Napo Runa] against the whites. From the psychological point of view, it is interesting to see that the Quijos don't rise up against the missionaries but rather are influenced by the white colonists. With the arrival of the soldiers, they flee without resisting. They have lost confidence in themselves, a fact which one notes with the unrest at the beginnings of the [twentieth] century. (Oberem 1980:116)

As this passage shows, Oberem foresaw the continual loss of indigenous culture in Upper Napo and the final assimilation of indigenous people to mestizo society as peasants (they would finally become, in Whitten's [1985] terms, "whitened"). Oberem argues that 1892 would be the last time the Napo Runa would resist the dominant system. This error of predicting the demise of native groups was common among twentieth-century ethnographers (even Franz Boas predicted the demise of the Kwakiutl). While some groups do in fact "disappear," the much repeated trope of disappearing worlds perhaps justifies the anthropological desire to appropriate rather than promote and interact. By predicting the demise of the people we study, we actually help create, unwittingly, the reality we loathe (Taussig 1993). Instead of portraying their struggle for cultural survival and self-determination, and our own intersubjective commitment to those goals, we create representations of our anthropological subjects as if they were already gone.

Oberem's account diminishes how the Napo Runa view their history of struggle; Oberem severs the current generation from that past. Far too often people in Ecuador and abroad negate the Napo Runa view of history by asserting that the Napo Runa are "immigrants" from the highlands or are not proper "Amazonians" (see Steward and Métraux 1948). More recently Taylor's otherwise stimulating piece in the prestigious *Cambridge History of the Native Peoples of the Americas* continues this stereotype in arguing that Amazonian Quichua speakers are "assimilated," *manso* (weak), and "generic" natives with "linear and periodized historical ideologies very different from those of the 'traditional' groups of the region" (1999:237). As I have shown, the people of Napo speak in a different voice. They speak through the voice and poetics of pachacutic—destroying, recuperating, and transforming society and history.

Conclusion

As Rival and Whitehead argue, we need to clearly distinguish indigenous historicity from modern Western historicity: "Differing approaches to native historicity may thus lead to an attempt to understand the historical experiences of those who have undergone domination and colonization, or what these historical events mean today, or even temporality from a native perspective" (Rival and Whitehead 2001:10, 11). In writing this book I have learned something important about historicity, the "cultural proclivities that lead to certain kinds of historical consciousness" (Whitehead 2003:xi). In this sense the Napo Runa and Western notions of historicity are quite distinct. Western historicity is founded on the proposition that history unfolds with an imaginary space dominated by lineal schemes of time and that the events it comprises are separated from the action of historical thinking itself (Whorf 1941). The Napo Runa, however, subscribe to a different scheme of historicity and historical action that I have glossed as pachacutic. The events of 2001 clearly show that, for the Napo Runa, "historicity is not an adjunct to cultural sensibility and practices but rather is constitutive of them" (Whitehead 2003:xix).

I demonstrated, for example, that Napo Runa historical thinking is dominated by kinship and the circulation of substance between the generations. The circulation of breath—one of the essential substances of consanguineal and affinal relations—is in itself a microcosm for larger temporal schemes. History is never divorced from inner power or from thought affectivity. Just as in the mythical narrative about the jaguar analyzed previously, the events and people of historical times surge to the present when the Runa, through their thoughts, words, dreams, or ritual action, establish an affective and experienced relationship with them. Such actions create links of temporal affinity and form the basis of the way people conceptualize their personal and collective power.

I have argued that, through the actions and resistance against modern colonial forms in the 2001 uprising, the people of Upper Napo were able to reenergize kinship affinity with the great warrior Jumandy, a proposition untenable from the Western historical, social, and cosmological perspective. The symbolic forms of Napo historicity have created a form of psychological revitalization resonating with the origins and beginnings of indigenous self-determination in Upper Napo.[6] Through kinship and mythical-historical realities, the power and substance of Jumandy has revived and recirculated to assist the Napo Runa in their struggles.

Glossary of Quichua Terms

Apamama: A strong, powerful woman.

Apayaya: A strong, powerful man.

Asua: A fermented food beverage of usually low alcohol content. For festive occasions, stronger and more flavorful varieties are produced. Also pronounced *aswa* or *asa*.

Auya (pl., auyaguna): Relatives created through marriage; complementary to *ayllu*.

Ayllu (pl., aylluguna): A group of substance-related people who usually but not always live together. The term can convey a nuclear family, an extended family, or even more distant kin relations; in addition, it can be used as a synonym for *muntun* to imply a residence group.

Ayllu-Muntun: A group of substance-related people who live together; literally, "a pile or bunch of consanguines."

Bura: The final stage in Napo Runa ritual marriages; the term derives from the Spanish *boda* but has become part of the current Quichua language.

Cachiwa: A potent distilled sugar-cane alcohol (called "aguardiente" in Spanish) used for ritual purposes and thought to contain divine energy.

Cachun (pl., cachunguna): Son's wife or brother's wife.

Cari: The term can mean "man" or, sometimes, "strength."

Cari parti: The man's side in a wedding.

Cari-warmi: Man-woman.

Causai: Life force; the term is used as an analogue to *culture*, as in "Runa causai" (the Runa way of life).

Churi: Son.

Cumpa: Diminutive of *compadre*.

Cushi: Happy.

Cuti: Again.

Iyai: Thought.

Izhu: The great flood of mythical times; also a future happening.

Llakina: To love.

Llakirina: To be sad.

Lugar: From the Spanish term for "place," the Quichua word refers to space-time; a synonym of *pacha*.

Mama: Mother.

Mana cari: Lack of masculinity.

Marcachuri: Godson.

Marcamama: Godmother.

Marcaushushi: Goddaughter.

Marcayaya: Godfather.

Masha (pl., mashaguna): Daughter's husband/sister's husband.

Muntun (pl., muntunguna): Literally denoting a "pile" or "bunch" of relations, the term means a group of aylluguna living together in a specific place and can designate a household, a group of households, or a community.

Ñaña: Sister with female ego.

Pacha: Space-time, world.

Pachacutic: "The World Again"; the term refers to a transformation of time-space to a better or regenerative state of new life.

Pani: Sister with male ego.

Quixos or **Quijos:** The pre-Hispanic and early colonial cultural group that controlled the highlands between the Andes and the Upper Napo region of Amazonia. They spoke Quechua as a lingua franca as well as their own languages. This group, through complex processes of transculturation with Zaporan peoples, became the Napo Runa. Some ethnographers and travelers refer to the Napo Runa as the Quijos Quichua or Quijos.

Rancia: The term connotes a person of North American or European heritage.

Runa: The Quichua word for "human," it is used in some contexts to designate an indigenous person; it can also mean "man" (pl., *runaguna*).

Samai: Literally meaning "breath," the term is used to talk about the soul, too. All living things—spirits, plants, trees, special foods, and living rocks—have samai.

Sasina: Taboo; the term refers to fasting and other prohibitions tied to couvade and shamanic rituals.

Shungu: Heart.

Sinzhi: Strong; the term connotes spiritual hardness.

Sinzhi runa: Strong man.

Sinzhi warmi: Strong woman.

Supai: Spirit.

Tucuna: Transformation or to become.

Turi: Brother with female ego.

Unai: Mythical space-time.

Ushai: Power as defined by the Napo Runa; it cannot be divorced from its synonym, *yachai* (knowledge).

Ushushi: Daughter.

Vinillu: A clear, sweet, and strong manioc wine made with special yeasts and used mainly for festive purposes.

Warapu: A fermented beverage consisting of manioc and ripe bananas and usually stronger than other kinds of asua.

Warmi: Woman.

Warmi-cari: Woman-man.

Warmi parti: The woman's side in a wedding.

Wasi: House.

Wauki: Brother with male ego.

Wawa: Child.

Yachac: Shaman or healer.

Yacu: Water or river.

Yaya: Father.

Notes

Introduction

1. *Napo Runa* refers to one of several Amazonian Quichua dialects and ethnicities in Ecuador. There are salient and crucial differences among Amazonian Quichua speakers (see Whitten 1976, 1985) that fall beyond the scope of this work. It is estimated that Amazonian Ecuador contains 70,0000 Quichua speakers (Wibbelsman 2003:xx). Ecuador is a strongly indigenous nation, and indigenous peoples dominate Ecuador's rural sectors. A July 2001 estimate posits that 28 percent of Ecuador's total population is indigenous (Wibbelsman 2003:377).

2. To protect the identities and privacy of research consultants, I have replaced most of the names with pseudonyms and have created fictional (but culturally appropriate) names for all the places I mention. Because those who are familiar with my affiliations with particular families in the Upper Napo region will be able to identify participants in these pages, I have tried to keep negative or possibly controversial information to a minimum.

3. I use the Quichua alphabet of Orr and Wrisley (1981:154) with the exceptions of the letters *w* for *hu* and *k* for *qu*. These changes make many Quichua words easier to follow for English speakers. The letters used are thus *a, b, c, ch, d, g, w, i, j, l, ll, m, n, ñ, p, k, r, s, sh, t, ts, u, y, z,* and *zh*. Although a "unified" alphabet exists for Quichua, it is more representative of highland dialects and distorts many words in Napo Quichua. While the unified dialect also uses *w* and *k* (e.g., "Kichwa"), it does not include some letters that are necessary to the Napo dialect. Also, because of the influence of Spanish, the Quichua vowel *u* is sometimes pronounced as *o*, but these sounds are generally interchangeable (as in, e.g., *chonta*).

4. In presenting the material in this book, I employ a strategy used by Marx (1977), who organizes his translation of nineteenth-century capitalism through the "philosophy of internal relations" (Ollman 1976). The basic idea of this approach is that factors or forms we normally think of as externally related are in fact elements of a larger whole. As Ollman writes, "every factor which enters into Marx's study . . . is a definite social relationship" (1976:14). There are two senses in which Marx talks about relations, "Relation" and "relation" (ibid., 14–17). The former are specific

social factors (e.g., capital). The latter are the connections among such factors (e.g., production and consumption). In *Capital* Marx (1977) uses both notions to describe how the individual parts (forms) of the system articulate and are transformed by the whole. Describing Napo Runa notions of value presents me a problem similar to the one Marx faced. The chapters dealing with the life cycle (childhood, marriage, and maturation) concentrate on Relations—namely, particular Napo Runa social forms. Other chapters deal with the larger social configurations of value (kinship and exchange), or relations.

5. I use *alienation* in the sense found in Ollman (1976). I do not mean that gifts cannot be "detached" from people—detaching things in the gift context creates significant relations. Alienation is different, however, for it describes a process whereby things are exchanged, yet significant social and moral relations are not created (Gregory 1997:79).

6. The weakness of this model (Gregory 1982) is that it does not identify the subordinate processes by which dominant processes occur in the Dumontian sense of hierarchies of value. Gregory's contribution was to help us see how gift modes locate value in the reproduction of people, an emphasis that is subordinate to the production of things in capitalist contexts.

7. In this regard my perspective is contrary to the thinking of Appadurai (1986, 1997), who has consistently argued that commodities are universal bearers of value and that value lies squarely in the domain of "things." Similarly I am critical of Bourdieu (1977, 1990), too, who assumes that the individual and individualistic motivations such as calculation are universal social constructs (Piot 1999). Bourdieu's formalism (as seen in concepts such as "cultural capital") is too tethered to the logic of capitalism to be effective in translating the value concepts of many of the world's subaltern peoples. As Marx showed clearly (1972), commodity forms, capital, and individualism are interrelated process that alienate labor and allow the accumulation of value in capitalistically defined social spheres.

8. One might posit weaving as a metaphor for intersubjectivity itself, a theme found in many cultural realities in which "human relationships are like nets, chains, many-stranded ropes, knotted cords, strings, or paths" (Jackson 1998:192). Among the Runa, these relations are implicit. Accounts where weaving is more overtly emphasized as social process include Guss 1989 and Urton 2003.

9. The traditional term in the anthropological literature is *manioc beer*. While *brew* may not be the right word to describe asua, I have decided on it because it simply means "a beverage made by brewing." *Beer* implies carbonization and the use of malt and hops (all of which are absent from asua).

10. Consciously organizing and participating in groups is a modern mode of social action, not a universal. The Durkheimian metaphor is a modern, Western theory of social action that orders lives and consciousness. Society is an abstraction, an invention that schools, newspapers, institutions, television, and other forms of communication and exchange make real and sustain (see Tocqueville 1990; Anderson 1992).

Among the Runa, there are no real "imagined communities" (Anderson 1992) that exist over and above individuals; only the relations themselves constitute such communities. Hegel says much the same thing in regard to political "corporations" in the *Philosophy of Right* (see Avineri 1972:164–65). More research is needed regarding the anthropological history of the concept of social groups in relation to the state.

11. The term *transculturation* was first used by the Cuban Fernando Ortíz in *Contrapunto cubano del tabaco y el azúcar* (1940). While Ortíz's use of the term carries with it a complexity I am not prepared to discuss, contemporary usages of this notion stress the mutual exchange and sharing of people, identities, relations, and things across social boundaries.

12. For example, conviviality was often mentioned in many of the papers and panels dealing with Native Amazonian peoples at the 2003 American Anthropological Association annual meetings in Chicago.

13. Love is a complex concept, for it is a dominant symbol of Christianity and the Western world. As Trawick's (1990:92) study of love in Tamil shows, Western notions can impede our understanding of similar concepts in other cultures or cause us to look the other way. I think this dynamic of intersubjective "cultural interference" explains some of the difficulties of studying and translating notions of emotional states across cultures. Indeed, it took me years to realize the subtle differences between my own notion of love and the analogous Runa concept.

14. To borrow Santos-Granero's (2000) terms, conviviality specialists can be labeled "doves" and those working on predation, "hawks." These figurative associations are a nice way of drawing out the contrasts of the theoretical concerns defining these opposing schools of thought.

15. All translations from Spanish materials are my own.

Chapter 1: Sinzhi Runa

1. Bloch proposes that such implicit perceptions are based on highly complex, integrative, image-based cognitive processes in which practical and experiential knowledge is organized not by linear logical-sentential abstractions but rather by "highly complex and integrated networks or mental models most elements of which are connected to each other in a great variety of ways" (1992:130).

2. The Runa distinguish Runa chickens, the large, brightly colored free-range chickens that hunt their food, from the awallacta, or white chickens, which are more domesticated and must be fed. It is interesting that domestic animals are distinguished through notions of race (*raza*), while forest animals are not.

3. The famous nineteenth-century anthropologist E. B. Tylor defines couvade as a "quaint custom" in which "the father, on the birth of his child, makes a ceremonial pretense of being the mother, being nursed and taken care of, and performing other rites such as fasting and abstaining from certain kinds of food or occupation, lest the new-born should suffer thereby" (1888:254). See also Métraux 1949, Rivière 1974, and Rival 1998 for a more thorough discussion and critique. Considerations of space

prevent me from reviewing all the relevant literature here, but I view the couvade as a rite of parenthood and not just of fatherhood.

4. As numerous colleagues have pointed out, many Amazonian peoples do not have meaningful complexes of child castigation. Indeed, more comparative research is needed regarding child rearing and childhood in Amazonia.

5. This idea of desire and energy regulation is central to Bororo practices regarding the treatment of plants, animals, and food and has been eloquently described by Crocker (1986).

6. Barry Lyons (2003) has discussed in detail the meaning and use of *cariyana* among Quichua speakers in the Andean region of Chimborazo. Lyons translates *cariyana* as "to act like a man" and "to get male" (2003:3). His analysis points to the problem of the essentialist versus processual notions of identity and gender states.

7. Belaunde's (2000:216) fascinating discussion of gender among the Airo-Pai of Amazonian Peru allows for a different conceptualization of gendered social forms. Belaunde shows that the genders are conceptualized in terms of the relationship between two birds, the oropendola and the green parrot; although each has its unique productive capacities, the two live together convivially as "the union of gendered and autonomous persons who raise their children together" (2000:216). Complementarity and the combination of differences are emphasized.

Chapter 2: The Poetics of Social Form

1. I take the translation of *tucuna* as "transformation" from Whitten and Whitten (1988:42). Much of this chapter is inspired by Norman Whitten's thought concerning beauty's relation to shamanic forces.

2. Like their Greek counterparts, Amazonian myths are some of the most imaginative and clever stories around—and among the most difficult to decipher. They display an elegant symbolism and aesthetics that have yet to be acknowledged by the literary world. In addition, the social principles of kinship transformation are elegantly contained within these tales.

3. While historical documents and anthropologists have shown that the Runa are an *ethnic* group that came into being during the colonial period, Runa people themselves tell a different history of their origins. Shape-shifting, not ethnicity, underlies the Runa philosophy of life. As Whitten and Whitten write: "When a Runa gleans knowledge of the spirit world from a shaman, s/he learns of animate essences of inanimate substances, of spiritual essences that may be acquired by human beings, and of the transformations that permeate these and other spheres of social existence. . . . As a person seeks to establish order in one realm of life, s/he draws information from another realm, thereby effecting a clear consciousness of transformation as the basis of all continuity and change" (1988:30).

4. Janis Nuckolls (1996, 2000:244) has argued that Amazonian Quichua poetics and storytelling have much to teach us about the relation of language to cognition. She shows that analogical thinking and an iconic linguistic feature called "sound-

symbolism" bring nature to life and allow speakers to transform into the things they describe. An example of a sound-symbolic word in Lucas's narrative is the use of *tun* to describe the rising water. *Tun* conveys the image of a sudden covering of a large space, as would happen when the sky is covered by dark clouds during an imminent thunderstorm. Other sound-symbolic features used in the narrative are *umbas,* a term that conveys a willful and calm silence, *awai* (meaning "up") to convey fast growth, and *tian,* which conveys the action of rolling over and over.

5. While structural considerations are crucial to myth analysis, I wish to emphasize that myth telling is a form of social action and conviviality. As the volumes of books on narratives, myths, and oral culture reveal, mythical and narrative analyses are not often coupled with detailed ethnographies of the social forms that create them, flow through them, and are transformed by them. I think that it is fairly trivial to try to define shape-shifting as "form" or "action"—or to simply repeat the truism that narratives are both. To confront shape-shifting in narrative and myth is to confront the essential questions of Napo Runa social life and personhood.

6. Regina Harrison has provided examples of Amazonian Quichua women singing about their transformation into powerful forest spirits (*supai*), man-woman beings (*cari-warmi*), snakes (*ucumbi*), and other forms. One aspect of this feminine shape-shifting is that it provides women the means to attract their men, who are often away from the home for a variety of reasons. Women use magic (*simayuca*) and the power of song to attract men. Just by thinking of their men, women are able to force their men to return to them. These songs of extreme emotion manifest themselves as knowledge and power (see Harrison 1989:168–69).

7. See my essay in *Millennial Ecuador* (Uzendoski 2003) for a fuller analysis of evangelical Protestantism in Upper Napo.

8. Taussig (1993:xvii) shows that mimesis is the transference of power from an original to a "copy," a composite of both "sympathetic" and "contagious" magic in which the representation elicits the power of the represented (as a substance flow). Mimesis, in the Napo Runa case, seems to fit when describing the logic of shape-shifting. See also Taussig 1987 (134).

9. I thank Tod Swanson for showing me this myth.

10. As Walter Benjamin (1968) demonstrates, modern art forms are defined by mechanical reproduction for the "masses," a divorcement of art from ritual (and cosmological meaning), and a loss of "aura" (the way works of art come alive in relation to the viewers).

Chapter 3: Ritual Marriage and Making Kin

1. For example, wedding rituals might be described as fractal reflections of the most salient and defining relations in Napo Runa society. Fractality "reproduces the whole, something different from a sum as it is from an individual part. . . . It is an instantiation of the elements themselves" (Wagner 1991:163).

2. Visual imagery is also important in this (and all phases) of bura dancing. Writes

Macdonald, "The costumes visually demonstrate the opposition and balance inherent in reciprocity. The basic contrast involves red and white, representing respectively the *warmi* and *cari partis*" (1979:120).

Chapter 4: The Transformation of Affinity into Consanguinity

1. I realize that the term *adoption* creates distortions when applied to other cultural forms. I use it in a descriptive sense. A more accurate term to describe Runa adoption is "apasha iñachina" (to take and rear).

2. Blanca Muratorio (1998) has recently focused on the way Napo Runa grandmothers see sexuality and bodily appearance through the changing attitudes of their daughters and granddaughters. She points out that the grandmothers make an issue of women's "reputations" within their in-law's house(s) and within the community in general. A woman's "performance in her in-laws' home, however, is also a test of her mother's and grandmother's own competencies in shaping her selfhood at an early age. Women's reputations must be tested continuously and are done so publicly by both women and men" (Muratorio 1998:412). Muratorio argues that good women are viewed as hardworking and productive, like the active, quick-moving bird the pichiwarmi. A bad woman is talked about as lazy or *carishina* (like a man). Muratorio reports one grandmother complaining, "Now women are only good to sleep with their husbands; they are keen to show their buttocks to men. Then, they become very upset when their husbands beat them up under the pretense they thought they had married a hardworking woman" (in ibid., 414).

3. "Although the term *gumba* seems to derive from *compadre-comadre* . . . I see no particular reason to suppose that this dimension of social organization is taken from the *compadrazgo* system of Hispanic culture" (Whitten 1976:139).

4. For example, Bloch and Guggenheim try to define compadrazgo specifically as an institution with an ideological core that associates women to men as pollution is associated with spirituality. Ritual parenthood (associated with men) is thus superior to the natural and "polluting" powers of feminine reproduction; feminine birth is co-opted through ritual acts by men. They write, "The ideological core of *compadrazgo* and baptism consists in the denial of biological birth and of the ability of women to produce 'legitimate' children by first declaring childbirth to be polluting and then by replacing it with a ritual re-enactment of birth which involves giving other parents" (Bloch and Guggenheim 1981:384). While this may be one particular representation of compadrazgo within a specific cultural context, it is not universally applicable, and it is especially inaccurate when applied to the Runa notion of compadrazgo relations. This kind of approach still appears in the literature in the form of Shapiro and Linke's (1996) "pseudo-procreation" theory, which implies that men everywhere co-opt the "natural" powers of women and replace them with their own "spiritual" powers. As I demonstrated in chapter 1 with the Runa couvade, however, rituals of birth exhibit complementarity, with both men and women taking on "procreative" and "pseudo-procreative" (i.e., "ritualistic") forms of action.

5. Wagner formulates a similar distinction for Daribi clan relations. He writes: "Thus, the principle by which clans are defined is that of exchanging wealth. This is symbolized by the sharing or giving of meat; members of a clan 'eat meat together,' while those of other clans 'give meat' or 'are given meat.' . . . Marriage is a form of exchange, and clan members by definition share exchange relationships; that is, they contribute to each other's bride prices and share in the distribution of the wealth received through exchange by one another" (Wagner 1967:145).

6. While the kinship forms of the Napo Runa share many affinities with Andean systems, they strike me as Amazonian. That is, the Napo Runa limit hierarchy mainly to the domestic sphere of parent-child relations and do not allow it to extend outward toward external entities, such as a class of sacred beings (the Inca), *cargos* (i.e., officials), or the state (see Clastres 1989; T. Turner 1984, 1996). Such dominating structures are features of Andean kinship, whereby the local is conceptually and socially subordinated to external forms. In Napo, however, affinity is conceptualized as dangerous and potentially predatory; affines must be domesticated through reciprocity.

Chapter 5: Meat, Manioc Brew, and Desire

1. Social relationships are not determined by a need to "satisfy" desire, as Dean asserts when he writes that "cultural value is deeply embedded in the lived experience of desire" (1995:100). Desire brings into relief the problem of subjectivity itself and what constitutes a living, feeling, desiring person in relation to society. The study of desire relates directly to Michael Jackson's statement that an "intersubjective" anthropology seeks to "recover the sense in which experience is situated *within* relationships and *between* persons" (1996:26).

2. For example, Geertz (1973:42) wrote about the problem of the "universal" and the "specific" in anthropology; his point is that loose, "indeterminate" traits are not as interesting as richly dense and specific cultural practices. It is useful to think of Geertz's point when looking at desire.

3. Sahlins writes, "But then, the capitalist economy had made a supreme fetish of human needs in the sense that needs, which are always social and objective in character, had to be assumed as subjective experiences of bodily affliction" (1988:44).

4. Attesting to the common "humanity" that humans and animals share within the social sphere, these words are also used in reference to giving nourishment to animals and to the interactions of animals as consuming subjects (Descola 1996a; Viveiros de Castro 1998).

5. The best example of this principle in the ethnographic literature is the Bororo division of *aroe* and *bope* as metaphysical properties of the cosmos that reside within the body and productive practices (see Crocker 1986).

6. Gow emphasizes this point: "There is no place in production for unmarried adults. Unmarried adults are under no obligation to do much work in the houses of their parents or other kin and often do very little, but they are expected and constantly

urged to marry. This is a fact of crucial importance in understanding the economy of food production in these communities. The unmarried adult does not produce, or produces very little and sporadically, because he or she has no one for whom to produce. The unmarried are fed because they are kin to others who are producing, but these providers cannot demand any return, for demand is prohibited in relations between adult kin" (1989:572).

7. Many of the world's cultures have long recognized fermentation as a spiritual event reflecting the presence of vital energy and the unseen forces of life itself (see Buhner 1998). Moreover, fermented beverages have both unique nutritional and healing properties ignored by modern Western science (ibid., 62–166). In addition, alcohol, which often bears a negative or base connotation in the modern West, has throughout history been seen as a manifestation of "spirit," not as a "drug." As Buhner writes, "The widely publicized negative effects of alcohol come from . . . the separation of alcohol from its original plant context. In traditional fermentations and the cultures that use them, the negative side effects of alcohol are never found" (1998:141). I have found Buhner's insights to be valid when looking at asua, although perhaps there is some romanticizing involved. However that may be, we often forget that living organisms (yeast) produce fermented beverages through a process of reproduction and "feeding." In this sense asua is more than the "cooked"; it is the "fermented," a product of life and reproduction itself.

8. Much of the relevant literature either sees things and people in Amazonia as one continuous sphere of communication (Clastres 1989) or views Amazonian societies as "economies of people" (Rivière 1983–84; T. Turner 1979). Both approaches miss complexities in the way things are used in personification. For example, a recent article by Lorrain in the "economy-of-people" tradition argues that "all male productive activities are self-contained: none of them depends on labor or equipment provided by women" (2000:300). While this statement may be true in the context of a hunting trip (assuming that the men do not eat), it is certainly not viable from a holistic perspective in which productive activities focus on the domain of people and not things—in other words, the domain of social reproduction.

9. Eating dirt may be an unexpectedly common sign of subversion among Native Amazonians and other cultures that live in close association with the land. There is little discussion of the practice in the anthropological literature, but in Gabriel García Márquez's *One Hundred Years of Solitude,* the consumption of dirt as subversion of social values constitutes an important aspect of the character Rebeca. During my research I observed children eating such things as soap, dirt, and stolen food. I heard people say that the perversion in such acts was that the kids ate alone (sapalla micusha tiyashca). One small boy, for example, was beaten repeatedly for eating his mother's washing soap. Children who stole other people's chickens were looked upon both as being bad children and as having bad parents. The point of concern is the loss of respect in the community. As one man put it, "I have raised my children so that they only work for what we eat and do not bother what is someone else's.

This way we live well and no one can speak badly about us." A bad reputation will cause the loss of future respect relations centered on the upbringing and marriage of one's children, as in ritual kin and, more importantly, affines. "Perverse" children do not find good spouses, so they prevent the household from prospering in terms of relational value.

Chapter 6: The Return of Jumandy

This chapter is based on an essay entitled "El Regreso del Jumandy: Historicidad, Parentesco, y Memoria en Napo," which was initially presented at the First Encounter of Ecuadorian Studies, Latin American Studies Association, June 2002, in Quito, Ecuador. It was subsequently presented at the 2003 American Anthropology Association annual meetings in Chicago as part of the symposium Ambiguous Others: Indigenous American Conceptualizations and Transformations of Alterity.

1. These processes of transformation are often described as ethnogenesis but are perhaps also glossed as "ethnodissolution." Ethnogenesis can be defined as "a creative adaptation to a general history of violent changes" (Hill 1996:1; see also Schwartz and Salomon 1999). As Hill has argued, ethnogenesis is not the formation of new ethnic groups but rather "the synthesis of people's cultural and political struggles to exist as well as their historical consciousness of these struggles" (1996:2). For the synthesis I describe here, power and the presence of substance flow obviate any notion of ethnicity.

2. The plaque bearing this inscription was not present in January 2004, perhaps because the municipal government of Tena was having it reconditioned.

3. I have found that many indigenous leaders in Ecuador explicitly challenge racial and ethnic constructs as hegemonic tools of the oppressors, thus associating race with the problem rather than the solution. This is not to say that race does not exist, however. Indeed, its oppressive force is felt and experienced every day in ways that make it one of the most real categories of indigenous experience.

4. In one of this chapter's scenes, indigenous and mestizo subjects consume *chicha* (a fermented corn beverage) while laughing, singing, and dancing. The people celebrate a collective victory against the authorities and colonial oppression. Anger is a marked feature. They "alternated each verse with outbursts of laughter . . . [and] stamped the floor violently. . . . The song spread to all the groups in the street and to the outer *chicha* bars" (Arguedas 1978:102). It is no coincidence that the central trope of this emotional outburst, and of the novel itself, is the river, which stands for a timeless cosmological, social, and affective flow of substance.

5. While I find Viveiros de Castro's (2001) model insightful, it does not address in great depth the specific processes by which consanguinity is constructed from affinity. I have gone to great pains to show the specific symbolic and productive mechanisms by which people become ayllu in Upper Napo.

6. Common origins, argues Godelier, constitute a sacred part of the human condi-

tion. He writes, "There can be no human society without two domains: the domain of exchanges . . . and the domain in which individuals and groups carefully keep for themselves, then transmit to their descendants or fellow believers, things, narratives, names, forms of thinking. For the things that are kept are always 'realities' which transport an individual or group back to another time, which place them once again before their origins, before the origin" (1999:200).

References

Abercrombie, Thomas A. 1998. *Pathways of Memory and Power: Ethnography and History among an Andean People*. Madison: University of Wisconsin Press.

Allen, Catherine. 1988. *The Hold Life Has: Coca and Cultural Identity in an Andean Community*. Washington, D.C.: Smithsonian Institution Press.

Amariglio, Jack, and Antonio Callari. 1993. "Marxian Value and the Problem of the Subject: The Role of Commodity Fetishism." In *Fetishism as Cultural Discourse*. Ed. Emily Apter and William Pietz. 186–216. Ithaca, N.Y.: Cornell University Press.

Anderson, Benedict. 1992. *Imagined Communities: Reflections on the Origins and Spread of Nationalism*. New York: Verso.

Arguedas, José María. 1978. *Deep Rivers*. Trans. Frances Horning Barraclough. Austin: University of Texas Press.

Appadurai, Arjun. 1986. "Introduction: Commodities and the Politics of Value." In *The Social Life of Things: Commodities in Cultural Perspective*. Ed. Arjun Appadurai. 3–63. Cambridge: Cambridge University Press.

———. 1997. *Modernity at Large: Cultural Dimensions of Globalization*. Minneapolis: University of Minnesota Press.

Århem, Kaj. 1981. *Makuna Social Organization: A Study in Descent, Alliance, and the Formation of Corporate Groups in the Northwest Amazon*. Uppsala, Sweden: Acta Universitatis Upsaliensis.

Avineri, Shlomo. 1972. *Hegel's Theory of the Modern State*. London: Cambridge University Press.

Barrera, Augusto. 2001. "'Nada sólo para los indios.' A propósito del último levantamiento indígena." *ICONOS* 10:39–47.

Basso, Ellen. 1995. *The Last Cannibals: A South American Oral History*. Austin: University of Texas Press.

Belaunde, Luisa Elvira. 2000. "The Convivial Self and Fear of Anger amongst the Airo-Pai of Amazonian Peru." In *The Anthropology of Love and Anger*. Ed. Joanna Overing and Alan Passes. 209–20. London: Routledge.

Belzner, William, and Norman Whitten. 1979. *Soul Vine Shaman*. Recording dated

Nov. 6, 1976. Booklet published by the Sacha Runa Research Foundation, Occasional Paper no. 5. New York: Crawford.

Benjamin, Walter. 1968. "The Work of Art in the Age of Mechanical Reproduction." In *Illuminations / Walter Benjamin.* Ed. Hannah Arendt. Trans. Harry Zohn. 217–52. New York: Shocken Books.

Bird-David, Nurit. 1990. "Giving Environment: Another Perspective on the Economic System of Gatherer-Hunters." *Current Anthropology* 31 (2): 189–96.

———. 1992. "Beyond 'The Original Affluent Society': A Culturalist Reformulation." *Current Anthropology* 33 (1): 25–47.

Bloch, Maurice. 1992. "What Goes without Saying: The Conceptualization of Zafimaniry Society." In *Conceptualizing Society.* Ed. Adam Kuper. 127–46. London: Routledge.

———. 1998. *How We Think They Think: Anthropological Approaches to Cognition, Memory, and Literacy.* Boulder, Colo.: Westview.

Bloch, Maurice, and S. Guggenheim. 1981. "Compadrazgo, Baptism, and the Symbolism of a Second Birth." *Man,* n.s., 16:376–86.

Bloch, Maurice, and Jonathan Parry. 1989. "Introduction: Money and the Morality of Exchange." In *Money and the Morality of Exchange.* Ed. Maurice Bloch and Jonathan Parry. 1–32. Cambridge: Cambridge University Press.

Bohannan, Paul. 1955. "Some Principles of Exchange and Investment among the Tiv." *American Anthropologist* 57:60–70.

———. 1959. "The Impact of Money on an African Subsistence Economy." *Journal of Economic History* 19:491–503.

Bourdieu, Pierre. 1977. *Outline of a Theory of Practice.* Cambridge: Cambridge University Press.

———. 1990. *The Logic of Practice.* Stanford, Calif.: Stanford University Press.

Brown, Michael F., and Eduardo Fernández. 1991. *War of Shadows: The Stuggle for Utopia in the Peruvian Amazon.* Berkeley: University of California Press.

Buhner, Stephen Harrod. 1998. *Sacred and Herbal Healing Beers: The Secrets of Ancient Fermentation.* Boulder, Colo.: Brewers Publications.

Campbell, Alan Tormaid. 1989. *To Square with Genesis: Causal Statements and Shamanic Ideas in Wayãpí.* Edinburgh: Edinburgh University Press.

Canciones indígenas en los Andes ecuatorianos: el aillu y el Ciclo Agrícola. 1996. Quito: Abya-Yala.

Chiriboga, Manuel. 2001. "El levantamiento indígena ecuatoriano de 2001: una interpelación." *ICONOS* 10:28–33.

Clastres, Pierre. 1989. *Society against the State: Essays in Political Anthropology.* New York: Zone Books.

———. 1998. *Chronicle of the Guayaki Indians.* Trans. and with a foreword by Paul Auster. New York: Zone Books.

Confederation of Indigenous Nationalities of Ecuador. 1993. "Political Declaration of Ecuador's Indigenous Peoples: The Fourth Congress of the Confederation of

Indigenous Nationalities of Ecuador." http://www.mtnforum.org/resources/
library/conai93a.htm. Accessed February 7, 2005.

Crocker, Christopher J. 1986. *Vital Souls: Bororo Cosmology, Natural Symbolism, and Shamanism.* Tucson: University of Arizona Press.

Damon, Frederick. 1980. "The Kula and Generalised Exchange: Considering Some Unconscious Aspects of the Elementary Structures of Kinship." *Man,* n.s., 15:267–93.

———. 1983. "Muyuw Kinship and the Metamorphosis of Gender Labour." *Man,* n.s., 18:305–25.

———. 1990. *From Muyuw to the Trobriands: Transformations along the Northern Side of the Kula Ring.* Tucson: University of Arizona Press.

———. 2002a. "Invisible or Visible Links?" *L'Homme* 162:233–42.

———. 2002b. "Kula Valuables: The Problem of Value and the Production of Names." *L'Homme* 162:107–36.

Dean, Bartholomew. 1995. "Forbidden Fruit: Infidelity, Affinity, and Brideservice among the Urarina of Peruvian Amazonia." *Journal of the Royal Anthropological Institute,* n.s., 1:87–110.

———. 1998. "Brideprice in Amazonia?" *Journal of the Royal Anthropological Institute,* n.s., 4:345–47.

Descola, Philippe. 1992. "Societies in Nature and the Nature of Society." In *Conceptualizing Society.* Ed. Adam Kuper. 107–126. London: Routledge.

———. 1996a. "Constructing Nature: Symbolic Ecology and Social Practice." In *Nature and Society: Anthropological Perspectives.* Ed. Philippe Descola and Gísli Pálsson. 82–102. London: Routledge.

———. 1996b. *The Spears of Twilight: Life and Death in the Amazon Jungle.* Trans. Janet Lloyd. New York: New Press.

Devereux, George. 1967. *From Anxiety to Method in the Behavioral Sciences.* The Hague: Mouton.

Dumont, Louis. 1977. *From Mandeville to Marx: The Genesis and Triumph of Economic Ideology.* Chicago: University of Chicago Press.

———. 1980. *Homo Hierarchicus: The Caste System and Its Implications.* Chicago: University of Chicago Press.

———. 1982. *On Value.* Oxford: Oxford University Press.

———. 1986. *Essays on Individualism: Modern Ideology in Anthropological Perspective.* Chicago: University of Chicago Press.

Fausto, Carlos. 2000. "Of Enemies and Pets: Warfare and Shamanism in Amazonia." *American Ethnologist* 26(4): 933–56.

Foletti-Castegnario, Alessandra. 1993. *Quichua Amazonicos del Aguarico y San Miguel.* Los pueblos indios en sus mitos. Quito: Abya-Yala.

García, Fernando. 2001. "¿Un levantamiento indígena más? A propósito de los sucesos de febrero 2001." *ICONOS* 10:34–38.

———. 2002. "Política, estado y movimiento indígena: nuevas estrategias de negociación en tiempos de la dolarización." Paper presented at the First Encounter of Ecuadorian Studies (LASA), Quito, Ecuador, July.

García Márquez, Gabriel. 1991. *One Hundred Years of Solitude*. Trans. Gregory Rabassa. New York: HarperPerennial.

Geertz, Clifford. 1973. *The Interpretation of Cultures*. New York: Basic Books.

———. 1986. "Making Experience, Authoring Selves." In *The Anthropology of Experience*. Ed. Victor Turner and Edward Bruner. 373–80. Urbana: University of Illinois Press.

Gell, Alfred. 1992. "Inter-tribal Commodity Barter and Reproductive Gift-Exchange in Old Melanesia." In *Barter, Exchange and Value*. Ed. Caroline Humphrey and Stephen Hugh-Jones. 142–68. Cambridge: Cambridge University Press.

Godelier, Maurice. 1997. "American Anthropology as Seen from France." *Anthropology Today* 13:3–5.

———. 1999. *The Enigma of the Gift*. Trans. Nora Scott. Chicago: University of Chicago Press.

———. 2000. *Cuerpo, parentesco, y poder: perspectivas antropológicas y críticas*. Quito: Abya-Yala.

Goulet, Jean-Guy. 1994. "Dreams and Visions in Other Lifeworlds." In *Being Changed: The Anthropology of Extraordinary Experience*. Ed. David E. Young and Jean-Guy Goulet. 16–38. Peterborough, Ont.: Broadview.

Gow, Peter. 1989. "The Perverse Child: Desire in a Native Amazonian Subsistence Economy." *Man* 24:567–82.

Graeber, David. 2001. *Toward an Anthropological Theory of Value: The False Coin of Our Own Dreams*. New York: Palgrave.

Graham, Laura. 1995. *Performing Dreams: Discourses of Immortality among the Xavante of Central Brazil*. Austin: University of Texas Press.

Gregory, C. A. 1982. *Gifts and Commodities*. London: Academic.

———. 1997. *Savage Money: The Anthropology and Politics of Commodity Exchange*. Amsterdam: Harwood.

Guha, Ranajit. 1983. *Elementary Aspects of Peasant Insurgency in Colonial India*. Delhi: Oxford University Press.

Guss, David. 1989. *To Weave and Sing: Art, Symbol, and Narrative in the South American Rain Forest*. Berkeley: University of California Press.

Harrison, Regina. 1989. *Signs, Songs, and Memory in the Andes: Translating Quechua Language and Culture*. Austin: University of Texas Press.

Heckenberger, Michael J. 1998. "Manioc Agriculture and Sedentism in Amazonia: The Upper Xingu Example." *Antiquity* 72 (277): 633–48.

Hendricks, Janet. 1993. *To Drink of Death: The Narrative of a Shuar Warrior*. Tucson: University of Arizona Press.

Hill, Jonathan D. 1988. "Introduction: Myth and History." In *Rethinking History and Myth: Indigenous South American Perspectives on the Past*. Ed. Jonathan Hill. 1–18. Urbana: University of Illinois Press.

————. 1996. "Introduction: Ethnogenesis in the Americas: 1492–1992." In *History, Power, and Identity: Ethnogenesis in the Americas: 1492–1992.* Ed. Jonathan Hill. 1–19. Iowa City: University of Iowa Press.

Hudleson, John Edwin. 1981. "The Expansion and Development of Quichua Transitional Culture in the Upper Amazon Basin." Ph.D. diss., Columbia University.

Hugh-Jones, Stephen. 1992. "Yesterday's Luxuries, Today's Necessities: Business and Barter in Northwest Amazonia." In *Barter, Exchange, and Value: An Anthropological Approach.* Ed. Caroline Humphrey and Stephen Hugh-Jones. 42–74. Cambridge: Cambridge University Press.

Humphrey, Caroline, and Stephen Hugh-Jones. 1992. "Introduction: Barter, Exchange, and Value." In *Barter, Exchange, and Value: An Anthropological Approach.* Ed. Caroline Humphrey and Stephen Hugh-Jones. 1–20. Cambridge: Cambridge University Press.

International Indigenous Peoples Summit on Sustainable Development. 2002. The Kimberley Declaration. Khoi-San Territory, Kimberley, South Africa, August 20–23. http://www.iwgia.org/sw217.asp. Accessed February 7, 2005.

Isbell, Billie Jean. 1978. *To Defend Ourselves: Ecology and Ritual in an Andean Village.* Austin: University of Texas Press.

Jackson, Michael. 1989. *Paths toward a Clearing: Radical Empiricism and Ethnographic Inquiry.* Bloomington: Indiana University Press.

————. 1996. "Introduction: Phenomenology, Radical Empiricism, and Anthropological Critique." In *Things as They Are: New Directions in Phenomenological Anthropology.* Ed. Michael Jackson. 1–50. Bloomington: Indiana University Press.

————. 1998. *Minima Ethnographica: Intersubjectivity and the Anthropological Project.* Chicago: University of Chicago Press.

Karsten, Rafael. 1998 [1920–21]. *Entre los indios de las selvas del Ecuador.* Quito: Abya-Yala.

Kingman, Eduardo. 2001. "La ciudad como reinvención: el levantamiento indígena de enero de 2000 y la toma de Quito." *ICONOS* 10:68–77.

Knauft, Bruce. 1997. "Gender Identity, Political Economy, and Modernity in Melanesia and Amazonia." *Journal of the Royal Anthropological Institute,* n.s., 3:233–59.

Kohn, Eduardo. 2002a. "Infidels, Virgins, and the Black-Robed Priest: A Backwoods History of Ecuador's Montaña Region." *Ethnohistory* 49 (3): 545–82.

————. 2002b. "Natural Engagements and Ecological Aesthetics among the Avila Runa of Amazonian Ecuador." Ph.D. diss., University of Wisconsin–Madison.

Kuper, Adam. 2003. "The Return of the Native." *Current Anthropology* 44 (3): 389–402.

La Fontaine, J. S. 1985. "Person and Individual: Some Anthropological Reflections." In *The Category of the Person: Anthropology, Philosophy, History.* Ed. Michael Carrithers, Steven Collins, and Steven Lukes. 123–140. Cambridge: Cambridge University Press.

Lathrap, Donald W. 1970. *The Upper Amazon.* New York: Praeger.

Leach, E. R. 1961. *Rethinking Anthropology*. London: Athlone.

Lévi-Strauss, Claude. 1969. *The Elementary Structures of Kinship*. Boston: Beacon.

Lorrain, Claire. 2000. "Cosmic Reproduction, Economics, and Politics among the Kulina of Southwest Amazonia." *Journal of the Royal Anthropological Institute* 6 (2): 293–310.

Lukács, Georg. 1967. "Reification and the Consciousness of the Proletariat." In *History and Class Consciousness*. Trans. Rodney Livingstone. 83–222. London: Merlin.

Luna, Luis Eduardo, and Pablo Amaringo. 1991. *Ayahuasca Visions: The Religious Iconography of a Peruvian Shaman*. Berkeley, Calif.: North Atlantic Books.

Lyons, Barry. 2003. "To Act Like a Man: Masculinity, Authority, and Resistance in the Ecuadorian Andes." Paper prepared for the 2003 meeting of the Latin American Studies Association, Dallas.

Macas, Luis, Linda Belote, and Jim Belote. 2003. "Indigenous Destiny in Indigenous Hands." In *Millennial Ecuador: Critical Essays on Cultural Transformations and Social Dynamics*. Ed. Norman Whitten Jr. 216–41. Iowa City: University of Iowa Press.

Macdonald, Theodore. 1979. "Processes of Change in Amazonian Ecuador: Quijos Quichua Indians Become Cattlemen." Ph.D. diss., University of Illinois–Urbana.

———. 1999. *Ethnicity and Culture amidst New "Neighbors": The Runa of Ecuador's Amazon Region*. Boston: Allyn and Bacon.

Marx, Karl. 1972. "The Grundrisse." In *The Marx-Engels Reader*. Ed. Robert Tucker. 221–93. New York: Norton.

———. 1977 [1887]. *Capital*. Vol. 1. New York: Vintage Books.

Mauss, Marcel. 1990 [1925]. *The Gift: Forms and Function of Exchange in Archaic Societies*. Trans. I. Cunnison. London: Cohen and West.

Mayer, Enrique. 1977. "Beyond the Nuclear Family." In *Andean Kinship and Marriage*. Ed. Ralph Bolton and Enrique Mayer. 60–77. Washington, D.C.: American Anthropological Association.

———. 2002. *The Articulated Peasant: Household Economies in the Andes*. Boulder, Colo.: Westview.

Métraux, Alfred. 1949. "The Couvade." In *Handbook of South American Indians.*. Ed. Julian Steward. Vol. 5:369–74. Washington, D.C.: Smithsonian Institution.

Morris, Brian. 1987. *Anthropological Studies of Religion*. Cambridge: Cambridge University Press.

Mosko, Mark S. 1995. "Rethinking Trobriand Chieftainship." *Journal of the Royal Anthropological Institute*, n.s., 1:763–85.

Munn, Nancy. 1986. *The Fame of Gawa: A Symbolic Study of Value Transformation in a Massim (Papua New Guinea) Society*. Durham, N.C.: Duke University Press.

Muratorio, Blanca. 1987. *Rucuyaya Alonso y la historia social y económica del Alto Napo, 1850–1950*. Quito: Abya-Yala.

———. 1991. *The Life and Times of Grandfather Alonso: Culture and History in the Upper Amazon*. New Brunswick, N.J.: Rutgers University Press.

————. 1998. "Indigenous Women's Identities and the Politics of Cultural Reproduction in the Ecuadorian Amazon." *American Anthropologist* 100 (2): 409–20.

Narby, Jeremy. 1998. *The Cosmic Serpent: DNA and the Origins of Knowledge.* New York: Putnam.

Nuckolls, Janis B. 1996. *Sounds Like Life: Sound-Symbolic Grammar, Performance, and Cognition in Pastaza Quechua.* New York: Oxford University Press.

————. 2000. "Spoken in the Spirit of Gesture." In *Translating Native Latin American Verbal Art: Ethnopoetics and Ethnography of Speaking.* Ed. Kay Sammons and Joel Sherzer. 223–51. Washington, D.C.: Smithsonian Institution Press.

Oberem, Udo. 1980. *Los Quijos: historia de la transculturación de un grupo indígena en el oriente ecuatoriano.* Otavalo, Ecuador: Instituto Otavaleño de Antropología.

Ollman, Bertell. 1976 [1971]. *Alienation: Marx's Conception of Man in Capitalist Society.* Cambridge: Cambridge University Press.

Orr, Carolyn, and Betsy Wrisley. 1981. *Vocabulario Quichua del Oriente.* Quito: Instituto Lingüístico de Verano.

Ortegón, Diego. 1989 [1577]. "Relación del estado en que se encuentra la Gobernación de Quijos y la Canela." In La *Gobernación de los Quijos (1559–1621).* Ed. Cristóbal Landázuri. 417–37. Iquitos, Peru: IIAP/CETA.

Ortíz, Fernando. 1940 [English-language trans., 1978]. *Contrpunto cubano del tabaco y el azúcar.* Caracas: Biblioteca Ayacucho.

Osculati, Gaetano. 2000 [1846–48]. *Exploraciones de las regiones ecuatoriales: a traves del Napo y de los rios de las Amazonas.* Quito: Abya-Yala.

Overing, Joanna. 2000. "The Efficacy of Laughter: The Ludic Side of Magic within Amazonian Sociality." In *The Anthropology of Love and Anger.* Ed. Joanna Overing and Alan Passes. 64–81. London: Routledge.

Overing, Joanna, and Alan Passes. 2000. "Introduction: Conviviality and the Opening Up of Amazonian Anthropology." In *The Anthropology of Love and Anger.* Ed. Joanna Overing and Alan Passes. 1–30. London: Routledge.

Palacio, José Luis. 1991. *Muerte y vida en el río Napo.* Quito: CICAME.

Parameshwar Gaonkar, Dilip. 2001. "On Alternative Modernities." In *Alternative Modernities.* Ed. Dilip Parameshwar Gaonkar. 1–23. Durham, N.C.: Duke University Press.

Parkinson, William. 2002. *The Archaeology of Tribal Societies.* Ann Arbor, Mich.: International Monographs in Prehistory.

Piot, Charles. 1991. "Of Persons and Things: Some Reflections on African Spheres of Exchange." *Man* 26:405–24.

————. 1999. *Remotely Global: Village Modernity in West Africa.* Chicago: University of Chicago Press.

Pitt-Rivers, Julian. 1957. "Ritual Kinship in Spain." *Transactions of the New York Academy of Sciences* 20:424–31.

————. 1977. *The Fate of Shechem: or, The Politics of Sex: Essays in the Anthropology of the Mediterranean.* Cambridge: Cambridge University Press.

Reeve, Mary Elizabeth. 1985. "Identity as Process: The Meaning of Runapura for Quichua Speakers of the Curaray River, Eastern Ecuador." Ph.D. diss., University of Illinois–Urbana.

Rival, Laura M. 1998. "Androgynous Parents and Guest Children: The Huaorani Couvade." *Journal of the Royal Anthropological Institute*, n.s., 4:619–42.

———. 2002. *Trekking through History: The Huaorani of Amazonian Ecuador.* New York: Columbia University Press.

Rival, Laura M., and Neil L. Whitehead. 2001. "Introduction." In *Beyond the Visible and the Material: The Amerindianization of Society in the Work of Peter Rivière.* Ed. Neil L. Whitehead and Laura M. Rival. 1–18. Oxford: Oxford University Press.

Rivière, Peter. 1971. "Marriage: A Reassessment." In *Rethinking Kinship and Marriage.* Ed. R. Needham. 57–74. London: Tavistock.

———. 1974. "The Couvade: A Problem Reborn." *Man*, n.s., 9:423–35.

———. 1983–84. "Aspects of Carib Political Economy." *Antropológica* 59–62:349–58.

———. 2000. "The More We Are Together . . ." In *The Anthropology of Love and Anger.* Ed. Joanna Overing and Alan Passes. 252–67. London: Routledge.

Sahlins, Marshall. 1988. "Cosmologies of Capitalism: The Trans-Pacific Sector of the World-System." *Proceedings of the British Academy* 74:1–51.

———. 1993. "Good-bye to Tristes Tropes: Ethnography in the Context of Modern World History." *Journal of Modern History* 65 (1): 1–25.

Salomon, Frank. 1986. *Native Lords of Quito in the Age of the Incas.* Cambridge: Cambridge University Press.

Salomon, Frank, and George L. Urioste. 1991. *The Huarochirí Manuscript: A Testament of Ancient and Colonial Andean Religion.* Austin: University of Texas Press.

Sammons, Kay, and Joel Sherzer. 2000. "Introduction." In *Translating Native Latin American Verbal Art: Ethnopoetics and Ethnography of Speaking.* Ed. Kay Sammons and Joel Sherzer. xi–xx. Washington, D.C.: Smithsonian Institution Press.

Sánchez-Parga, José. 1997. *Antropo-logicas Andinas.* Quito: Abya-Yala.

Santos-Granero, Fernando. 1986. "Power, Ideology, and the Ritual of Production in Lowland South America." *Man* 21:657–79.

———. 1991. *The Power of Love: The Moral Use of Knowledge amongst the Amuesha of Central Peru.* London: Athlone.

———. 2000. "The Sisyphus Síndrome, or the Struggle for Conviviality in Native Amazonia." In *The Anthropology of Love and Anger.* Ed. Joanna Overing and Alan Passes. 268–87. London: Routledge.

Santos Ortíz de Villalba, Juan. 1993. *Quichua Amazonicos.* Los pueblos indios en sus mitos. Quito: Abya-Yala.

Schneider, David M. 1968. *American Kinship: A Cultural Account.* Englewood Cliffs, N.J.: Prentice-Hall.

Schwartz, Stuart B., and Frank Salomon. 1999. "New Peoples and New Kinds of

People: Adaptation, Readjustment, and Ethnogenesis in South American Indigenous Societies (Colonial Era)." In *The Cambridge History of the Native Peoples of the Americas*. Ed. Frank Salomon and Stuart B. Schwartz. Vol. 3, South America (pt. 2): 443–501. Cambridge: Cambridge University Press.

Selverston-Scher, Melina. 2001. *Ethnopolitics in Ecuador: Indigenous Rights and the Strengthening of Democracy*. Foreword by Luis Macas. Miami: North-South.

Shapiro, Warren, and Uli Linke, ed. 1996. *Denying Biology*. New York: Rowman and Littlefield.

Shiguango Dahua, Luis Carlos. 2002. "El levantamiento indígena en la provincia de Napo." Document prepared for the First Encounter of Ecuadorian Studies (LASA), Quito, Ecuador, July.

Simson, Alfred. 1883. "Notes on the Napo Indians." *Journal of the Anthropological Institute of Great Britain and Ireland* 12:21–27.

Siskind, Janet. 1973. "Tropical Forest Hunters and the Economy of Sex." In *Peoples and Cultures of Native South America*. Ed. Daniel Gross. 226–40. New York: Natural History.

Slater, Candace. 2000. *Entangled Edens: Visions of the Amazon*. Berkeley: University of California Press.

Steward, Julian, and Alfred Métraux. 1948. "Tribes of the Peruvian and Ecuadorian Montaña." In *Handbook of South American Indians*. Ed. Julian Steward. Vol. 3:535–656. Smithsonian Institution.

Strathern, Marilyn. 1988. *The Gender of the Gift*. Berkeley: University of California Press.

———. 1992. "Parts and Wholes: Refiguring Relationships in a Post-Plural World." In *Conceptualizing Society*. Ed. Adam Kuper. 75–104. New York: Routledge.

Taussig, Michael. 1987. *Shamanism, Colonialism, and the Wild Man*. Chicago: University of Chicago Press.

———. 1993. *Mimesis and Alterity: A Particular History of the Senses*. New York: Routledge.

Taylor, Anne Christine. 1993. "Remembering to Forget: Identity, Mourning, and Memory among the Jivaro." *Man* 28:653–78.

———. 1996. "The Soul's Body and Its States: An Amazonian Perspective on the Nature of Being Human." *Journal of the Royal Anthropological Institute* 2 (2): 201–15.

———. 1999. "The Western Margins of Amazonia from the Early Sixteenth Century to the Early Nineteenth Century." In *The Cambridge History of the Native Peoples of the Americas*. Ed. Frank Salomon and Stuart B. Schwartz. Vol. 3, South America (pt. 2): 188–256. Cambridge: Cambridge University Press.

Tessmann, Günter. 1999 [1930]. *Los indígenas del Perú nororiental: investigaciones fundamentales para un estudio sistemático de la cultura*. Quito: Abya-Yala.

Tocqueville, Alexis de. 1990 [1840]. *Democracy in America*. Vol. 2. New York: Vintage.

Todorov, Tzvetan. 1982. *The Conquest of America*. Trans. Richard Howard. New York: Harper and Row.

Tomoeda, Hiroyasu. 1993. "The Concept of Vital Energy among Andean Pastorlists." In *Redefining Nature: Ecology, Culture, and Domestication*. Ed. Roy Ellen and Katsuyoshi Fukui. 187–212. Oxford: Berg.

Trawick, Margaret. 1990. *Notes on Love in a Tamil Family*. Berkeley: University of California Press.

Turner, Edith. 1997. "The Reality of Spirits." *Shamanism* 10(1). Available at http://www.shamanism.org/articles/957283797.htm. Accessed Sept. 8, 2002.

Turner, Terence. 1979. "Kinship, Household, and Community Structure among the Kayapo." In *Dialectical Societies: The Gê and Bororo of Central Brazil*. Ed. David Mayberry-Lewis. 174–217. Cambridge, Mass.: Harvard University Press.

———. 1984. "Dual Opposition, Hierarchy, and Value: Moiety Structure and Symbolic Polarity in Central Brazil and Elsewhere." In *Différences, valeurs, hiérarchie: textes offerts à Louis Dumont*. Ed. Jean-Claude Galey. 335–69. Paris: Éditions de l'École des Hautes Études en Sciences Sociales.

———. 1988. "Commentary: Ethno-Ethnohistory: Myth and History in Native South American Representations of Contact with Western Society." In *Rethinking History and Myth: Indigenous South American Perspectives on the Past*. Ed. Jonathan D. Hill. 235–81. Urbana: University of Illinois Press.

———. 1995. "Social Body and Embodied Subject: Bodiliness, Subjectivity, and Sociality among the Kayapo." *Cultural Anthropology* 10 (2): 143–70.

———. 1996. "Social Complexity and Recursive Hierarchy in Indigenous South American Societies." *Journal of the Steward Anthropological Society* 24:37–59.

Turner, Victor. 1967. *The Forest of Symbols: Aspects of Ndembu Ritual*. Ithaca, N.Y.: Cornell University Press.

———. 1969. *The Ritual Process: Structure and Anti-Structure*. Ithaca, N.Y.: Cornell University Press.

Tylor, E. B. 1888. "On a Method of Investigating the Development of Institutions, Applied to Laws of Marriage and Descent." *Journal of the Royal Anthropological Institute* 17:245–72.

Urton, Gary. 2003. *Signs of the Inka Khipu: Binary Coding in the Andean Knotted-String Records*. Austin: University of Texas Press.

Uzendoski, Michael. 1999. "Twins and Becoming Jaguars: Verse Analysis of a Napo Quichua Myth Narrative." *Anthropological Linguistics* 41 (4): 431–61.

———. 2003. "Purgatory, Protestantism, and Peonage: Napo Runa Evangelicals and the Domestication of the Masculine Will." In *Millennial Ecuador: Critical Essays on Cultural Transformations and Social Dynamics*. Ed. Norman Whitten Jr. 129–53. Iowa City: University of Iowa Press.

———. 2004a. "The Horizontal Archipelago: The Quijos Upper Napo Regional System." *Ethnohistory* 51 (2): 318–57.

———. 2004b. "Manioc Beer and Meat: Value, Reproduction, and Cosmic Substance among the Napo Runa of the Ecuadorian Amazon." *Journal of the Royal anthropological Institute* 10:883–902.

Uzendoski, Michael, Mark Hertica, and Edith Calapucha. Forthcoming. "The Phenomenology of Perspectivism: Aesthetics, Sound, and Power in Women's Songs from Amazonian Ecuador." *Current Anthropology.*

Valeri, Valerio. 1994. "Buying Women but Not Selling Them: Gift and Commodity Exchange in Huaulu Alliance." *Man* 29:1–26.

Van Gennep, Arnold. 1965 [1908]. *The Rites of Passage.* London: Routledge and Kegan Paul.

Viveiros de Castro, Eduardo. 1992. *From the Enemy's Point of View: Humanity and Divinity in an Amazonian Society.* Chicago: University of Chicago Press.

———. 1996. "Images of Nature and Society in Amazonian Ethnology." *Annual Review of Anthropology* 25:179–200.

———. 1998. "Cosmological Deixis and Amerindian Perspectivism." *Journal of the Royal Anthropological Institute*, n.s., 4:469–88.

———. 2001. "GUT Feelings about Amazonia: Potential Affinity and the Construction of Sociality." In *Beyond the Visible and the Material: The Amerindianization of Society in the Work of Peter Rivière.* Ed. Neil L. Whitehead and Laura M. Rival. 19–44. Oxford: Oxford University Press.

Wagner, Roy. 1967. *The Curse of Souw: Principles of Daribi Clan Definition and Alliance in New Guinea.* Chicago: University of Chicago Press.

———. 1974. "Are There Social Groups in the New Guinea Highlands?" In *Frontiers of Anthropology.* Ed. Murray Leaf. 95–122. New York: Van Nostrand.

———. 1977. "Analogic Kinship: A Daribi Example." *American Ethnologist* 4:623–42.

———. 1981. *The Invention of Culture.* Englewood Cliffs, N.J.: Prentice-Hall.

———. 1986. *Asiwinarong: Ethos, Image, and Social Power among the Usen Barok of New Ireland.* Princeton, N.J.: Princeton University Press.

———. 1991. "The Fractal Person." In *Big Men and Great Men: Personifications of Power in Melanesia.* Ed. Maurice Godelier and Marilyn Strathern. 159–73. Cambridge: Cambridge University Press.

———. 2001. *An Anthropology of the Subject: Holographic Worldview in New Guinea and Its Meaning and Significance for the World of Anthropology.* Berkeley: University of California Press.

Warvin, Marqués de. 1927 [1993]. "Leyendas tradicionales de los indios del oriente ecuatoriano." In *Indianistas, Indianófilos, Indigenistas: entre el enigma y la fascinación, una antología de textos sobre el "problema" indígena.* Ed. Jorge Trujillo. 677–92. Quito: Abya-Yala.

Weismantel, Mary. 1995. "Making Kin: Kinship Theory and Zumbagua Adoptions." *American Ethnologist* 22 (4): 685–709.

Whitehead, Neil L. 2002. *Dark Shamans: Kanaimà and the Poetics of Violent Death.* Durham, N.C.: Duke University Press.

———. 2003. "Introduction." In *History and Historicities in Amazonia*. Ed. Neil L. Whitehead. vii–xx. Lincoln: University of Nebraska Press.

Whitten, Norman E., Jr. 1976. *Sacha Runa: Ethnicity and Adaptation of Ecuadorian Jungle Quichua*. Urbana: University of Illinois Press.

———. 1985. *Sicuanga Runa: The Other Side of Development in Amazonian Ecuador*. Urbana: University of Illinois Press.

———. 1988. "Commentary: Historical and Mythic Evocations of Chthonic Power." In *Rethinking History and Myth: Indigenous South American Perspectives on the Past*. Ed. Jonathan D. Hill. 282–306. Urbana: University of Illinois Press.

———. 1996. "The Ecuadorian Levantamiento Indígena of 1990 and the Epitomizing Symbol of 1992: Reflections on Nationalism, Ethic-Bloc Formation, and Racialist Ideologies." In *History, Power, and Identity: Ethnogenesis in the Americas: 1492–1992*. Ed. Jonathan D. Hill. 193–218. Iowa City: University of Iowa Press.

———. 2003. "Introduction." In *Millennial Ecuador: Critical Essays on Cultural Transformations and Social Dynamics*. Ed. Norman E. Whitten Jr. 1–45. Iowa City: University of Iowa Press.

Whitten, Norman E., Jr., and Arlene Torres. 1998. "General Introduction: To Forge the Future in the Fires of the Past: An Interpretive Essay on Racism, Domination, Resistance, and Liberation." In *Blackness in Latin America and the Caribbean*. Ed. Norman E. Whitten Jr. and Arlene Torres. Vol. 1:3–33. Bloomington: Indiana University Press.

Whitten, Norman E., Jr., and Dorothea S. Whitten. 1984. "The Structure of Kinship and Marriage among the Canelos Quichua of East-Central Ecuador." In *Marriage Practices in Lowland South America*. Ed. Kenneth M. Kensinger. 194–220. Urbana: University of Illinois Press.

———. 1988. *From Myth to Creation*. Urbana: University of Illinois Press.

Whitten, Norman E., Jr., Dorothea S. Whitten, and Alfonso Chango. 1997. "Return of the Yumbo: The Indigenous Caminata from Amazonia to Quito." *American Ethnologist* 24 (2): 355–91.

Whorf, Benjamin. 1941. "The Relation of Habitual Thought and Behavior to Language." In *Language, Culture, and Personality: Essays in Memory of Edward Sapir*. Ed. Leslie Spier, A. Irving Hallowell, and Stanley S. Newman. 75–93. Menasha, Wisc.: Sapir Memorial Fund.

Wibbelsman, Michelle. 2003. "Appendix: General Information on Ecuador." In *Millennial Ecuador: Critical Essays on Cultural Transformations and Social Dynamics*. Ed. Norman Whitten Jr. 375–88. Iowa City: University of Iowa Press.

Wright, Robin M. 1998. *For Those Unborn: Cosmos, Self, and History in Baniwa Religion*. Austin: University of Texas Press.

Index

adoption, 11–12, 22, 97, 110–11, 159–60, 176n1
affinal relationships, 22, 92–93, 95–117, 159–62. See also *auya; cachun; masha*
aguardiente (strong liquor), 10, 111, 140. See also drinking
alienation, 45; defined, 172n5. See also capitalism; commodities
alternative modernities, 152. See also anthropology: humanistic approaches to; communitarianism; value: politically constituted
Amazonian region, 52–53, 79, 117, 126–27, 143, 159, 161, 177n6, 178n8
American Anthropological Association Code of Ethics, 13–14
anacondas, 30, 127–28, 133–34, 140–41, 159
Andes region, 15, 52–53, 56–57, 79, 111, 145, 159, 165, 177n6
anger, 1, 16–17, 73, 94, 99, 103–5, 147–51, 157–59, 160–61, 179n4
anthropology: ethics in, 13–14; humanistic approaches to, 20–21, 155–56; writing in, 154–56
Arguedas, José María, 19, 21, 151, 157–58, 179n4
art, 22, 67, 175n10. See also beauty; Napo Runa: aesthetic principles of; Napo Runa: music of; Napo Runa: mythology of
Atchei, 20, 158
auya (relatives by marriage), 111–12, 115. See also affinal relationships
aya (wandering spirit), 37–38, 47–48. See also death
ayllu, 11–12, 18; as depicted in women's

songs, 57; expansion and intensification of, 108, 112, 159; life cycle of, 101–3; Napo Runa concept of, 63–67, 115, 159; transformations of, in marriage, 72, 80–81, 92–93, 95–96, 101, 159. See also *auya; muntun;* substance

Barraclough, Francis, 19
beauty, 41, 87–89, 155. See also Napo Runa: aesthetic principles of
Belaunde, Luisa Elvira, 160–61, 174n7
Benjamin, Walter, 175n10
bilingual education, 12, 149–50
Bird-David, Nurit, 113
birds, 55–57, 72
birth, 25, 28–32, 126, 138, 142, 143
Bloch, Maurice, 5, 25, 173n1
blood (*yawar*), 19, 33, 36, 47. See also body; substance
Boas, Franz, 165
body: adoption as constituted in, 110–11; of children, 25–26, 27–28, 30–33, 34–35, 42–43, 126–27, 134; drinking and, 140–41; gendering process of, 42–49; kinship theory within, 25–49, 67–68; love and, 27; of men, 37, 43–44, 133–34; organs of, 27, 30, 40–41, 55, 133, 138–39; shape-shifting nature of, 43, 54, 134; site of shamanistic action, 57; the soul and, 36–40, 48–49; subjectivity of, 54, 61, 143; of women, 27–28, 126, 134, 138–39, 142–43
Bohannan, Paul, 97–98
Bourdieu, Pierre, 172n7
bride price, 95–96

Buhner, Stephen, 178n7
bura (wedding), 71, 75–94, 98, 109, 175n2. *See also* marriage

cachun (daughter-in-law), 73, 95; service obligations of, 103–5; reputation of, 103–5, 112, 176n2. *See also* affinal relationships
Campbell, Alan, 57, 59
Canelos Quichua. *See* Pastaza Runa
Capital (Marx), 2–3, 171–72n4
capitalism, 2, 3, 10, 172n5, 172n7; desire and, 177n3; Ecuadorian transformations of, 147–48, 152, 158–59; indigenous views of, 152–57; individualism within, 45. *See also* alternative modernities; commodities; value
cargo cults, 147–48
causai (life force), 34, 37–39, 51, 60, 127, 149
Christianity, 36, 51, 57–60, 106, 109, 141, 175n7
Chuquín, Carmen, 6
circulation, 18, 22, 38, 96, 111, 113–15, 139–41. *See also* exchange; value
Clastres, Pierre, 20, 28, 61–62, 131, 158–59, 178n8
coca (plant), 140–41
Coca (city), 64, 108
Colombia, 64
commodities: as dominant, 154, 155; gifts and, 77–78, 152–53; notion of, 2–5; as objects of desire, 120, 143; women seen as, 95–96, 119. *See also* capitalism; value
communitarianism, 153–57
compadrazgo (ritual kinship). *See* Napo Runa: *compadrazgo* among
complementarity (masculine-feminine), 22, 46–48, 57, 79, 92, 122, 137, 143, 174n7, 177n6. *See also* feminine strength; masculinity
Confederation of Indigenous Nationalities of Ecuador (CONAIE), 153. *See also* indigenous federations; uprisings
conviviality: concept of, 2, 16–17, 68, 94, 120, 139, 142, 173n12, 173n13; humor and death, 61–63; in political actions, 144, 158–59, 179n4; as power, 160–61, 166; of remembrance, 151, 164–66; of the warrior, 151, 157–58. See also *llakina*

couvade, 31–32, 105, 110, 173n3, 176n4
Crocker, Christopher, 122, 174n5, 177n5

Damon, Frederick, 2, 3, 17, 18, 70, 142
dancing, 86–87, 91, 93
Daribi (group from Melanesia), 116, 177n5
death, 38, 55–56, 61–63, 157–58
De la Torre, Luz María. *See* Torre, Luz María de la
Descola, Philippe, 2, 37–38, 126, 142–43, 177n4
desire, 22–23; bodily nature of, 40–41; children and, 27–28, 38–40; feminine notions of, 128, 142; food and, 120–21, 130, 174n5; masculine notions of, 136–38, 141–42; spirit world and, 128; as theoretical concept, 119–20, 141, 177n1; value and, 113; in women's songs, 56
dollarization, 147–48, 158–59
doves, 55–57
drinking, 43–44, 58, 74, 77–78, 94, 109, 118–19, 136–37, 139–41, 178n7
duality, 52, 79, 82–83
Durkheim, Emile, 5

Ecuador, 6, 12–13, 23, 140, 147–48, 151–57, 165, 171n1
ethnicity, 14–15, 145, 156, 171n1, 174n3, 179n1
ethnogenesis, 147, 179n1
exchange, 18, 95–96, 107–8, 112; generalized, 98; substance and, 115–16, 159; thought and, 150–51, 157–60. *See also* circulation; value

femininity: desire and, 128, 142; strength of, 22, 48, 54–57, 135, 157, 176n2. *See also* complementarity; gender; labor
fieldwork, 6–14, 20–21, 155
fishing, 11, 79. *See also* Yacu Warmi (water woman)
Fitzcarraldo (Herzog), 135, 155–56
flood. *See* Izhu

García, Fernando, 151
gardens, 126–27. *See also* labor, production
Geertz, Clifford, 13, 177n2
gender, 21–22, 25, 74, 174n6, 174n7, 176n2; as

defined by labor, 121–25. *See also* complementarity; femininity; masculinity
gifts: commodities and, 77–78, 95–96, 152,
154; exchanged among kin, 112; theory of,
2, 3, 22, 90, 112–15; use of, to transform
relationships, 90, 109, 152. *See also* commodities; personification; value
Godelier, Maurice, 2, 3, 156, 179n6
"going native," 13. *See also* fieldwork
Goulet, Jean-Guy, 21
Gow, Peter, 112, 119–20, 139, 141–43, 177n6,
178n9
Gregory, Christopher, 2, 3–4, 96, 172n5,
172n6
groups, 63, 172n10. *See also* individualism
Guss, David, 68

Harrison, Regina, 53, 175n6
Herzog, Werner, 135, 155–56
Hill, Jonathan, 144, 179n1
historical consciousness, 23, 144–45, 152,
162–66
house (*wasi*), 42, 122, 131–32. See also *ayllu;
muntun*
Huaorani, 77
Hudleson, John, 15
hunting, 76–77, 78–79, 122–23, 127–31, 138

indigenous federations, 145, 153–57
indigenous self-determination, 23, 145,
151–57, 165–66, 179n3. *See also* uprisings
individualism, 45, 120, 143, 172n7, 172n10
Izhu (great flood), 51–54, 61, 67, 162, 164,
174n4

Jackson, Michael, 6, 172n8, 177n1
jaguars, 35, 43, 134, 162–64
Jesuits, 93–94
Jumandy, 144–47, 149–51, 162–64, 166

Karsten, Rafael, 56
Kimberley Declaration, 154–55
kinship, 2, 4, 15, 22, 159; Andean vs. Amazonian, 177n6; historical consciousness
and, 144–45, 150–51, 164–66; humor and,
60–61; mythological patterning of, 51–53,
117, 174n2; shape-shifting nature of, 63–66;

siblingship as model for, 66–67, 105, 108;
sociality and, 156, 159–60; thought and,
160–61, 162–64, 166; value and, 48–49.
See also adoption, affinal relationships,
*auya, ayllu, cachun, compadrazgo, masha;
muntun;* Napo Runa; substance
Kuper, Adam, 156

labor: in adoption, 110; of *cachun* and
masha, 99–105; exchanges of, among *auya,*
112; exchanges of, between *compadres,*
108, exchanges of, between spouses, 131,
139–40; as gendered, 121–25, 137, 142;
Marx's notion of, 2; Napo Runa notion
of, 121–22; power and, 131; value and, 114;
in weddings, 72, 77, 95. See also *minga;*
production; value
La Fontaine, Jean, 26
Lathrap, Donald, 126
liminality, 70, 72–75, 82, 86, 92
llakina (love), 22, 27, 35, 160, 173n13; in
exchange, 113, 114; food and, 76, 84, 91;
in kinship, 107, 112; as power, 55, 150–51,
157–62. *See also* conviviality; sadness
Lower Napo, 2, 56, 64–65, 77, 108
Lyons, Barry, 47, 174n6

Macdonald, Theodore, 71, 88, 90, 175n24
manioc. *See* gardens; production; *see also*
manioc brew
manioc beer. *See* manioc brew
manioc brew, 10, 22–23, 55, 172n9; as defined
by *samai,* or spirit, 137–39; outsiders' views
of, 89, 135; production of, 135–38; role of,
in weddings, 74, 84, 91, 93–94
marriage, 11–13, 15–16, 22, 57, 68, 70–94,
177n6; without permission, 98–101. *See also*
kinship; Napo Runa: marriage practices of;
substance
Marx, Karl, 2–3, 172n7; on the individual, 45;
philosophy of internal relations, 171–72n4
masculinity: dominance of, 22, 46–48, 174n6;
desire and, 136–38, 141–42; hunting and,
76–77, 90; origins and, 67; weakness of,
48, 56. *See also* complementarity; gender;
labor
masha (son-in-law), 69, 90, 95; reputation

of, 104–5, 112; service obligations of, 100–105
Mauss, Marcel, 90, 137–38
Mayer, Enrique, 95, 96
mestizos, 14–15, 108, 145, 148–49, 156, 164–65
Métraux, Alfred, 32
military, Ecuadorian, 148–49, 151
millennial cosmology. See *pachacutic.*
Millennial Ecuador (Whitten), 152, 175n7
mimesis: of the anaconda, 30, 133; defined, 175n8; in gardening, 126; in humor, 61–62; of thought, 160–61
minga (work party), 7–8, 112, 118
mountain creators, 51–53
muntun (group), 12, 15, 63–66, 114–15; combinations of, in marriage, 72, 92–93; life cycle of, 101–3, 159. See also *ayllu*
Muratorio, Blanca, 65, 104, 162–63, 176n2
music. See Napo Runa: music of
myth. See Napo Runa: mythology of

names, 61, 69, 90, 109. See also Napo Runa: kinship terminology of
Napo Quichua. See Quichua: Napo dialect of
Napo River, 148
Napo Runa, 1, 4, 6, 10–11, 171n1; adolescence among, 32–35, 174n4, 178n9; adoption among, 110–11; aesthetic principles of, 22, 51, 52–53, 57, 64, 67–68, 164, 165, 174n4; alliance relationships among, 111–12; birth practices of, 28–32, 141–42, 176n4; *compadrazgo* among, 22, 32, 106–10, 112, 142, 176nn3–4; cuisine of, 73–74, 76–78, 89–90, 93, 118–43, 150, 178n7; death, notions of, 55–56, 112, 157–62; gender theory of, 45–48; humor, 33–34, 60–63, 94, 95, 103–4; identity models of, 14–15; kinship terminology of, 63–68, 102–3, 105, 107, 110, 111–12; marriage among, 69–94, 95–106, 159; music of, 22, 54–57, 72, 74, 77, 80, 91; mythology of, 51–54, 112, 126, 133–34, 161–64, 174n2, 174n4, 175n5; sexuality among, 44–45, 53, 71, 88, 91, 128, 133–35; soul, concept of, 36–40; value theory of, 112–17; will, concept of, 41–45, 55, 161. See also Quijos
Neubauer, Renault, 6
Nuckolls, Janice, 52, 174n4

Oberem, Udo, 145, 164–65
Ollman, Bertell, 171n4, 172n5
Osculati, Gaetano, 25, 35, 88–89, 140
Otavalo Region, 6, 56
Overing, Joanna, 2, 16–17, 60, 67, 161

pachacutic, 23, 144–45, 164, 165, 166. See also Izhu (great flood); uprisings
pactachina (fulfillment of agreements), 71, 74–75, 98
Parameshwar Gaonkar, 152
Passes, Alan, 2, 16–17
Pastaza Runa, 37–38, 51, 62
personhood: 25–49, 48, 86, 87, 92–93, 175n5
personification, 3, 93, 95–97, 137–38, 141–43, 152, 178n8
Piot, Charles, 4, 26, 112
Pitt-Rivers, Julian, 107
Plato, 38–39, 42
The Power of Love (Santos-Granero), 160
predation, 2, 16–17, 59, 173n14; in humor, 62–63; love and, 157–59; shape-shifting and, 68
production, 4, 17, 22, 70, 97, 117, 178n8; in manioc-based society, 126–27; mythological principles in, 152; of people, 141–43; postmarriage, 101, 102; as socially defined, 152; for weddings, 74–79, 92–93. See also labor; value
punishment. See Napo Runa: adolescence among
Puyo (city), 64, 148

Quichua language, 171n3; Amazonian dialects of, 6, 15, 37, 56, 171n1, 174n4; Napo dialect of, 7, 10, 14, 36–38, 52–53, 60–61, 107, 120–21, 132, 174n4; unified dialect of, 149
Quijos/Quixos (indigenous group), 89, 145–47. See also Napo Runa
Quito, 6, 144, 152, 163

ritual, 22, 69–70, 74, 79, 95, 101, 109–10
Rival, Laura, 32, 113, 134, 166, 173n3
Rivière, Peter, 17, 92, 107, 134, 173n3, 178n8
Runa Paju (modern Napo Runa music), 77, 91, 134

Sacha Warmi (forest woman), 128, 142. *See also* substance: animal combinations of

sadness (*llakirina*), 55–56, 85–86, 93, 159

Sahlins, Marshall, 120, 153, 177n3

Salomon, Frank, 6, 56–57, 111, 179n1

samai (breath/soul substance), 18, 22, 32, 68, 110–11, 140, 160–61; of the body, 36–38, 43, 54; as defining of historical consciousness, 149, 166; as defining of meat and manioc, 137–39; love and, 160–61; shamans and, 37, 58. See also *causai* (life force); substance; *ushai* (power); *yachai* (knowledge)

Sammons, Kay, 21

Sánchez-Parga, José, 140

Santos-Granero, Fernando, 16–17, 160, 173n14

self-determination. *See* indigenous self-determination

shamanism, 37–38, 110–11; anger and, 161; love and, 161–62, 163; magical objects of, 134–35; principles of, 50–51, 54, 57–60, 66, 68, 174n3. *See also* shape-shifting

shape-shifting, 22, 50–68, 157, 161–62, 164, 175nn5–6, 175n8; defined, 54

Shiguango-Dahua, Luis Carlos, 150–51

Sherzer, Joel, 21

soul. See *samai*

Strathern, Marilyn, 3, 4, 18, 26, 40

subalternity, 23, 155

subjectivity, 3–4, 6, 21, 23, 53, 154, 165, 172n8

substance, 18–19, 21–22, 177n1; adoption and, 110–11, 133–34; animal combinations of, 43, 54–57, 61, 133–34, 140–41, 157, 162–64; historical consciousness and, 144–45, 150–51, 164, 166, 179n1; kinship combinations of, 18, 68, 95, 105–7, 110–12, 115–16, 159–62; sexuality and, 133–35; transformation, defined by, 174n3. See also blood; kinship; *samai*

Swanson, Tod, 175n9

tapuna (request), 71–74, 98

Taussig, Michael, 156, 165, 175n8

Taylor, Anne Christine, 162, 165

Tena (city), 14, 63, 145, 148–49, 179n2

Tessman, Günter, 44

thought, 160–66

tocadur (violinist), 74, 80, 85, 91. See also *bura* (wedding); Napo Runa: music of

Torre, Luz María de la, 6

transculturation, 15–16, 145

translation, 20–21, 37, 155–56

tree of life (myth), 50–51, 52–53

tucuna (transformation), 50–51, 174n1, 174n3. *See also* Napo Runa: mythology of; shape-shifting; shamanism; substance; *ushai* (power)

Turner, Terence, 40, 145, 152, 178n8

Turner, Victor, 70, 74, 139

twins (culture heroes). *See* Napo Runa: mythology of

Upper Amazonia, 2

Upper Napo (region), 67, 90, 108, 145, 160, 165

uprisings, 23, 65, 144–59, 162–64. See also *pachacutic*

Urioste, George, 56–57

ushai (power), 50, 54, 56, 134–35, 161; *pachacutic* and, 144–45; as present in Christianity, 59

value: conversions of, 97–98; conveyances of, 97–98; gifts and, 102; in giving and reciprocity, 107–8, 113–15, 117, 164; marriage and, 71, 93, 96, 98; metamorphosis of, 95, 116, 141–43; mythological principles of, 152; Napo Runa theory of, 112–17; politically constituted, 1, 144, 152–57, 158–59, 165–66; reproduction, as created through, 48–49; social context as transforming, 77–78, 159; spheres of, 97–98, 109, 137, 142; theory, 1–4, 17, 22, 171–72n4, 172n5, 172n7. *See also* capitalism; circulation; commodities; exchange; gifts; labor; personification; production

Villalba, Juan Santos Ortíz de, 56

vinillu (manioc wine), 55

virsaru (drummer and chanter), 74, 80–86, 87–88, 77, 91. See also *bura* (wedding); Napo Runa: music of

Viveiros de Castro, Eduardo, 2, 16, 38–40, 117, 122, 177n4, 179n5

Wagner, Roy, 5, 18, 21, 63, 70, 116, 175n1, 177n5

Warvin, Marqués de, 162–64

weaving, 5, 63, 172n8

Weismantel, Mary, 110–11

Whitehead, Neil, 59, 162, 166

Whitten Dorothea, 50, 62, 133, 174n1, 174n3

Whitten, Norman, 37, 41, 50, 62, 68, 106, 133, 144–45, 152, 171n1, 174n1, 174n3

Whorf, Benjamin, 160

Wibbelsman, Michelle, 171n1

women's songs. *See* Napo Runa: music of

yachai (knowledge), 37, 50, 55, 127, 134

Yacu Warmi (water woman), 128, 142. *See also* anacondas; substance: animal combinations of

Michael Uzendoski, an assistant professor of anthropology at Florida State University, has won two Fulbright awards for study in Ecuador (1994, 2002). His publications include "The Horizontal Archipelago: The Quijos Upper Napo Regional System," which appeared in *Ethnohistory,* and "Manioc Beer and Meat: Value, Reproduction, and Cosmic Substance among the Napo Runa of the Ecuadorian Amazon," published in the *Journal of the Royal Anthropological Institute.*

▶ ▶ ▶ ▶ *Interpretations of Culture in the New Millennium*

Peruvian Street Lives: Culture, Power, and Economy among Market Women of Cuzco   *Linda J. Seligmann*

The Napo Runa of Amazonian Ecuador   *Michael Uzendoski*

The University of Illinois Press
is a founding member of the
Association of American University Presses.

———————————————

Composed in 10/13 CC Galliard
with ITC Galliard display
by Jim Proefrock
at the University of Illinois Press
Designed by Dennis Roberts
Manufactured by Maple-Vail
Book Manufacturing Group

University of Illinois Press
1325 South Oak Street
Champaign, IL 61820-6903
www.press.uillinois.edu